From The Library of

Ex Libris

Merle Steven McClung

A RHODES RETROSPECTIVE

Volume II: My Career, Revised Edition

BY MERLE McCLUNG

DEDICATION

T his memoir is for three memorable role models from Montevideo, Minnesota:

(1) Martha McClung, my mother, who valued the opportunities public education made possible for her seven children,

(2) Oliver Rekow, Republican banker, who selflessly helped me and so many others in Montevideo, and

(3) Claude Dziuk, my English teacher at Montevideo Public High School, who lit the educational fires of scores of students, including mine, with his inspirational teaching.

Book Cover and Coriolanus Plate from The Library Shakespeare (3 vol.), Illustrated by Sir. John Gilbert, George Cruikshank and R. Dudley, London: Mackenzie circa 1900.

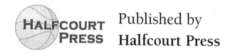 Published by
Halfcourt Press

Design:
Concepts Unlimited
conceptsunlimited@estreet.com
www.ConceptsUnlimitedInc.com

Editing:
David T. Kennedy
dave@dkennedy.io
dkennedy.io

ISBN-13: 978-0-69262-831-7 (pbk)

First Printing, 2015
Revised, January 2024

Printed in the United States of America

TABLE OF CONTENTS
Vol II

A RHODES RETROSPECTIVE
Vol. II: My Career

Players, by Merle McClung

BY MERLE McCLUNG

FOREWORD
BY JEFFREY ZORN

As Merle McClung's memoir continues, a pun or double entendre might come into the minds of many readers: The words "Harvard Center" apply with equal force to Merle as athlete and public intellectual. (A friend for forty-five years, I cannot call him "McClung" here.)

The second volume of *A Rhodes Retrospective* finds Merle still playing basketball at a very high level in Birmingham with the Miles faculty team, slowing down in late middle age in Denver (though memorably kicking John Elway's behind), and then hitting athletic retirement prematurely as health problems mount. Merle's hoops stardom serves him well on many levels, gaining him as a teenager much-needed recognition and confidence, seeing him through elite university education at Harvard and Oxford and developing in him the character that will win admiration and deep respect wherever he goes.

A consummate team player, Merle masters early-on the balance between self-assertion and self-sacrifice in a basketball game. If he gets his as the center, both out on the floor and at the rim, the opposition has to adjust. Its defensive spacing warps to contain Merle's potent offense, and now his passing skills come to the fore. Merle is an agile, unselfish ballplayer and, as Volume II shows in strikingly close connection, an agile, unselfish thinker—about matters from school philosophy to real estate, intimate personal relationships and dying with dignity.

The other "Harvard Center" refers to the Harvard Center for

Law and Education, where Marian Wright Edelman detects Merle's talent and brings him aboard as staff attorney. Edelman, founder of the Children's Defense Fund and the first black woman ever certified to practice law in Mississippi, gets Merle's career flying. As he details the first, fascinating cases he works on, we see Merle wrestling with issues of political philosophy that look back to his time at Miles College and forward to his advocacy of the civic standard for public education in the United States.

Note then how Merle's sharp criticisms of the test-based "reform" movement in U.S. education demonstrate an insider's expertise. Completing the analogical loop here, his critique recalls the disdain of real athletes for statistical analysis of their games by geeky non-players. Like clueless owners of sports franchises, business-model school reformers are seduced by the veneer of objective, empirical control on otherwise mysterious goings-on. Numbers numb, Merle suggests, when we have no feel for the game and only the vaguest sense of purpose beyond "winning."

One last prefatory note: Keep your eyes on how Merle handles adversity in this volume. It takes a man of his power and depth to face up to limitation and failure with the forthrightness explicated herein. Rejection stings; physical misery saps our best energies; death awaits impatiently. Merle faces it all undaunted and unflinching, giving readers of his *Rhodes Retrospective* one more pleasure to savor: a heroism to emulate in the hard times we all must face.

THE LITTLE PRINCE

All my childhood years have passed since
I first read about the Little Prince
And it's only now I have come to sense
Numbers are matters of inconsequence.
We grow up to run down roads near and far
Never quite satisfied with where we are
Busying ourselves with forms of pretense
Rather than that which makes a difference.
We find a lonely space, the land of fears
Next to that secret place, the land of tears.
The Prince's rose and his sheep in a box
Form the heart of the fox's paradox:
We can find the essential if we try
To see what's invisible to the eye.
The flower we bless with care and duty
Becomes uniquely dressed in true beauty.
Thus the Little Prince sees our common faults
A children's tale to benefit adults.

John Usher Monro, 1912-2002: A Committed Yankee Goodhead

Chapter 18

JOHN MONRO & MILES COLLEGE

Perhaps the most valuable result of all education is the ability to make yourself do the thing you have to do, when it ought to be done, whether you like it or not.—Thomas Henry Huxley

Despairing at the prospect of fighting in what I considered an immoral war, I wrote a letter to former Harvard College Dean, John Monro, then directing the Freshman Studies Program at Miles College in Birmingham, Alabama. His dramatic career decision a few years earlier to step down from one of America's most prestigious deanships for a humble position at a small unaccredited black college in Birmingham, Alabama had attracted substantial media attention. I probably have a copy of the letter buried somewhere in a box in my basement, but remember the opening to be something like, "Dear Dean Monro, I would not be writing you this letter if President Johnson had not ended student deferments. My plan had been to finish my three year program at Harvard Law School, but I think I could do more good assisting you at Miles College than fighting in the rice paddies of Vietnam." A more likely alternative to being drafted, I continued, would be to refuse induction into the army. I could not claim conscientious objector status because I believed that some wars like World War II were necessary.

My new plan was to do everything legal that I could to avoid having to make that ultimate decision. My draft board in Montevideo, Minnesota probably would reject my application for a teaching deferment, but as a matter of law the board would have to consider my request if I was teaching at Miles College. It was possible that the time it would take to deny my application, and my right to appeal that decision, would take me to my 26th birthday—the cut off age for draft eligibility. If not, I would be in dramatic Coriolanian "I will not do it" civil disobedience mode.

Fortunately for me, Mr. Monro said that he in good conscience could write a letter to my draft board as he agreed that I could do more good at Miles College than in Vietnam. As Mr. Monro's part time administrative assistant and full time Social Studies teacher in his Freshman Studies Program at Miles College, I had a unique up-close look at the man I came to respect more each day.

After months of melodramatic anguish, my draft dodging plan worked as my last appeal expired only a few days after I turned 26. Score one for man's plans, but I was totally surprised that my experience at Miles would turn into one of the best in my life. Part of that experience is summarized in an article I wrote for the *American Oxonian*: "Miles College: A Chance for Birmingham's Black Student?" (April, 1970).

John Monro at Miles College

The following is my 7/11/2003 response to a survey Toni-Lee Capossela asked me and others to complete as research for her superb comprehensive biography *John U. Monro: Uncommon Educator* (2012):

I am pleased to hear that my article in the *American Oxonian* (Vol. LVII, No.2, April 1970, pp 348-54) is helpful. The *American Oxonian* is the official publication of and for American Rhodes Scholars and other Americans who studied at Oxford University.

Sometime in 1968 President Johnson ended student deferments. Being opposed to the Vietnam War, I was looking for a constructive alternative when a friend suggested I contact John Monro about teaching at Miles College. My December 1968 letter to Monro stated that I would not be writing if I did not need a teaching deferment, but perhaps I could be useful teaching English or Social Science in his program at Miles. Monro responded with an offer to teach and also work part time as his administrative assistant preparing reports for the Ford and other foundations. I accepted the offer and started work for Monro at Miles in January 1969.

I was preparing a report to the Ford Foundation one day in Mr. Monro's office when I heard him utter an uncharacteristic curse and looked up to see him crumple a paper and toss it into his wastebasket. When I asked, he said it was just another hate letter. I retrieved the unsigned paper with his permission, and read: "Such nigger lovers like you behind all this racial trouble does not help because we in the South will overcome too. And when the revolution and shooting starts you may be in the top 10. We don't have any more use for you damn Yankees than we do these damn niggers."

I asked Monro how often he received such. He replied something like, "All the time, but I have more important things to worry about," and continued preparing for his English class.

I think Mr. Monro spent as much time, or perhaps even more, than we did in preparing for class. On many occasions he mentioned how important it was for him to be in the classroom teaching so he could better direct the Freshman Studies Program. I remember at staff meetings the English and Social Studies teachers would share ideas as well as exercises they had prepared for their classes, and Mr. Monro would similarly share his.

I don't remember specific ideas or suggestions, but he treated us as equals in this sharing process. We were free to use or not use materials shared at staff meetings in our classes. I also remember at times he would go on and on about some particular problem or approach, and often we would lose interest long before he did. Perhaps Jeff or Rick can elaborate on some of this.

Although I was in a unique position as John Monro's administrative assistant as well as teaching both English and Social Studies classes in his program and admired his commitment, energy, sincerity, courage and character in general, I did not feel close to him as a friend might. I don't know if he had many close friends at Miles, but everyone I knew admired and respected him for reasons just mentioned. My impression was that John was totally dedicated to his work at Miles and never questioned his decision to leave his prestigious position at Harvard to work at a small black college in the South. Some of us, however, wondered if it might have been much harder for his wife, Dottie, to make the transition. I can't comment on this because I only met her a few times in social settings, but she is undoubtedly an important part of the story that you may want to explore.

Looking back more than thirty years later, I can say that my time at Miles College was one of the best that I have experienced. A large part of this can be attributed to the friends I met at Miles, especially Jeff, Rick, Prentiss and Denny who comprised the core of our faculty basketball team. Now we are scattered across the country, but still stay in touch and have occasional reunions to reminisce about our time at Miles College.

This response probably has more words and less useful information than you need, but I write at some length because it is flattering to have someone ask. And also because I think it important for someone to do a thoughtful biography of John Monro. So I hope you are able to find the material you need, and am looking forward to reading the finished product. —Merle

Carpetbagging Honkies from Harvard

The academic and social challenges of trying to educate poor black students in Birmingham, Alabama in troubled times was the focus of Mr. Monro's team of untested young, mostly white, English and Social Science teachers. "Carpetbagging honkies from Harvard" in the colorful terminology supplied by Prentiss Willson, who was on our team and therefore describing himself as well. Given the enormity of the challenge, I wondered what was the most important thing one can acquire from a college education? The answer seemed obvious: critical thinking. Of course there are many valid formulations of the ultimate value of a college education, but it seemed to me that the most important outcome of a successful college education is the ability to think critically. Although I did not make the connection directly at the time, this conclusion is based on my personal experience at Harvard College and elaboration on the implications of the civic standard first considered in my third year paper at Harvard Law School in 1972.

Today, I would refine the primary purpose of most colleges as "learning critical thinking and empathetic application," since both are necessary to Make Our Democracy Work well (see Chapter 11).

The primary outcome of critical thinking became the focus of the course materials I designed for my social studies classes. A large part of the appeal and challenge of Mr. Monro's Freshman Studies Program was encouraging his teachers to design courses and materials to fit the specific needs of our students. Designing materials of course was more difficult than teaching from a pre-scribed curriculum, but most of us welcomed the challenge. I was particularly impressed with the innovative teaching techniques devised by Rick Voigt for his social studies classes and Jeff Zorn for his English classes. I think it fair to say that all of us were dedicated and put in long hours preparing for our classes, but we found time for relief from our teaching responsibilities at Miles.

Miles College Faculty Basketball Team

The relief came in the form of—yes—you guessed it—basket-ball. Once again I was very happy to have left basketball behind me in Cambridge, especially since I wanted to improve my tennis game—which like my classrooms offered new challenges. Rick Voigt and Jeff Zorn and I played regularly on some tennis hard courts near the campus that were enclosed within the ubiquitous chain link fencing so common in marginal areas. Soon we were joined by Harvard graduates Prentiss Willson, Denny Reigle and Frank Martin—all northern honkies working in other Miles College programs. We were close enough in tennis ability and com-petence to enjoy competitive sets in the humid Birmingham evenings. But what they enjoyed more than the tennis was—basketball and soon our group morphed into the Miles College Faculty basketball team. Occasionally we would play against some regulars on the all black Miles College basketball team, but "The Golden Bears" had their own competitive basketball program, and so we joined a Birmingham industrial league for competition. Initially skeptical, I soon was immersed in the most fun I have ever had playing basketball.

The joy was partly due to the wacky group of right wing white teams making up the Birmingham industrial league (including the Fairfield cops and Auburn faculty teams). Plus we were a wacky group in our own right, with long hair and attitude so different from our straight-laced crew-cut opponents. The unique experiences of playing against this contingent of modern day Hotspurs was memorable not only during the games, but reliving them later at upscale Birmingham restaurants such as Catfish King (All you can eat: $3.95). Everyone on the team had his favorite stories to tell about the encounters and over time the stories became more outrageous and unrecognizable. We still tell them to this day, over forty years later, since Prentiss Willson has organized us into regular biennial reunions—partly with his Exclusive Resorts carrot which he generously shares with us plebeians. We were so busy playing basketball and teaching in Birmingham that a team picture was never taken, but see "team" photo on page 18 at May 2005 reunion in Telluride.

Bottom line realization for me: all the basketball teams I have played with over a lifetime were enjoyable and rewarding experiences, but the Miles College Faculty basketball team was more so because there were so few good alternatives for our free time. We were a bunch of northern white hippies living and working within a friendly black circle surrounded by mostly hostile whites in what to us was a foreign country. We were forced together to enjoy each other's company in a way that would not be possible in a more normal setting. In a more normal setting, I would not have purchased an iguana (hard to resist since it was "For Sale, Only $19.95") as a wedding gift for Prentiss and Carolyn. And in my defense, a reasonable person could not have foreseen that the iguana would escape its box during the reception, thereby scaring and scattering the wedding guests. The curious little girl, who had unfortunately opened my gift box, later persuaded her parents to let her keep the iguana (for some incomprehensible reason, the newlyweds did not want it); so as far as I know she and her pet iguana lived happily ever after.

Not all Birmingham whites were hostile. A national newspaper at the time ran a positive story about how much progress Birmingham was making to erase the ugly memories of church children being bombed, and dogs and fire hoses and worse being turned on peaceable black protesters. Denny Reigle, a Harvard Business School graduate who was working with President Lucius Pitts and Vice President Richard Arrington (later mayor of Birmingham) in the Miles College Development Office, arranged for an invitation to an upscale Mountain Brook mansion where our progressive white Birmingham hosts were anxious to introduce us to several eligible white southern belles. Oh, my, what a memorable experience that was when Jeff met his "Mrs. Robinson!"

If not before, I now realize the extent to which the most important events in a person's life are the result of chance, not plan or choice. I did not plan on being a Harvard graduate, much less a Rhodes Scholar. I did not plan to teach at a small black college in Birmingham, Alabama. I did not intend to live most of my life in Colorado. None of these eventualities was even conceivable when I was making plans for my life. Where and when we were born, our parents, our careers, our friends, our mates and almost everything before and after today will owe more to chance than plan. Even seemingly insignificant events like missing a plane or eating the wrong thing for breakfast can turn our lives around. See, for example, "September 11—My Story of Missing the Last Train to the World Trade Center," Jacque Gonzales (10/4/13); also, a 2001 movie *Serendipity,* and similar theme in movie about missing a MTA train (title?).

Therefore I reach a sobering yet challenging conclusion: realizing that our good fortune is not necessarily deserved is the first step to becoming the kind of empathetic and critical thinking citizens necessary to making our democracy work. There is no logical basis for thinking we are inherently better than our fellow citizens or worldwide counterparts. There but for the grace of Chance (God), whatever you believe, go I. So lend a hand to others when you can, and hitch your wagon to something greater than yourself—like the civic standard and the golden rule. For more reflections on Choice & Chance see Chapter 26.

Vietnam & the Draft

A serendipitous conclusion to my draft dilemma offers further material for reflection on Choice v. Chance. I managed to stretch out my legal appeals until a few days after I turned 26, but that was not the end of my life-altering experience with the Vietnam war. The individual choices the Vietnam War forced upon our generation are now part of our DNA, even today more than fifty years later, as reflected in the following e-mail exchange on January 7, 2015. John Austin Sletten was an All-Conference fullback on our 1961 MPHS (Montevideo Public High School) football team; now the author of *Football Season 1960* about our championship season, and also of *Deceit, Chaos* and several other mystery thrillers.

Merle to John Sletten: "Your story about your father is compelling. What a great man he must have been. Regret that I never knew him. What courage it must have taken for a decorated Air Force Colonel in Montevideo to take a stand against the war and set an example of independent thinking for his son. I know that independent thought was not often rewarded among his generation in Montevideo.

Did you know Roger Anderson? An outstanding MPHS athlete perhaps a year or two younger than you. I heard from a classmate that Roger had volunteered and been killed in Vietnam. I always think of Roger when I remember those troubled times and wonder if it would have made a difference to either of us if we could have discussed Vietnam over a beer or two. I found his name on the Vietnam War Memorial in Washington D.C., and wept."

John's reply to Merle: "Yes. Roger Anderson played on our football team my senior year…One day, I think in December 1970, Dad called me and told me he just received word that Roger was killed in Vietnam. That he had just graduated law school at Valparaiso and had the same deferment as me (3A) but volunteered to go into the Army. He went to OTS and received his commission as a Second Lieutenant (the most likely to get killed in action (Infantry) leading raw troops through the jungles). That was Roger—gung ho. I understand that he was shot through the neck by a sniper leading his patrol through the bush.

He is buried near my maternal grandparents

(Austin, right behind the lecture podium where my Dad gave many Memorial Day speeches). Roger was an Ace. I do know he was quite a track star—of course, long distance running. Every time I visit Sunset I stop by his grave, take two steps back and salute. I've been to the Wall many times in D.C., tracing my fingers through his initials. The first time I, too, wept."

Few in our generation do not have classmates or friends who were killed or wounded in that misconceived war. The critical thinking at the root of the civic standard is essential to distinguishing wars worth fighting from those that are not; a continuing obligation for all citizens as our country moves from one war to the next after failing to find better solutions.

Of course, one serendipitous event in our lives can lead to another and that in turn to others in endless waves—even if not to the extent of a butterfly flapping its wings in Brazil last year impacting our lives today.

Summer Jobs

Other personal examples are the unique summer jobs I acquired as a result of my fortuitous admission to Harvard. Summer jobs as tutor to John P. Chase's son and my two Yale Summer High School stints have already been described in *ARR Vol. I*; two others merit comment. I was among the law school students that the Office of Economic Opportunity (OEO) hired in the summers of 1968, 1969 and 1970 to inspect its VISTA summer employment program for disadvantaged youth around the country. I was assigned to inspect programs in New Orleans, Pittsburgh, St. Louis, Dallas, Houston, Austin, Newark and Washington D.C. Like my counterparts, I found no evidence of fraud in these programs; only some that were better than others and a few that were so impressive we could recommend them as possible models for other cities.

In the summer of 1971 before my third year at Harvard Law School, the Boston law firm Sullivan & Worcester hired me as one of the summer interns it might mold into full time S&W associates the following year. I found S&W and its work interesting, but not enough to want to spend my entire life in a glass tower with other lawyers, so at my exit interview that summer I asked if working half-time with S&W would be an option. The S&W partner was shocked and said definitely not. If I could work half time everyone would want to do so, and then what would happen to the traditional quid pro quo money culture of the firm? Big law firms offer a highly compensated future, but in return want your body and soul—full time. Perhaps a fair tradeoff for most, but not the right one for me, or for Goodhead luminaries such as Marian Wright Edelman.

Miles "Team" reunion in Telluride in 2005.
From left to right: Rick Voigt, Jeff Zorn, Merle McClung, Prentiss Willson, Dennis Reigle

THE PROPHET

From Near East to Far West there came someone
With vision nourished on Mount Lebanon.
The Prophet wrought of Kahlil Gibran's hand
Brought insight to dwellers of every land.

You cannot hold love like gold in a chest
Love possesses not, nor will be possessed.
Let love flow free like a stream or river
Uncontrolled by receiver or giver.

In your love let there be spaces to soar
As the sea moves between each soul shore,
Or like the lute with each string all alone
Blending into one harmonious tone.

Make your house a mast, not an anchor
That ties your passion to the shore.
For comfort enters a guest, becomes master,
Lulls you to sleep, and invites disaster.

Though you may house your children as they grow
Their souls dwell in the house of tomorrow
That even in dreams you cannot visit,
So give all your love for their benefit.

Only that which today gives you sorrow
Can provide true delight come tomorrow.
The deeper your being is carved with pain
The more joy thereafter you can contain.

Some give neither of their self nor their wealth
Their fear of need harms more than need itself.
Their thirst will not quench as hard as they try
Thus their full well might as well be dry.

All those who bake bread with indifference
Feed just half their hunger in consequence.
To labor with love should be our work goal
For then we keep pace with earth's secret soul.

Our body's death is not the final rest
But as the eagle must leave the nest
Before it can fly across the sun
The soul flies when the body's work is done.

For to die frees breath from restless tide
That it may expand ethereal wide
At the mountain top you begin to climb,
Being free to dance outside the chains of time.

Life and death are one like river and sea
Merging through the gates of eternity
When the soul is freed of body's life span.
So said the Prophet of Kahlil Gibran.

Marian Wright Edelman: The Ultimate Goodhead

Chapter 19
MARIAN WRIGHT EDELMAN & HCLE

A child mis-educated is a child lost.—John F. Kennedy

Upon graduation from HLS in 1972, I had two offers in hand. One was from the large and prestigious law firm of Morrison Foerster ("Mofo") in San Francisco, and the other was from Marian Wright Edelman at the Harvard Center for Law and Education in Cambridge. The classic choice: private practice or public service. Private practice was lucrative, but the first years were lost in a competitive sweat shop far removed from client contact or significant responsibility. Public service was definitely not lucrative but usually offered client contact and substantial responsibility from day one.

Morrison Foerster

I was flattered that Mofo made me the offer on the strength of Prentiss Willson's recommendation without the usual requirement of exhaustive interviews with the firm. See Prentiss's rationale for doing so in his Foreword to *Volume I of ARR*. Almost everyone emphasized how Harvard contacts and the HLS brand name would open doors closed to others, but the offer sans interview floored me—as I am sure was the intent of Prentiss and Mofo. Actually, the offer was a clever move by Prentiss and Mofo. Immediately Mofo was at the top of my nonexistent list of firms to consider.

What other law firm could compete with that offer plus the opportunity to work in the same firm as one of my best friends in one of the most attractive cities in the U.S.? Actually Mofo's risk was low. My credentials would be a plus for Mofo and if I proved to be a dud, the normal partnership path would weed me out as a matter of course. I did not interview with any law firm; Mofo was the obvious choice if I had wanted a traditional legal career.

Marian Wright Edelman

Marian's offer was also flattering because someone at the Harvard Center for Law and Education (HCLE) told me that Marian only offered staff attorney positions to experienced attorneys and I was the first that Marian had offered a position to right out of law school. Perhaps in my case Marian considered my two years' experience teaching at Miles College in Birmingham, Alabama an acceptable substitute given HCLE's law and education specialty, and my third year paper on second generation desegregation problems demonstrated commitment to a key HCLE cause.

Mofo versus HCLE, money versus responsibility, San Francisco versus Cambridge, the classic tough choices, but not tough for me because a lucrative law firm career had never been my goal. I could hardly believe that I had the opportunity to work for Marian at HCLE and was eager to validate her choice by contributing substantially on the big class action law reform case she assigned me, as described below, but first some background on Marian excerpted from *childrensdefense.org*:

Marian Wright Edelman, founder and president of The Children's Defense Fund (CDF), has been an advocate for disadvantaged Americans for her entire professional career. A graduate of Spelman College and Yale Law School, Ms. Edelman began her career in the mid-60's when, as the first black woman admitted to the Mississippi Bar, she directed the NCAA Legal Defense and Educational Fund office in Jackson, Mississippi. She served as Director of the Center for Law and Education at Harvard University (1970-1972) and has been Director of CDF since 1973. A MacArthur (genius) Fellow, in 2000 Mrs. Edelman received the Presidential Medal of Freedom, the nation's highest civilian award, and the Robert F. Kennedy Lifetime Achievement Award for her writings.

The first education case that Marian assigned me followed a call for help from Lewis Randa whose alternative Life Experience School was about to be closed down by the Town of Sherborn in Massachusetts. After meeting with Lewis, I researched local law and represented the school at a special town hearing to try to reverse the closure. Twenty-three years later during a Boston visit Sharon invited me to tour her daughter's school—a serendipitous occasion as it turned out to be the Life Experience School and I was surprised when Lewis immediately recognized and thanked me for "saving his school." An exaggeration, of course, but I was not about to argue the point.

Greenhouse v. Greco

The first law reform case that Marian assigned me surpassed all my expectations. *Greenhouse v. Greco* was a class action law reform lawsuit brought by black Catholic students and their parents against their Diocese for discriminatory closing of black Catholic schools and their subsequent exclusion from nearby white Catholic schools. My first case thus raised novel issues of Church and State, racial discrimination and more, and within a few months I was seated at plaintiffs' table in a federal district court in Louisiana as a second to an experienced litigator, Benjamin Lamberton, of The Lawyers Committee for Civil Rights (LCCR) based in Washington D.C. As a national back-up center in education law issues for legal services attorneys around the country, a legal services attorney and black plaintiffs had requested HCLE (and LCCR) support in the case. Ben welcomed my participation, and together we filed motions, wrote briefs and initiated and responded to depositions and other discovery. I was learning quickly about class action and law reform lawsuits that raised novel constitutional issues during one of the most troubled times in our nation's history.

The strength of our democracy is illustrated by a Congress prodded by a determined President to enact the Legal Services Corporation that would help translate the noble ideals of our constitutional democracy from theory to practice. Now in our courtrooms the weak can seek justice against the mighty through attorneys funded by the federal government. This newfound possibility of practice matching ideals drew thousands of legal services attorneys (like Jon Asher, HLS '70) into low paying careers in the decades since. For decades before, the lofty ideals of the Bill of Rights existed primarily in theory only as the poor could not afford the legal counsel necessary to clarify and enforce their rights. But now in 1972 the practice was starting to match President Johnson's original 1964 OEO theory since the Nixon administration and a bipartisan Congress passed the Legal Services Corporation Act which provides attorneys for the poor.

Legal Services attorneys across the country started to file many class action and/or "law reform" cases. In *Greenhouse v. Greco* we returned the favor by naming HEW, the Department of Justice and the IRS as additional defendants on the theory that they enabled school lunches and other federal assistance to the Diocese pursuant to written contracts that the Diocese would not discriminate on the basis of race. It is no wonder that almost every year funding for the Legal Services Corporation, especially back up centers like HCLE which in an effort to make the biggest bang for the buck filed many class action and/or law reform suits, was in jeopardy. The attack under the Nixon administration was led by Howard Phillips, and he became a household name within our circles as our nemesis. Phillips and nearly half of Congress pointed to the absurdity of "the government financing litigation against itself," but the rights of the poor were illusory without such funding.

My brother, Mark, the missionary combines his fundamentalist religion, as do many of his colleagues, with right wing politics and can be counted upon in his sermons and life to criticize the separation of church and state guarantees of the Constitution. In their minds, it is outrageous for the courts to deny their right to equal treatment under the law by denying them funding for their private religious schools. And like a broken record their complaints echo throughout legislative halls across the country, and every year they try to find new ways around the separation. Today the cutting edge is via charter schools which try to escape what they see as onerous federal, state and local regulations by claiming to be private, but still arguing for the right to equal dollars for their schools (see Privatizers in Chapter 4 of *ARR Volume I*). The battle rages on across the country because some courts have fallen for this charade (public when pursuing dollars, but private when taxpayers want oversight of their dollars)(like the Greedheads who can have it both ways when their "too big to fail" banks fail—heads they win, tails we lose). Other courts have recognized the charade for what it is and have held that taxpayer dollars cannot be used to support private religious schools. So far I have been unsuccessful in convincing Mark that he and his colleagues are on the wrong side of this issue— because with public dollars come public control. *Green-house v. Greco* is a case in point.

At a preliminary hearing Bishop Charles Pascal Greco's demeanor demonstrated his profound resentment at being called to answer for his actions in a federal court. Ben started to put his first question to Bishop Greco, but the Bishop interrupted in angry defiance, "In the Catholic Church there are two kinds of excommunication—de jure excommunication where the party is given an impartial hearing and permitted to state his case; and ipso facto excommunication—as when anyone sues their Bishop." Total silence in the courtroom. I started to smile since I was not a believer and thus immune to the threat. But then I turned to look at the faces of the black Catholic parents we were representing. They were stunned. Excommunication for them was no small matter; in fact it would be hard to imagine anything worse for serious Catholics like our black clients. I needed to absorb this fact if I was going to represent them properly.

The federal district judge (Nauman S. Scott) immediately called for all parties to meet him in his chambers. We did not have to argue the point. Even the private high-powered defendant's attorney, Camille Gravel, quickly agreed that the Bishop's comment was inappropriate and had exceeded his authority. The judge instructed the defense attorney to so advise his client, and soon an agreement was reached to strike the Bishop's chilling comments from the record. I felt guilty about my personal reaction so removed from my clients' reality and was thankful that it had not been vocal or otherwise observable to the parties.

Massachusetts Bar Exam

An unwelcome surprise was waiting in my mailbox when I returned to Cambridge: I had failed the Massachusetts Bar exam. In my absorption in *Greenhouse v. Greco* and the lofty Constitutional issues raised by the case, I had shortchanged my bar preparation. I had assumed that I would pass the bar exam as a matter of course. HLS also assumed such for its graduates, and therefore offered no special courses designed to prepare for the bar exam (unlike some state law schools where passing the bar was a major part of, some say the only, curriculum). The number of HLS graduates failing the Massachusetts Bar must have been minute, but now I was one of them. This was an embarrassing moment of self-appraisal. I had forgotten that I am not as smart as many think I am. My success in the academic world since grade school had been forged out of hard work. Others could successfully coast, but I did not share their natural brilliance. If I was going to succeed or even survive in the legal world, I would have to work longer and harder than others. I vowed to never forget this fact again. I put in the long and hard hours I had not the first time and consequently passed the Massachusetts Bar exam on my second try.

Harvard Center for Law and Education

How embarrassing that in trying to validate Marian's confidence in hiring me by earning my stripes in *Greenhouse v. Greco*, I had in fact failed her as well by failing the bar exam. Marian was very gracious and offered welcome support by saying something about being stronger in the broken places. Perhaps a cliché but a welcome one at the time and in fact, as is often the case, the cliché proved true. I worked long and hard not only because I loved my work at HCLE, but also because I did not want to fail again. The renewed effort paid off. Soon many organizations asked permission to reprint my publications on different aspects of law and education and I was invited to speak at so many conferences that I had to turn many down.

I realized that I had turned the competence corner when one day a fellow HCLE attorney told me she had overheard senior staff attorney, Roger Rice say, "Eric thinks he knows everything; Merle does." Actually Roger's comment was more a dig at Eric than a compliment for me. Given my earlier failure, I was not inclined to dismiss Roger's comment, but recognized it as simply reflecting an ongoing clash of personalities. Eric Van Loon was a bright, neatly-groomed, cheerful WASP in charge of HCLE publications; Roger a full-bearded, intense radical responsible for Latino (including ESL) issues. Our senior HCLE colleague, Nick Flannery, nailed it when he said, "Roger looks like Jesus." Not the ubiquitous photo-shopped kindly Jesus of traditional Christianity (as depicted in my early drawing reproduced at page 33 of *Volume 1 of ARR*), but the grittier Jewish version.

Debra P. v. Turlington

My overlap with Marian at HCLE was short as she succeeded in attracting sufficient foundation support to found and direct The Children's Defense Fund in Washington D.C. Like Bill Bradley in national politics, Marian was already a respected celebrity in the national civil rights world by the time she was thirty. Decision time for me again. Assuming that Marian would want me, I could join the team she was assembling for CDF in Washington D.C. or remain at HCLE under new leadership. I chose the latter, but often wondered what my life would have been like if I had decided otherwise. The reason I decided to stay at HCLE was I could not imagine a job better than the one I had. I was completely absorbed in my research and publications and starting to develop a national reputation as an expert in many testing and other "classification" issues. This development peaked when my publications and recommendations were cited and implemented in *Debra P. v. Turlington* (the challenge to Florida's competency testing program) and other cases. I summarized my various work on competency testing in the 1979 *Fordham Law Review* article titled "Competency Testing: Legal and Educational Issues."

I contended among other issues that high stakes competency tests required (1) adequate notice, and (2) curricular and instructional validity in order to be fair and legal. The trial court's decision in *Debra P. v. Turlington* in 1979 upheld Florida's testing program, but ruled that students had not been given adequate notice and ordered the state not to use the test as a diploma requirement until the 1982-83 school year. The case was appealed to the U.S. Fifth Circuit Court of Appeals which affirmed the lower court's four-year delay on using the test as a prerequisite for graduation. Also, "We hold that the State may not constitutionally so deprive its students unless it has submitted proof of the curricular validity of the test."

In "Implications of a Landmark Ruling on Florida's Minimum Competency Test" in *Kappan* magazine (Phi Delta Kappa, September 1981), Professor W. James Popham and Elaine Lindheim elaborate: "The U.S. Fifth Circuit Court of Appeals ruled that, when students are required to pass a test to receive their high school diploma, the test must be fair; i.e., it must cover materials that have actually been taught. If a test is not fair, using it to determine who graduates is a violation of the equal protection and due process clauses of the U.S. Constitution. Neither the plaintiffs nor the defendants intend to appeal the case to the U.S. Supreme Court. Thus the circuit court ruling will play an important role in future lawsuits challenging minimum competency tests."

"The trial court and the appeals court agreed that a competency test should have content validity. That is, the test should measure a representative sample of the universe of situations that the test purports to measure. The trial court contended that the Florida competency test had content validity, but the appeals court ruled this contention "clearly erroneous." The appeals court argued that "an important component of content validity is curricular validity." Using expert testimony, the appeals court defined curricular validity as "things that are currently taught." The appeals court ruled that the state had failed to demonstrate that the test actually measures what is taught in Florida schools."

"Merle S. McClung, who has written extensively on the legal implications of competency testing, first introduced the concept of curricular validity. In 1978 McClung defined this type of validity as "a measure of how well test items represent the objectives of the curriculum." Curricular validity, McClung observed, could be established by comparing test objectives with course objectives. In a sense, then, curricular validity depends on the extent to which a test matches the schools' curricular intent."

"The appeals court said that "fundamental fairness requires that the state be put to test on the issue of whether the students were tested on material they were or were not taught." Obviously, the appeals court was using McClung's concept of instructional validity but was calling it curricular validity."

Sidetracked

Then I got sidetracked. The deputy director position at HCLE became available and I thought it a logical next step in my law and education career. I applied for the position, but an African American staff attorney got the job instead and I began to wonder if there would always be a cap on my public service career because I was a white man with elite credentials. I did not disclose my impoverished SES origins out of pride and principle, but thought I had earned the deputy director position because of the impact I was starting to make in challenging discriminatory competency testing programs and helping to design more equitable alternatives. Darrell, on the other hand, was younger than I and had not published or litigated in his brief work as a staff attorney for HCLE. It was clear to me that Darrell, who came from a middle class background, got the position because he was an African American, and that seemed to me unfair.

I began to consider alternatives, including private practice before I had gone so far down "the other road" at the classic fork that it was too late to go back. When the Law and Education Center in New Jersey advertised for a new director, I flew down to Newark for an interview. I was so focused on the preventive law potential of the LECNJ that I did not ask questions about continued funding for LECNJ—which probably was their chief concern. They hired an attorney from D.C. with no education law background, but more "seasoned" than me.

In retrospect, Director Bob Pressman made the right call in choosing Darrell for the deputy director position. Darrell had "people-person" strengths that I did not, and with an engaging personality was better suited than I to deal with the personnel, fund-raising and other workaday responsibilities of the deputy director position. In other words, Darrell was more qualified than I for that position. My strength, however, was in researching, writing and speaking about equal education opportunity in K-12 public schools. The deputy director position would have detracted from work where I had the most impact. But at the time this obvious fact did not occur to me; and I moved forward somewhat bitter and very concerned about "a glass ceiling" on my career as an elitist white in public service unless I disclosed and traded on my low SES background. Wherever I went in the non-profit world, would people always see me as an elitist white male unless I went against my personal values and self-promoted my SES history? Like Coriolanus, the very thought of it was repulsive to me at the time. "I will not do it, lest I surcease to honor mine own truth, and by my body's action teach my mind a most inherent baseness."

Getz & Glass

I knew I must have achieved some national prominence when Jon Getz and Gene Glass published an article criticizing my involvement in the competency testing movement ("Lawyers and Courts as Architects of Educational Policy," *High School Journal,* January 1979). We got into a pissing contest in print, as evident in my response: "Lawyers, Courts and Educational Policy: The Real Case of Minimal Competency Testing—A Response to Getz and Glass," *High School Journal*, March 1979. Part of the problem was my call for curricular validity and instructional validity before any competency testing program with potential injury like diploma denial could be considered fair and legal. I had made the mistake of treading on other people's professional turf—the educators and psychometricians responsible for developing and implementing the APA standards and defensible education policy generally. I proposed the concepts of curricular and instructional validity because the APA standard of content validity did not deal adequately with the problems raised by high stakes competency testing. I assumed that specialists in the psychometric field could and would refine my concepts into more sophisticated and defensible standards. After all, what could be more sensible than requiring some kind of match between curriculum and test, and between instruction and test, before denying diplomas to students who had progressed through school under different standards and assumptions? Also, who would argue that adequate notice of such a momentous change in policy was not important, as well as adequate phase in periods, before denying students diplomas as a result of a competency test? The answer seemed to be those who had their feathers ruffled by an upstart young Harvard attorney who was doing the job they should have done earlier on their watch.

Cambridge

My position as staff attorney at HCLE was also attractive because Marian had given me a small but uniquely workable private office tucked into the alcoves of the top floor of 61 Kirkland Street, a beautiful turn-of-the-century mansion owned by Harvard. I could walk to work from my one bedroom apartment at 11 Everett Street or equal distance to enjoy the perpetual chaos that is Harvard Square. And finally start to take advantage of the many university activities that my studies and busy schedule had prohibited as a student. As an officer of Harvard, I had a pass to all Harvard athletic facilities, including the Blodgett swimming pool in the new athletic complex on the Boston side of the Charles, and dining privileges at the elegant Harvard Faculty Club. I was starting to renovate and furnish the 1,030 square foot two bedroom condominium at 61 Garfield Street in Cambridge that I had purchased in late 1976 for $30,500 with only five percent down—a very conservative decision that I later regretted since the alternative had been a magnificent Victorian triplex on Garden Street only three blocks from Harvard Square. But the sellers were asking $110,000, and even with two tenants to help pay rent in a triplex free of rent control, I hesitated at what at the time seemed an enormous sum. My little condo doubled in value within three years, but so too the triplex, and today is certainly worth over $2 million in Harvard's pricy housing market. Would've, could've, should've.

After Marian left to direct the Children's Defense Fund in D.C., I lost my fine alcove office when HCLE, under the new leadership of Nick Flannery, moved to the architecturally significant but ugly, almost windowless Larsen Hall on Appian Way. Fortunately this stay was short lived when Nick and senior attorney Bob Pressman finalized better space in Gutman Library just down the street. Gutman was a modern building with boring small offices, but close proximity to Harvard Square meant I could catch lunch in the square while enjoying the street musicians and other aspects of the 24/7 chaos in Harvard Square.

These were happy days for me. I could still walk to work from my renovated condo at 61 Garfield Street. My publications on the legal implications of competency testing programs were attracting nationwide attention as many states which were considering or already moving forward with competency testing programs of their own contacted me. I was getting invitations to speak at so many state and national education conventions that I had to turn many down. Bob Pressman, the new director of HCLE who labored tirelessly and thanklessly for years representing plaintiffs in *Morgan v. Hennigan*, the Boston school desegregation case (1972-1985), encouraged me to accept these invitations as an experiment in the kind of preventive law practice I was advocating.

Fortunately, Gutman Library also housed the offices of Mark Shedd, soon to be appointed Connecticut Commissioner of Education. Several times I had accepted Mark's invitation to join his Harvard Ed School classes to talk about competency testing and other law and education issues and we became friends. When

Mark moved to Hartford as the new Chief State School Officer for the State of Connecticut, he offered me $100 a day to assist him and his Board of Directors at the Connecticut State Department of Education (CSDE). For a guy who once worked for a milkman for $1 a day, the pay was almost unbelievable. Bob Pressman accepted my proposition for half-time work at HCLE so I could devote the other half to CSDE. Bob was somewhat skeptical of my contention that I could be more effective doing preventive law on the inside than litigating from the outside, but agreed to give me a chance to prove my point.

Until I accepted the half-time consulting position at the CSDE, I had no need for a car. At the time (before I purchased the condo at 61 Garfield Street) I was living in a one bedroom apartment, West Gate #1, at 11 Everett Street at the north end of HLS, my first residence since leaving the comforts of Harvard Yard, but a big step up in being my first rented residence. The apartment on the first floor of a turn of the century stucco building suffering from deferred maintenance was somewhat dark but served my purposes as a single guy: an easy walk into Harvard Square and my office at the Kirkland Street mansion and later at Gutman Library, and a rent-controlled bargain at only $205 a month. I was feeling quite wealthy with my first full time salary of $12,000 a year as a staff attorney at HCLE. Years earlier in Montevideo Ollie Rekow had told me that he thought that a $10,000 annual salary was a reasonable aspiration and enough for any young professional. Passing time with the young man who was installing my first telephone in my apartment at 11 Everett Street, I asked how much he made as a Bell Telephone employee. I was shocked when he said $18,000 a year—but he quickly explained that he had to attend a six week training program in order to qualify for that salary. I was too shocked to tell him that I had spent four years at Harvard College, two years at Oxford University and three years at Harvard Law School to qualify for my $12,000 annual salary. Sobering, yes, but I had no debt, and $12,000 was more than enough to cover my modest expenses.

My apartment was just across Everett Street from a new HLS parking structure. One of many perks as a Harvard employee and officer was a low-cost parking sticker for this structure. Somewhat giddy now that I was rich with a $100 a day contract with CSDE, I answered an ad placed in the *Boston Globe* by a young California woman who had recently moved to Boston. She was selling her two-tone metallic green 1972 low-mileage Mustang Grande 8 cylinder muscle car for substantially below book value because her Boston apartment did not have parking. I told her I would buy her Mustang if it passed a mechanic's inspection, and it did ("like new" the report glowed, and so did I). Months later shortly after I started to date a beautiful woman who was working full time at CSDE, I couldn't wait to show off my fancy car. Sharon did not even notice. I could have been driving an old Rambler, and she wouldn't have noticed—or cared. Unfortunately, others noticed. Over the next four months Cambridge teenagers, seduced by my hot Mustang, stole it three times from the HLS parking garage. It seemed like they had possession of my car more than I did. The last time in ripping out the ignition they caused considerable damage to the leather dashboard and the Mustang was no longer as attractive to me as to the kids who seemed to have it more than me anyway. I sold the Mustang for about what I had paid for it and purchased a used 6 cylinder Plymouth Scamp. I was not surprised when Sharon did not notice my change in "wheels" when I next picked her up at her Hartford house for dinner and a movie.

Preventive Law

Earlier I had explained to Bob Pressman that the Connecticut SDE work was an opportunity to experiment with the preventive law specialty I conceived after David Gordon at the California State Department of Education invited me to help California SDE design its competency testing program according to the ideas advanced in my publications. With Dave's steadfast help, we and his colleagues developed a model competency testing program at California SDE which was approved by its board of directors (and I like to believe prevented California from undergoing the same kind of expensive and time-consuming litigation like *Debra P. v. Turlington* which undermined Florida's questionable program). I was amazed that Dave and I and his California SDE colleagues had accomplished at almost no expense to California taxpayers what was taking years to litigate in Florida. The state legislators and state departments of education and their boards were not bad guys, just overworked and understaffed trying to do their best in a difficult political situation. State after state was enacting competency testing programs in the wake of the alarmist "A Nation at Risk" report of President Reagan's Commission on Public Education (1983). That report incorrectly stated that U.S. public education was failing and assumed the wrong purpose of education by stating that enhanced accountability for public schools was necessary for the country to compete in the global economy. Today Diane Ravitch is courageously leading the overdue counterattack on these myths that have waylaid intelligent education reform for decades (see Chapter 4 of *Vol I of ARR*).

I concluded that other states were similarly handicapped and disposed, and published an article in the January 1981 *Journal of Law & Education*: "Preventive Law and Public Education: A Proposal." An early draft of the article had come to the attention of

Allan Odden at the Education Commission of the States (ECS) located in Denver, Colorado. Allan was a brilliant young "quant" busy creating a little fiefdom within ECS. Allan had a proposal for me when we later overlapped on a panel in Boston discussing competency testing. Why not join him at ECS to do the preventive law work I had advocated in the article? Allan was sure that we could tap funds at various foundations where he had good contacts to create a preventive law and education center at ECS. I would be the director of a center designed around the preventive law ideas I was advocating. This was very appealing because at the time I was nursing wounds inflicted by being rejected for the deputy director position at HCLE.

After Allan Odden and I in late 1978 submitted a proposal for a preventive law and education center at ECS, we followed up with oral presentations to the two foundations that expressed interest: The Carnegie Corporation in New York City and the Spencer Foundation in Chicago. Both agreed to an initial two year grant to cover the cost of my salary as director, a staff attorney, an administrative assistant/secretary, and related costs associated with setting up the new preventive Law & Education Center (LEC) at ECS. The contract signed by the foundations, ECS and me specified that LEC would be a preventive law center to carry out the work I had already started on competency testing programs with the California State Department of Education and various other states. So within a few months, with Allan's help, I had a tailor-made job to direct my own preventive law center.

Leaving Harvard & Cambridge

I had mixed feelings about leaving the Harvard environment I had come to love after so many years living in Cambridge. I was starting to enjoy the benefits of Harvard's diverse cultural offerings. My Oxford friend, Keith Stevenson, and his wife, Catherine, now lived in the North End, and for years we looked forward to the annual undergraduate Gilbert and Sullivan productions, as well as the diverse offerings of the Loeb Theater. A nice fringe benefit of being an officer of Harvard University was that I could impress dates and treat my friends to an occasional meal at the Harvard Faculty Club. On the athletic front I scored great seats for another Montevideo HLS graduate, Frank Gniffke (RIP, Frank), and me to witness Harvard's historic 29-29 "win" over Yale's football team in 1968. For personal workouts, I could swim in the new Blodgett pool anytime, and regularly joined a mixed group of about twenty town and gown tennis players who informally gathered across the street to play almost every evening at the Harvard Business School tennis courts. No need to schedule a match; just show up and ask one of the group to hit or play a set: "Tennis, anyone?" Members included John Greer, Jan Stewart, Mac Runyan, Carol "Caley" Roth, Joe Kelly, Mark Flannery and Jim Sheldon. Another frequent participant was Mike McCaskey, an HBS student who later inherited his family's responsibilities as owners of the Chicago Bears. The informal group also arranged with the Harvard Business School to reserve the courts for occasional tournaments, and highlights for me included a first place finish in mixed doubles with Jan and later with Vicky (photo p. 42), and another in singles in a narrow 7-6, 6-4 win against Mac Runyan.

While I enjoyed the competition, I discovered that I derived even more pleasure just from hitting balls–not trying to win anything, but just keeping the ball in play for as long as possible with a partner on the other side of the net; in other words, collaborative rather than competitive tennis. Fortunately Barbara Ruchames felt the same way, and we spent hours on the Harvard Business School

Author & Vicky: First Place, HBS Mixed Doubles

courts just hitting. Sometimes I fantasized about hitting with Barbara in a romantic way but she never seemed interested, even though at one point Barbara arranged for her elegant mother to draw my portrait and we enjoyed a pleasant talk while she did so. My guess is that Barbara and her mother were looking for a nice Harvard Jewish boy to complete the picture. In any case, when I left Cambridge Barbara gave me a soap-on-a-rope as a departing gift; I would have preferred a hug. The tennis group threw a big going away party and presented me with a framed fake *Boston Globe* front page headline: "McClung heads West, Cambridge mourns loss."

With Sharon's help, I sold my condominium at 61 Garfield Street for almost double what I had paid three years earlier, packed my bags into my boring but reliable 1972 Plymouth Scamp and headed west to Denver. In the rush to pursue my dream job, I forgot about the gypsy's curse: "May your dreams come true."

ALFERD

Fighting a snowstorm in seventy-four
Alferd Packer, a mountain prospector,
Proclaimed to his five prospecting friends:
"Our grub is gone, and we face our ends
Unless we soon take drastic action
That may not give all satisfaction."
"I'm sorry, but there's nothing else to be done,"
Sighed Colorado's most famous native son,
As he proceeded to eat them—one by one.

Al thought he had consumed the evidence
But his presence led to an inference
That all on the jury would understand:
How could he survive without some helping hand
And the endurance of five other men?
Men they knew they would never see again.

At his trial Al spoke with eloquence
Claiming circumstance proved his innocence.
"You must believe me, it's really no fun
To chew your friends into oblivion."
"They weren't my culinary preference
But starving is no time for abstinence."
"I actually prefer roast venison,
But I had to flesh out my skeleton."
"And while I do not mean to give offense,
Consider their contributory negligence.
It's possible the five wouldn't have been harmed

Had they the good taste to be fully armed."

The judge and jury considered what Al said,
Then sentenced him to hang by the neck until dead.
"On Friday you'll dance from the hangman's tree,
A small price to pay for your gluttony
And assault aggravated by irony:
"There were only five Democrats in this county"
The judge cried, "The best I recall,
And you, Alferd Packer, you ate them all."

More than foot in his mouth, Alferd confessed
Telling everyone which friend he liked best.
They say Al went to his eternal rest
Being denied his final meal request.
While it's not good to eat friends limb by limb
You still have to hand it to him.
It's no small feat, though somewhat grim,
To eat all without salt or cinnamon.

The moral of this story's plain to see
Even if you feel the proclivity
To put your friends into a recipe,
Some courts consider it a felony.

Author & ECS Education Panel

Chapter 20
EDUCATION COMMISSION OF THE STATES

May your dreams come true.—Ancient Gypsy Curse

The month before arriving in Denver, I had flown out to ECS to meet my new colleagues and arrange for housing. Perhaps thinking of the triplex near Harvard Square that I should have purchased years earlier when instead I played it conservatively by buying a $30,500 two bedroom condo, I told my realtor, Bob Jamison, that I wanted a triplex near ECS offices located at 1860 Lincoln Street in Denver. As a single guy I would only need one unit, but could leverage my investment by renting out the other two units. Initially discouraged by expensive run-down downtown triplexes near ECS, Bob Jamison found "a needle in a haystack" triplex in the single family neighborhood of upscale Montclair about eight miles east of ECS.

838 Leyden

It was a no-brainer—love at first sight. The 4,800 square foot 1894 Victorian 3-unit conversion at 838 Leyden Street in the Montclair subdivision of Denver had recently been renovated, each unit distinctive and attractive in its own way. I immediately offered the $155,000 asking price and caught the next plane back to Cambridge wondering which unit I should occupy. It was a tough choice. The developer/sellers had created a new third floor "A-frame" open concept unit that was spectacular with six skylights across the vaulted ceiling, contemporary maple-surround fireplace and new kitchen separating the front living area from the bedroom and bath at the back. Perhaps the best unit was on the second floor with two bedrooms, renovated kitchen and bathrooms and a working fireplace with carved period mantle. I chose the main floor two bedroom unit with refinished oak hardwood floors and fireplace, even though the kitchen and bathroom had not been updated, because of its easy in-out access. I priced the rental units a little below market value and never had a vacancy or tenant problem in the nine years I lived in the house. It was the perfect arrangement for me with built-in help and security when I was away on business trips.

838 Leyden

ECS Law & Education Center

In short order I hired Chris Char as my very competent administrative assistant/secretary, and Pat Lines, a former HCLE staff attorney. Pat might have appeared a strange selection for me since she made no secret about her conservative free choice bias, but I figured that her obvious brilliance more than made up for her politics, especially since she also was focused on civil rights for minorities and was very personable in dealing with others. I encouraged Pat to develop her own preventive law specialty and continued with my work on improved competency testing programs with David Gordon at the California Department of Education. My pet project was creating *Footnotes*, the new ECS LEC monthly news bulletin for ECS membership. Each consecutively numbered footnote had an update on some issue related to preventive law and I found it a fun distraction from my other LEC responsibilities. Each day when I was not traveling, I would skip lunch and play pick-up basketball at the YMCA about three blocks south of ECS offices.

All went well until it didn't. I should have been more tuned in to national politics and the role they would inevitably play at ECS. A year after I joined ECS in 1979, Ronald Reagan was elected President of the United States. Reagan's election transformed ECS when a conservative Board of Directors was appointed to oversee ECS and selected a very conservative new Executive Director of ECS. Robert Andringa was the polar opposite of Warren Hill, the pleasant elderly Goodhead who preceded him. Andringa struck me as a young type-A Hotspur after he introduced himself to the one hundred plus employees gathered to see their new executive director with the statement that he felt blessed by God to be chosen to lead ECS at such an opportune time in U.S. history. More of same before he asked us to bow our heads in prayer to our Lord and Savior Jesus Christ to lead us through the challenging months ahead. I was stunned. ECS staff was diverse, representing many religions, including at least twenty percent Jewish, and the blatantly Christian prayer clashed with ECS non-sectarian policy.

The change in leadership soon impacted me directly when Allan Odden asked me to prepare a package of materials explaining my ECS-LEC work for Andringa to review. Allan explained that one of the new directors on the ECS Board was Florida State Education Secretary Ralph Turlington who complained that I was responsible for his state competency testing program being overturned by the courts. Turlington wanted to know why I had found a home at ECS. I prepared the package with some confidence that it should appeal to most conservatives because it was designed to prevent litigation by assisting states to protect the civil rights of students in developing their competency testing programs. I heard nothing further for several weeks until Allan informed me that I would be offered the new general counsel position at ECS with a significant increase in salary and responsibilities. Allan was pleased as one of his own would now be inside the executive power circle at ECS and as such another feather in his expanding cap. I was stunned. The general counsel position would undoubtedly involve me in representing state interests in their never-ending battles with the federal government. I had been party to lawsuits against federal agencies as in *Greenhouse v. Greco* where we named HEW and the Justice Department as defendants for failing to enforce their non-discrimination agreements, but this change would make me part of the problem I had been fighting my entire career since HCLE. I immediately told Allan that I could not accept the general counsel position since my ECS-LEC contracts with the Carnegie Corporation and Spencer Foundation specified preventive law work with the states on competency testing programs.

Allan said he would discuss the problem with the powers that be. A few days later he informed me that there was no problem since he had contacted our program officers at both the Carnegie Corporation and the Spencer Foundation and they had agreed their funding could be used for the new general counsel position for me. I objected that Allan had done so without consulting me and said that the change would also violate the contract ECS had with me since I had left opportunities in Cambridge to pursue our specific contract agreement regarding preventive law for the states. I also told Allan that I thought his frequently stated view that the new ECS reorganization essentially abrogated all previous commitments, both formal and informal, was not defensible either legally or morally. Allan seemed surprised that I would not jump at the chance to improve my salary and status within ECS and I don't think he ever understood my contrary thinking. The ECS general counsel offer was a clever response to "the Turlington problem" I had created because redirecting my energies would also reinforce ECS' more important battles with the feds on behalf of state rights. "States' Rights" continues as the classic mantra of the right wing since the beginning of our republic, fighting the power of the federal government to intervene in state affairs. This is NOT what I had signed up for and I told Allan that if I wanted to be general counsel for a big corporation, I would do so in the private sector with a more competitive salary. The handwriting was on the wall. I needed a new job fast since I now had a mortgage to pay.

PICK-UP GAMES

At noon each day for exercise and sport
We skip lunch and head for the hardwood court.
Round up ten guys for pick-up basketball
No matter if short or tall, big or small
You are in if you love the game at all.

A blocked shot and fast break across the gym
Leading to a slam dunk right through the rim.
Stealing the ball and behind the back pass
Leap high for a reverse layup off glass.

Though we are in our thirties and forties
We dream new dreams and relive past glories
Greatly enhanced by fading memories.
The game so concentrates our energies
We soon forget our workaday worries.

The score is kept and fouls called by honor
So heads as well as bodies can get sore
Moving pick, travel, carrying the ball
Double dribble, charge, what a lousy call.
We laugh and yell and even scream and cuss
As if the outcome should matter to us.

And in the locker room after the game
The losing team will frequently complain
So we say don't feel bad since we agree
They played to the best of their ability
And if pressed we would probably admit
We now talk a better game than play it.

Ed Pendleton: Self-Made and Fun

Chapter 21
ED PENDLETON & PENDLETON LAND & EXPLORATION

The aim of education is the knowledge not of fact, but of values.
—Dean William R. Inge

(NOTE: Before interviewing Ed Pendleton for this chapter more than twenty years after I had been general counsel for Pendleton Land and Exploration, Inc. (PLE), I informed Ed that I would be writing about him both positive and negative as I now perceived our history together, and would not sugarcoat the narrative just because he was my friend. As expected, Ed said he had assumed that would be the case and signed a lawyer-client waiver to that effect.)

I had limited my job opportunities by not taking the bar exam when I arrived at ECS from Massachusetts. I would have to take and pass the Colorado Bar before a private Colorado law firm would hire me. Given my prior experience with the Massachusetts Bar, I knew I would have to undertake several weeks of intensive study to prepare for the Colorado Bar. Before accepting the ECS position, I had looked at the Colorado law governing reciprocity and thought my years of legal experience qualified me for Colorado reciprocity, but was denied it because of an interpretation that left me about four months shy of the required legal experience. To clarify my status, I made an appointment with an official at the Colorado State Bar office, and was told that there was an exception to the bar requirement for members of other state bars who represented only one client. So my work at ECS met Colorado requirements and so too would any general counsel position in private practice. In any case, I had figured that after a few years at ECS I would return to Massachusetts where I was already a member of the bar.

Washington Park Tennis Club

Now, however, return to the Boston area would be very difficult because I loved the Colorado climate, and my splendid Victorian house at 838 Leyden Street (photo p. 48) which I was beginning to fill with collectible books and valuable antiques. Also, I had made many new friends at ECS and at the Washington Park tennis courts. A diverse SES group of tennis enthusiasts, who played regularly in the beautiful setting of small ponds and big trees on the south side of the park formed the Washington Park Tennis Club. Membership was open to anyone who could pay the modest annual membership fee (about $30), and similar amounts to compete in the various tournaments the club organized on a monthly basis during tennis weather with the cooperation of Denver Parks and Recreation, and at the rented indoor Meadowcreek facility during winter months. The tennis was competitive at all USTA levels 3.0 through 5.5, but for most of us the related social life was more important. In fact, it was at Washington Park that I met Pam—who joined me in 4.5 mixed doubles and eventually shared my Victorian house with me. Members of the Washington Park Tennis Club included all socio-economic groups. What mattered to this diverse group was not SES, but how good your serve and backhand were.

WPTC members included Jean & Paul Thompson, Steve Wilkens & Judy Gerber, Howard & Karen Ellenstein, Mike &

Nancy Hallowell, Lee & Shirley Carlson, Len & Carrie Hierath, Steve St. Claire, Joannie Seay, Carrol Miller, Earl Christian, Dede Rodriguez, Milt Kahn, Patty McMickle, Mary Lou Clark, Bob Graham, Jan Cole, Tom Moss, Carole Loveseth, Art Haag, Chris Sargent, Kristen Padberg, Jim Collins, Arlene Taylor, Gary Foster, Karen Weaver, Sue Smith, Bill Sutherland, Judy Gilbert, Steve Behm, Connie Sutter and Kathy Corbett.

And of course Jenny Choker. Jen, a cute petite blonde, almost always lost close matches, even when leading 5-4 in the final set. I used to tease her about her "choking." She pretended to be upset with my teasing, but we all knew she loved the attention.

Merle, "So Choker, I see you choked away another match."

Jen, "Oh Merle! Stop it. You know my first name is not Choker."

Merle, "Choker's your middle name?"

Jen, "It's not my name at all; it's just what I do. It's so frustrating."

Merle, "You're too nice. You have to develop a killer instinct if you want to win. Take no prisoners."

Jen, "You think I'm not competitive enough?"

Merle, "You tell me."

Ed Pendleton

One day after my confrontation with Allan Odden, I found myself complaining to one of my basketball friends at the YMCA about my predicament. Ed Pendleton was also a regular at our lunchtime YMCA pickup games, and we often picked each other to play on the same team because we got along so well. I liked Ed because he was a feisty point guard always cracking jokes, including about how I should shoot less and set more picks for him. I did not know that Ed was the president of a privately held oil company, but now he knew what I did and told me what he did. I was surprised, but it would not have mattered if he had been homeless or a low level landman at an oil company since SES does not matter on the basketball court. Once again basketball was about to open doors for me. Without asking for a resume or further information about my background, Ed on the spot offered me the general counsel position at his corporation, Pendleton Land and Exploration, Inc. (PLE).

Merle, "Are you serious?"

Ed, "Absolutely."

Merle, "I need some time to think about it. Do you have any materials about your company that you can share with me?"

Ed, "More than you'd care to read, but they will be delivered to your office this afternoon. Take your time. I know it's a big decision. Just let me know when you have decided—and in the future, focus on rebounding and passing me the ball more often."

The materials arrived as promised, and I reviewed them and my options. I called Allan Talesnick, a friend who I had met years earlier when he and his lovely wife, Jane Michaels, had been proctor/advisors in Pennypacker Hall at Harvard College. Allan and Jane now lived only a few blocks away from me in an elegant Mediterranean style house on Sixth Avenue in upscale Hilltop. Both worked for big prestigious law firms, Allan for Holmes, Roberts and Owen; Jane for Holland & Hart. I had been just as fond of Jane as Allan ever since Jane years ago had fixed me up with Karen, a tall drop-dead gorgeous Boston University law student. I immediately concluded that Karen's outer beauty matched an inner one because when she opened the door to her modest Cambridge apartment on our first date, I observed the loving maternal relationship shown to her African-American little brother in wrapping up his homework assignment. Karen was so much the woman of my dreams that I was fumbling and nervous around her rather than projecting the cool confidence that most women want to see in their man. As a result, our relationship never had a chance to develop. Jane and Allan would divorce several years later and I tried to continue as friends with both, but that experience impressed upon me how difficult that can be. Anyway, I asked Allan, a securities specialist with energy experience, what he thought about the oil and gas industry. His one word response, "Gritty."

Reviewing Ed's materials, and contemplating the pros and cons over a long weekend, I accepted Ed's offer the following Monday. My reasoning in the end was simple. I could continue looking for a job with a better fit and if it didn't work out, I could start over with no downside disadvantage. One plus was that finally I would be making some real money in private practice rather than the artificially depressed salary of public service law.

Walking into PLE's impressive offices in a sleek black glass modern building (8085 South Chester Street) near the Denver Technological Center (DTC) my first day on the job, Ed greeted me in the reception area. He introduced me to his brother, Bill, who was one of two PLE vice presidents, saying that Bill would work out the details of my employment contract. Ed and I had not discussed the terms of my PLE employment as we just assumed that such would be worked out with no problems. Bill motioned me to sit across from his big executive desk in a spacious corner office. I sat, he told a few jokes, farted, laughed, farted again and told me to review the employment contract that had been prepared for me. I did so in the tainted air thinking that Allan should have warned me about the oil industry being "malodorous" as well as "gritty," and almost gagged when I came to the contract's annual salary provision: $42,000.

Merle, "Only $42,000? Have you looked at my resume?"

Bill, "We thought you'd be pleased. You state in your application that you have been making $35,000 at ECS. $42,000 is almost a fifteen percent raise."

I briefly considered negotiating for a higher salary, but decided that I could always do so after I had worked at PLE long enough to prove my value. I shrugged, signed the contract, Bill farted, laughed and introduced me to some other top level employees at PLE: Bev Pendleton, Ed's wife; Al Pendleton, Ed's eldest son; Louis Pendleton, Ed's other son; and Jack Deeter, Ed's brother-in-law and the second vice president. Welcome to the world of family owned and operated companies. Then introductions to a second level of employees including several who were identified as friends of Al and Louis. I could not resist commenting about the disproportionate number of absolutely gorgeous secretaries. "They all cost the same, might as well hire the pretty ones," Ed winked. This is going to be some kind of trip, I thought, and I can always get off at the next stop.

Then the unexpected: I really enjoyed the work—in large part because Ed and I continued the easy going friendship started at the YMCA. Ed was a fun boss and even during difficult times at the company retained his positive attitude and sense of humor. It was almost as if I were family too, except for one minor detail I was reminded of each time I deposited my paycheck. About 11:30 most mornings, Ed would stop by my office to invite me to join him to continue our regular pickup games at the YMCA. The downtown YMCA was a ten minute drive northwest on I-25 and then north on Lincoln Street for the remaining fifteen minutes and ten miles. We would play pickup games for about 90 minutes, shower and then retrace our drive back to the PLE offices. Total time out of office each time was about 2 ½ hours. We rode in style as Ed liked "well precisioned machines," such as his new Silver Shadow Rolls Royce and the "sorry Ferrari" that was in the repair shop more often than on the road. The one hour drive time was not wasted. Ed and I would talk business. Then to help make up for our noontime truancy, we would work for another hour or two after others exited at 5 pm.

Pickup Basketball Games

In the late 80's Ed Pendleton and I switched from the YMCA to the Colorado Athletic Club at Inverness, much closer to our office, for our pickup basketball games. As with pickup games across America at noon on any given weekday, businessmen of all ages trade their suits for basketball shorts - first team to score 10 points wins and gets to play the next team. "Losers" must sit to wait their turn to play again, so play can get intense to hold on to the court.

One highlight of our Inverness play was the day (2/11/93) when our pickup team twice beat a team of Denver Broncos, including the fiercely competitive John Elway, Tim Lukas and twin brother linemen Dave and Doug Widell. Elway could hardly believe that he and his professional athletes had lost to a bunch of amateurs, but hoops was our primary sport and our team included slender Ted Henderson who could drive hard to the basket or stop on a dime for jump shots (similar to Stephen Curry of the Golden State Warriors); heavyset John Baudelier (RIP Johnny, we hardly knew you) who could shoot the lights out from long range; and Randy Brooks, a late blooming natural with superb skills who would have been a welcome addition to almost any college team. To our delight, the usually cool Elway who so ably represented the Broncos with the Denver media for years, displayed a less engaging persona that day.

Another regular for Inverness pickup hoops was Steve Shraiberg, president and owner of Esprit Homes, who often brought along his general counsel, Al Blum, for support at the other guard position. A few years ago Steve sold part of his assisted-living real estate holdings to Shaquille O'Neill for a reported $85 million, and has contributed substantially to Jewish Goodhead organizations, so he is one of those rare Goodhead one-percenters. Steve occasionally would invite Pam and me for pick-up games at the basketball court inside one corner of his house in Greenwood Village. On one occasion Steve assigned one of the best players to team up with Pam for mixed doubles competition. Pam still tears up every time she describes Joe Clemons' (?) inspirational rendition of the National Anthem to mark the start of the competition. Since Pam is also a good athlete, she and her partner won the Third Annual Shraiberg Invitational and earned their place among the engraved names of past winners on the plaque next to the gymnasium door. I also remember the occasion, but not so fondly since Steve paired me with a woman who could hardly walk, much less shoot. So Steve, if you ever read this, you owe me—big time.

Occasionally some Denver Nuggets like Alex English, Fat Lever and Walter Davis would join our Inverness pickup games, thereby intensifying already rather intense play as everyone would try (unsuccessfully) to impress the pros with their best moves. Whether joined by pros or not, our pickup games were a great way to vent, joke, laugh, sweat and stay somewhat in shape.

Pendleton Variety

The mid-day break for pickup games left us re-energized for work upon return, and I think I got to know Ed as well as any employee could. As I reviewed oil and gas operating, seismic, employment, horse, ranch and sundry other agreements needing Ed's signature, I also got to know PLE business in detail. Unlike most small closely-held and other for-profit corporations that develop a niche and specialty in the market that they can exploit, Ed entered into a wide range of business agreements. Of course, true to its corporate name, most of Pendleton Land and Exploration's agreements involved either oil exploration or real estate acquisition. Rather than re-investment into PLE, most of the profits from PLE's oil and gas ventures were funneled into various private real estate investments, including the magnificent showpiece 2586 acre Shamrock Ranch in the Black Forest about twenty miles east of the Air Force Academy. Ed also owned the adjacent Bar X ranch, and a tony horse farm in Kentucky where he and his family showed three and five-gaited saddle bred horses. Ed hired his friend Chuck Doughdrill to pilot his Cessna for company business and family recreation.

One day I requested the Cessna because Ed had authorized me to settle an embarrassing lawsuit in Kansas where an angry landowner had sued PLE for fraud over a dispute about implementation of an oil and gas lease agreement. His lawyer's office was in a remote Kansas town far from the nearest viable airport in Wichita. Chuck told me that the plane was already taken as Bev had a reservation with her favorite hair dresser in Santa Barbara. So a one day trip turned into a three day trip as I arranged for the round trip commercial flight and rental car alternative.

This is not a dig on Bev. Bev is a devout Christian, and would have deferred to me had she known about the schedule conflict. She was also a hard worker; managing a Christian bookstore in addition to the various work she did for PLE. The luxurious life Bev led was encouraged by Ed who always referred to her as "my bride," she to him as "Eddie," and the two seemed as close as they had been since the day they married in Wichita about forty years earlier. After meeting with Ed the other day (6/24/14), Bev encouraged me to look up my ancestors on *ancestry.com*. I explained that there was no point since my so-called father was a deadbeat drunk adopted at birth by exploitive step-parents. "Not like you with your tony pedigree," I joked. "My father was a horse thief," Bev immediately responded. More laughs.

At the end of the year when I was sure that I had proven my value to PLE, I proposed to Ed that instead of a raise, I wanted, at the same $42,000 annual salary, a three day work week. I explained that I had enjoyed working with him at PLE more than expected, but realized that with all the family mouths to feed with overrides, I would never make any serious money at PLE. I told Ed that I valued my time more than his money, and needed more time to pursue my varied interests, including income property investments in Denver where I had a chance to earn multiples rather than percentages on my investments—just like he did with his various business ventures. I also said if there was an important meeting or emergency on one of my free days, I would drop everything to be there for him. Ed thought about my proposal for a minute or two, probably realized that I could make a multiple of what he was paying me if I wanted to work in a big law firm downtown (which I didn't), reached out to shake my hand, and said "deal." It was a win/win deal since I secured an unusual degree of freedom in a job I liked, and Ed secured a valuable employee who otherwise would have left for greener pastures. It was the main reason I stayed for ten years (1982-1992).

Denver Nuggets for Sale

Back at PLE Ed assigned me a variety of tasks. When the eleven individual owners of the Denver Nuggets tired of continued cash calls, they put the Nuggets up for sale for ten million dollars. Ed was interested and asked me to evaluate the potential investment. As a former hoopster and lifelong basketball fan, I loved the assignment. First I met with Carl Scheer, the Nugget's General Manager, who, after vetting Ed's business and apparent capability, agreed to meet with me in the concrete dome called McNichols Arena where the Nuggets played home games. In his spacious McNichols' office, Scheer opened spread sheets on a nearby table (no computers in 1984!), and I quickly discerned what troubled the Nuggets disparate ownership. The Nuggets finances were upside down. So too would be that of any prospective buyer who paid ten million dollars cash for the team (which by the way Ed did not have, but probably would have finessed by offering various PLE oil interests to the eleven owners and other wheeling and dealing). Not only were the Nuggets losing money, but the prospects were for them to lose even more because Alex English's contract was up the following season, and English certainly deserved a substantial increase in salary or else the Nuggets' best player would be playing for a team which could afford him. I immediately expressed my concern to Scheer who said that in the short term the Nuggets were locked into losses. But he said, the new owner probably would be wealthy enough to absorb the losses until revenues improved and the various tax advantages provided by the losses would absorb much of the pain. I tried to keep a straight face, but my limited hopes were dashed. Ed not only did not have $10 million cash to invest in the Denver Nuggets (less than the owners he wanted to replace), but he had plenty of tax losses with his current oil and gas operations.

Merle, "What are the prospects for increased revenues?"

Carl, "Not very good, I'm afraid."

Merle, "What about promotions to fill more seats at McNichols?"

Carl, "We have tried everything we can think of, and the numbers just do not work."

Merle, "Any long term prospect for turn around?"

Carl, "The best hope would be for a big NBA contract with a cable network that would televise many more games than the major networks can now manage."

Merle, "And the prospects for a big cable deal?"

Carl, "That question I am not qualified to answer, except to say current ownership has explored the possibility for years, and as you know have decided to sell."

Merle, "Who would be able to answer my question in detail?"

Carl, "The best man to do so would be Bill Daniels. As you can imagine, he's a very busy man, but I can try to pave the way for you."

Merle, "I'd appreciate that very much. I don't see how I can recommend that Mr. Pendleton purchase the Nuggets unless there is some realistic hope for a turnaround."

Bill Daniels greeted me warmly in his elegantly understated Cherry Creek offices. I had not been as nervous since interviewing for a Rhodes Scholarship many years before, but one of the most impressive individuals in Denver's history immediately put me at ease and soon we were talking about the prospects for cable TV and consequently for the Nuggets. Actually, he did most of the talking, and I most of the listening. Bottom line: Daniels was sure that the cable industry would dramatically change the finances of everyone within it; and the NBA and NFL would be among the first beneficiaries with big contracts with cable companies. He went into fascinating detail to support his conclusion, but I hardly heard because I had such a big question to ask.

Merle, "How long do you think this turnaround will take?"

Daniels, "That's the million dollar question. I'm one of the best positioned to predict, but it's hard because so many variables are involved."

Merle, "A year or two?"

Daniels, "Oh no, certainly not that fast, but perhaps six to eight years. I'm one of the more optimistic about the timetable. Most of my colleagues think more like a decade or two."

In language I proposed years later, I had walked into Bill Daniels office expecting a Greedhead, and walked out knowing a Goodhead. I also left with mixed feelings. Exhilarated that Bill Daniels was such a likable and impressive guy and had given me as much and more time than I needed to answer my questions. He had stopped calls for our meeting, ushered me into his office at the time agreed without making me wait as so often happens with businessmen who take advantage of their positions and never made me feel like I was wasting his time. Perhaps, probably even, those are the human qualities that made Daniels a cable TV plutocrat, since he too was a self-made man starting in Texas with a small bank account and a big dream. On the other hand, the interview had torpedoed any hope that we (Ed always insisted that we talk in "we" terms as a team, because "we" were all in it together, from receptionist to general counsel to president) had of purchasing the team. In reality, Ed was not in a position to carry the negative on a ten million dollar investment for a few months, much less a few years and much much less a decade or two. Now I was clearly out of my league, because I had never been involved in high finance and "funny money" except on my relatively small real estate deals. Perhaps there was a way to finesse the deal, but

Ed would know more about that than I.

I prepared a lengthy memo outlining my various interviews and financial projections, concluding that I did not see how it made sense for "us" to invest ten million dollars to purchase the Nuggets. I said that I was very sorry I had been forced to reach that conclusion because it would have been such a blast for us to own the Nuggets. I could picture myself in Scheer's spacious Mc-Nichols office helping Ed wheel and deal with the Nuggets and the NBA. And it would have been a blast, except not in the way I implied or Ed assumed. Usually I was straightforward with Ed in our various dealings but I could not tell him that I thought he would be a total disaster as the owner of the Nuggets. Ed loved the game as much as I, but unlike me he would not have been able to delegate authority to professionally oversee the Nuggets organization. He would delegate but then I thought he would interfere, especially in player selection, team development and all things a general manager is expected to do. I could see the headlines in the *Denver Post* and *Rocky Mountain News*: "Ed Pendleton, New Owner and General Manager of the Nuggets - tells astonished reporters he can be both." Ed asked some questions about the finances which I could answer truthfully and soon other matters required our attention.

The turn-around was much sooner than Bill Daniels predicted. Within a few years the cable companies made lucrative deals with the NBA. The Nuggets value consequently multiplied many times over. *Forbes.com* reports that when Stan Kroenke (net worth: $2.7 billion) bought the Nuggets in 2000, the team was worth $202 million. Denver Nuggets estimated team value today (summer 2014): $316 million.

If only Ed had ten million dollars to play with in 1984. Knowing Ed, he certainly would have shared his good fortune with his

General Counsel. Unfortunately for both of us, unforeseen and unpredictable political and economic events were about to turn our worlds upside down.

Oil & Gas Crash

The oil and gas industry which had been getting gradually worse each year since 1981 suddenly got much worse. Within months the price of a barrel of oil in 1986 dropped from about $35 to $8, and PLE's cost to produce a barrel was then about $12, so do the math and you understand the crisis. During our June 24, 2014 meeting, Ed explained why the price suddenly dropped, and why entire nations had conspired in an artificial decline in oil prices. According to Ed and later confirmed in more detail by his oldest son, Al Pendleton, who is a geologist, the Reagan administration wanted to reduce the world wide price of oil in order to undermine the Soviet Union. Secretary of State Kissinger and others persuaded the Saudis to substantially increase oil production which caused oil prices to plummet, which in turn undermined the economy of the Soviet Union, which in turn caused the Soviet Union to collapse leading to democratic reforms and the end of the Cold War era. With the Soviet Union thus weakened, President Reagan was confident enough of the result to make his historical demand, "Mr. Gorbachev, tear down this wall." Given the outcome, it is ironic that Ed was one of President Reagan's biggest fans; at one time Ed had been on one of Reagan's business advisory boards.

The above summary no doubt ignores a large part of this huge story, but what was relevant to Ed Pendleton and all his employees at PLE was that the artificially induced low price of oil on the international market undermined PLE and U.S. oil companies as well as the Soviet Union. Many oil and gas companies around the U.S. folded their tents and simply disappeared, especially the smaller companies which did not have the resources to survive a prolonged fall in oil prices. Ed Pendleton was one of the few who refused to call it quits by filing for bankruptcy, either for PLE or himself.

The collapse in oil prices caused real estate to follow in dramatic decline, and the U.S. economy stalled for several years. Ed faced serious financial problems since most of his net worth was tied up in oil and gas interests and extensive real estate holdings.

Shamrock Ranch for Sale

The biggest of these problems was the $1 million balloon payment that was due Mr. John Mark McLaughlin of Dallas, Texas who had sold and self-financed the Shamrock Ranch with a secured note from Ed. Ed had been meeting his annual contractual payments on a regular basis, but now it would not be easy to do so. Ed was a typical oil man used to taking big risks, and almost all of his cash was tied up in various oil projects which were suddenly in trouble. Not only was the oil and gas industry stalled, but also real estate for similar reasons. Almost all of Ed's net worth was in oil and his real estate, none of which was generating much cash at this point. The struggle to find a buyer for the Shamrock, or some way to find the cash to cover the mortgage payment, became intense. "We" obviously did not want to lose the Shamrock over the $1 million balloon payment when two years earlier we had the ranch under contract to a group of Texans for $35 million. That contract was subject to financing, which fell through due to the savings and loan crisis that cost taxpayers, according to the General Accounting Office, $132.1 billion dollars. (For details, see my introduction and play about the S & L scandal, "White Collar Time," in *Three Farces*.)

Ed tried everything he could think of to pay McLaughlin and stay afloat. Ed was a proud man, too proud many would say. I would say so if I believed that the subsequent pissing match with prospective buyers of the Shamrock Ranch was actually torpedoed because of a manure spreader—which incidentally cost me a $425,000 payday. Here's how it happened.

As part of his extensive efforts to save his beloved Shamrock Ranch, Ed agreed in writing to pay me a five percent commission if I found a buyer who closed on the ranch. I had plenty of time to do so because at the time I was working for Ed on a contract basis of $100 per hour, and was averaging only about seven or eight hours per week under the contract. As I would have done in a similar position, Ed did not sign an exclusive with a real estate agent or anyone else, but he did authorize several agents and friends to market the property on his behalf. I was grateful to be one of those given this opportunity, but think that Ed would have done the same for his secretary if she knew of a possible buyer.

After years of working with Ed on various aspects of the Shamrock Ranch, I probably knew more about the ranch than anyone but him, including details about the pending perfection of the water rights. The studies Ed had undertaken on the water rights proved that they would be far more valuable than the ranch itself. The Denver water rights attorney who I was working with to perfect the rights assured us that eventually the water rights would be perfected under Colorado law, but that was months and even years away. Months and years that Ed did not have. Since we had the Shamrock under contract for $35 million with a Texas group only months earlier, I had no doubt that the ranch was worth much more than Ed now would have to take for it. In fact, if I had deep enough pockets, I would have bought the Shamrock myself, and since I so truly believed in the value of the ranch, I found it easy to market the ranch to my friends and acquaintances. I prepared marketing materials and shared them with likely prospects, including some members of my Harvard and Oxford classes, but all passed on this great opportunity.

One friend I had met on the Inverness basketball court, who had deep-pocket clients for his financial firm, expressed some interest. Since Dave Snyder and his sidekick, Jason, were regulars at our pickup games at Inverness, it was easy for me to fan their interest in the Shamrock and I did so over the many months that followed. Finally I succeeded in getting Ed and Dave together to talk terms. The meeting was set for 2 pm on March 22, 1991, and Dave showed up on time—and then waited and waited in the reception room for Ed. Thirty minutes passed and Dave kept looking at his watch. I kept asking the receptionist to ring Ed again, saying Dave was about to leave. The receptionist was in tears, caught in the middle of a situation neither she nor I could control. It had happened many times before. Ed would keep potential partners waiting as a power play. At about 2:40 pm Dave said he was sorry, but he had another appointment, and started to leave. Ed suddenly appeared, apologizing profusely and explaining that he had been on a long distance call on another big deal.

My view is that it is more impressive to be on time for meetings as a show of respect and acknowledgement that other people's time is important too, and Ed's tactic seemed to me self-defeating, but Ed was the multi-millionaire and I was his part time employee. To my great relief, the damage seemed repaired, Ed and Dave agreed on an $8.5 million price. At the next pickup game at Inverness, Dave signed the contract on behalf of his Scandinavian clients, and that evening Ed did as well. I was elated, but also concerned because the contract finessed the touchy subject of personal ranch property to be included in the deal. My concern proved real as several attempts to reach agreement on a personal property attachment to the contract failed. At one point Ed said, "I hope the contract fails," and I was unsure as to whether this was truth or tactic, so I did not relay the comment to Dave. I tried to put Humpty Dumpty together again, but Dave and his clients were upset and no longer interested. After a later pickup game at Inverness when I asked Dave about what had happened, he said, "Ed shot himself in the foot."

Since I had lost a $425,000 pay day, I wondered over the years what Ed's view was and told Ed in advance that part of our June 24, 2014 meeting would be on this question. Since it had been such a big deal for me, I was surprised when Ed said that he did not remember signing a contract with Dave Snyder, much less a dispute about ranch equipment. To prime the memory pump, I said that the dispute was about a new manure spreader that Ed said he wanted to take to the new downsized ranch he planned to buy with the Shamrock proceeds. Again, Ed drew a blank. I gave Ed a reasonable explanation by saying that I knew at the time that he was negotiating with an Arapahoe County Commissioner (Tom Egert) for the sale of Shamrock water rights to the county, and of course I could understand that such a sale could bring more than the ranch itself. In the same position, I emphasized to Ed, I might have pursued that possibility as well. Still, Ed could not remember, and since his son, Al, joined us in Ed's office, I dropped the subject. Al's life, like mine, would have been very different if the contract with Dave Snyder had closed.

Had I been played? Did Ed sign the contract with Dave only to shop it for a better one?

Now it starts to make sense. Ed truthfully did not remember

the contract with Dave because it was not a real contract in his mind. The manure spreader was just an excuse to kill the deal – and I was just another partner he misused!

After a great deal of maneuvering to save his prized Shamrock Ranch, Ed ended up losing it. One account of this history can be found in *Shamrock Ranch: Celebrating Life in Colorado's Pikes Peak Country,"* by current Shamrock owner David A. Wismer, with Gary T. Wright (see pages 235-38, and 262-75). Like my memoir, Wismer's book on the Shamrock Ranch is a prepaid self-serving account of one man's life, and so needs to be read with a grain of salt. But one fact seems apparent. Although the northwestern corner of the Shamrock Ranch was eventually developed in the aftermath of the various wheeling and dealing that followed, under Mr. Wismer's stewardship the Shamrock is likely to maintain its core integrity as an important and uniquely beautiful Colorado landmark rather than being further subdivided into single family lots.

Hard Times

Over time Ed had trouble meeting PLE payroll. A few times he managed to secure bank loans just hours before paychecks were due. A less committed and proud man might have pulled the plug and filed for bankruptcy. Ed never did. One by one I would hear of Ed's employees being let go, including those who had been most key to PLE operations. I asked Ed about the difficulty of letting his employees go. He paused as if recalling the pain, and then said, "It's the hardest thing I ever had to do."

Almost all men and women are a mix of strength and weakness, good and bad and we all struggle with our dark sides. An honest biography or even summary of anyone's life should acknowledge such in an attempt to create a balanced picture. If Ed had a blind side, it probably was his treatment of his partners who rarely signed up for a second venture with him.

From my close proximity to Ed, I could see that not everyone was as impressed with him as I. I was surprised one day to overhear a partner warn a prospective investor, "Watch your pocketbook when Ed Pendleton is around." The comment reminded me of a similar one Ed made to me one day about a wealthy businessman who played pickup basketball with us at the Inverness Athletic Club, "I'd like to get into his pocketbook." Surprised, I looked at Ed who just smiled and winked—like it was a joke—or our little secret? I tend to be too trusting—too fast to give the benefit of doubt, because to do otherwise can be so counterproductive. But sometimes this philosophy can make me appear weak and even naïve. I probably spent more one-on-one time with Ed than any other PLE employee except his wife, Bev, but I rarely was present when Ed met with his partners, so I did not know about his interactions with them. I did not know what promises were made or implied or broken, but I did know that we had almost no repeat clients, and every new deal meant valuable executive and geologist time was wasted going from one oil company to another begging for the opportunity to make a presentation on the latest hot prospect PLE had to offer.

Perhaps it was simply that our partners were disappointed that PLE prospects hit too many dry holes to be profitable, but I thought I knew the answer or at least part of the reason for nonrenewals. Most of the contracts I had negotiated and/or drafted before were arms-length agreements between relatively equal parties. I was surprised at, what I thought, the PLE biased Oil and Gas Exploration Agreement and related Joint Operating Agreement, copies of which now crossed my desk for legal review as a matter of course before Ed signed. The standard agreement used in all sales seemed to me one-sided since PLE would make a ton if the prospect hit oil, but also made a significant amount even if it was a dry hole. It seemed to me that Ed had managed to take the risk out of an inherently risky business. In a typical deal PLE would collect a large sum up front and retain most of the Overriding Royalty Interest (ORRI) which was the plum in any deal since ORRI payments were paid right off the top with no need to absorb any of the expenses. PLE's partners on the other hand had most of the Working Interest in the wells, meaning that all expenses associated with any given well were deducted before any payment was made to the working interest. This was the risky part of drilling for oil; a duster meant no income, but substantial expenses that still needed to be paid. Difficult decisions often had to be made on marginal wells that produced oil and gas, but raised the question of whether the expense involved justified continued operation of the well. This was never an easy decision because so many variables were involved, like the price per barrel of oil (PPB) could and often did drop quickly and substantially, and the well might have unpredictable equipment failures.

One day on the way to the YMCA I told Ed that I would never sign such a lopsided agreement where one party made a profit even when the other partners did not. Ed explained that the PLE agreement was fairly standard in the industry, and represented a fair compromise for all involved given the initial pre-agreement investment the selling company had in any prospect (overhead, including secretaries, accountants and legal counsel, expenses to pay landmen to acquire leases and lease payments to landowners, seismic acquisition costs, etc.).

So if the terms of the agreement were not the reason for client non-renewal, what was? It was difficult to escape the conclusion that conflicts had arisen during the implementation of the agreements, and the conflicts were so serious that the clients resolved never again to enter another partnership with PLE. The oil and gas industry being the closed circle that it is and in fact quite incestuous as companies frequently need to pool resources to cover the enormous costs involved in oil and gas exploration, eventually the pool of possible partners dries up. Sooner rather than later, the companies also share stories about their good and especially their bad experiences with other oil and gas companies, and apparently there were not many of the former about PLE. I will never know the cause for non-renewals. From time to time I tried to discuss the subject with Ed, but it was not a subject he wanted to pursue. It was not my place or position to suggest more collaborative ways to work with partners so they would come back time and time again for more projects. I was a newcomer to the gritty world of oil and gas exploration; Ed had spent his entire career in it. Furthermore, even though we were friends and teammates, Ed was the multi-millionaire boss; I was the underpaid employee. But it seemed fairly obvious to me that playing nice in the sandbox with your partners would be a more sensible path in the long term. This was ironic because Ed was so personable and friendly in all other situations, and I was only one of many who frequently said, "Ed is such a people person" and "It's hard not to like Ed."

A STATE OF MIND

What would you call a state of mind
Where the eagle still rides the wind and sky
Swoops low to lake for fish it aims to find
Where the mountains climb three miles high
And send clear creeks cascading canyon walls
Over rock slides and then down water falls
To wide rivers that feed the plains below
Giving all life and hope a chance to grow
Into new dreams that will soar as high
As that eagle gliding the mountain sky.
Where the air stays cool and mild for everyone
Yet the sun shines bright in every season
And lights up the evening sky to close each day
More splendid than a fireworks display
Then setting light behind the highest peak
Inspiring awe so deep one dare not speak
So give silent thanks that here we can reside
For you can travel far and travel wide
But a finer place you will never find
In fact this state is more than just a state of mind
It's Colorado, and it's your state as well as mine.

McEdLaw Logo.

Chapter 22
AUTHOR AS CAPITALIST
& MATERIALIST

Getting and spending, we lay waste our powers —Wordsworth

As described more fully in my introduction to *Three Farces* (2014), after I was confident that I had proved my value to him at the end of my first year as general counsel to Pendleton Land and Exploration, Inc. (PLE), I proposed to Ed Pendleton that instead of a raise he give me a three day work week at the same salary. I explained to Ed that as a single guy with modest expenses, time was more important to me than an increase in salary. Ed agreed, probably realizing that I could make a multiple of what he was paying me if I wanted to work for a big law firm in downtown Denver (which I didn't). Later I did the same as general counsel to a multi-state collections company to secure a four day work week (see Chapter 23).

Almost everyone wants more free time until they have it. Then the question of what to do with that time hits full force. This chapter will summarize part of what I did with my negotiated free time under three headings: (1) Real Estate, (2) Collecting, and (3) Writing.

REAL ESTATE

This chapter describes my experience in purchase and management of Denver income property. I have always believed that the goal of financial independence is a praiseworthy one because with it comes personal freedom which is priceless. It is difficult to maximize your potential and joy in life if you are spending all of it working for someone else. In the United States the goal of achieving financial independence is within the reach of many motivated hard working individuals. I emphasize "many" because I know that poverty and discrimination conspire to make financial independence illusory for most, and therefore my statement is not a validation of the status quo which denies large numbers the equal opportunity to achieve financial independence.

In my case, my family and I had nothing, often not even enough to eat. I have experienced poverty up close and personal and see nothing about it that is noble. Poverty is a hateful scourge on our society, free market economy and constitutional democracy, and we need to do everything possible to minimize if not eliminate it forever. So I started with zero but was extremely fortunate to win the lottery several times. My basketball skills enabled me to win scholarships that in turn enabled me to earn impressive credentials that in turn led to relatively well-paying employment. Not everyone can be so lucky. With term time and summer employment supplementing my scholarships, I managed to graduate from Harvard Law School with three degrees and no debt. I cannot even imagine the burden on a graduate who is forced to make career decisions with six figure debt to repay before a positive net worth is even possible. We need to do better to minimize student debt, perhaps by expanding the federal Public Service Loan Forgiveness Program, and creating similar public service incentives.

I chose real estate as my tool because the leverage involved in a typical transaction makes multiple rather than percentage returns possible and even likely. Prime modern apartment buildings were beyond my economic reach, but I found that older apartment buildings around Cheesman Park in Denver could be purchased and break even for a ten percent down payment with the seller carrying the balance at ten percent interest-only payments. The increase in property value reflected increased rental income by improving the units and better management. If one could increase net income by ten percent, the return would be 100 percent on the ten percent investment due to leverage provided by the seller's loan. Losses, including depreciation of an appreciating asset, as my friend, Denny Reigle, informed me, could be deducted from my other employment income.

The trade-off of course for this potential high return is that managing tenants and repairs can be onerous. My approach was to hire a manager for each building by offering a discounted rent for normal duties, plus additional payment for extras like cleaning and renting a vacant unit. I eventually found a reliable highly skilled handyman, Carl Richell, who charged almost twice as much as most, but was well worth his $10 hourly rate. I told my managers, including Chris & John, a gay couple who rented at 1648 Ogden, that we would not discriminate against any tenants in renting apartments on any basis except for not being a good tenant (paying rent on time, not disturbing other tenants, etc.), and that tenants would treat us well if we treated them well (the golden rule). For the most part this Goodhead approach worked well, except a few rotten apples took advantage.

Over several years I acquired sixty-two units in six apartment buildings, the largest being the 21 unit Marquette at 14th and Downing. A listing of my real estate holdings:

ADDRESS	TYPE
1. 838 Leyden Street, Denver, CO	Owner-occupied 3 Unit Victorian House
2. 830 Leyden, Street, Denver	Single Family House
3. 1370 Gilpin Street, Denver	6 Unit Victorian House
4. 1648 Ogden Street, Denver	4 Unit Apartment Building
5. 15 Tregay Street, Silver Plume, CO	Single Family House
6. The Georgian, 1372-78 Franklin St.	Denver 8 Unit Apartment Building
7. 1436 Gilpin Street, Denver	10 Unit Apartment Building
8. 1446 Gilpin Street, Denver	10 Unit Apartment Building
9. The Marquette, 1364-68 Downing	Denver 21 Unit Apartment Building
10. Hartman Castle, 277 Cty Rd 50 Gunnison, CO	Victorian Restaurant Conversion & Single Family House on six acres

In my opinion, all the apartment buildings were suitable for conversion to condominiums given my earlier experience in Cambridge where my first purchase had been a condo conversion near Harvard Law School. And in fact the Marquette and the two Gilpin apartment buildings have been converted into condominiums (after I sold them).

I purchased the apartment buildings on a 3X10 formula: Building price based on ten times annual income, ten percent down, with Seller-carry financing for several years at about ten percent interest-only payments. I earned "sweat equity" by improving each unit when it was vacated by new paint, repairs, minor upgrades, etc. At first I painted and rented apartments by myself, but soon negotiated (a rent discount plus a commission for rentals and an hourly rate for extras like simple repairs) with a tenant in each building to manage that building.

I purchased 1648 Ogden, 1370 Gilpin and the Georgian using my savings as down payments. Then later after rental income had increased, I sold 50 percent interests in 1370 Gilpin to my Boston partner/friend, and in the Georgian to a Sacramento partner/friend, based on the 3X10 formula. I used the proceeds to buy the twin brick ten unit apartment buildings at 1436 and 1446 Gilpin Street about two blocks north of Cheesman Park. When the Denver rental market collapsed after 1988, my Sacramento partner opted out and I decided to sell all my real estate. I was burned out on managing my managers and related problems but I should have toughed it out. Bottom line: I made some money, but not the small fortune I would have if I had held on to the buildings for about four or five more years when Denver real estate almost doubled in value.

I learned the hard way that it is tough to be a Goodhead landlord when others do not play by the same rules. The most dramatic tenant example: a heavy-set 6-foot black man who claimed to be a former Marine, rented the studio apartment at 1436 Gilpin Street, and a few days later sued me for back injuries he claimed he had suffered when he fell off of a loose toilet seat. I called my manager, Jodie Gibson, to ask why she had not fixed the loose toilet seat as requested, and she explained that she had tried but the tenant had changed the locks on his door and would not give her a new key as required by our lease. My insurance company wanted to settle but I convinced them to let me defend myself in small claims court. My research indicated this tenant had previously extorted a settlement from a prior landlord and I was determined to stop his scams. He actually showed up for the hearing but the judge awarded me possession and back rent after he heard our respective stories. I was not able to collect on the judgment since the tenant immediately filed for bankruptcy and moved on (probably looking for his next victim).

15 Tregay, Silver Plume, CO

I purchased 15 Tregay one summer since I was charmed by this old blue collar mining town in the Colorado Rockies, one mile from upscale Georgetown and about a ninety minute drive on I-70 from Denver. My plan was to rent the house as an investment property, but negotiate rights to occupy it myself for a vacation week or two each year. The owner of 15 Tregay was a pretty young woman (hereafter "ET") who was selling the house without a realtor (FSO), and we agreed that $50,000 was reasonable for this charming house separated from city hall and a Victorian bandstand by Clear Creek. I considered an inspection condition in the contract, but ET assured me that everything was in working order. I rented the house to the first person who looked at it, charmed by the bighorn sheep looking down at the house from nearby cliffs, but a few months later she called to say that the furnace was dangerous. Sure enough, the propane furnace made a loud scary noise when it started its cycle and I had to replace the defective furnace. Live and learn, I thought and soon forgot about ET and her "concealment."

About two years later ET called me to ask if I would write a "good character" recommendation for her as part of a mortgage loan application. I said I could not do so in good conscience because her furnace concealment in my opinion did not indicate good character. To my surprise I was served with litigation papers a few weeks later. Surprised not only that ET would sue me given the circumstances, but also that an attorney had agreed to take her case. I filed a motion to dismiss and was surprised once again when the Denver District Court denied my motion. Once again I persuaded the agent for my insurance company to let me defend myself, even after he reminded me of that old saw, "A lawyer who defends himself has a fool for a client."

So at some expense and considerable time, I defended myself in a full-blown trial, complete with witnesses on both sides. I called my tenant who first had discovered the problem to explain her experience and also the guy who replaced the defective furnace. The case went on for much longer than needed, in large part because I kept trying to find new ways to say that I had no legal obligation to provide a good character recommendation, and such a recommendation would lose its value if obligatory. The judge showed a great deal of patience in letting me go on and on, and then dismissed ET's case and my counterclaim. What a waste of court time!

1436 Gilpin Street, Denver

Another anecdote about 1436 Gilpin underscores how crazy the landlord experience can be. A few months after I purchased the building, I received a non-compliance notice from the City of Denver. The notice stated that I was in violation of a Denver code requiring all apartment kitchens to have an exterior window. The requirement seemed absurd not only because eight of the one bedroom apartments in the building were unusually desirable for the area (900 square feet each, with original hardwood floors and a spacious dining room separating the kitchen from the closest windows), but also because the 1930's brick building obviously had met building requirements for over fifty years, or had been grandfathered as exempt from the subsequent kitchen window requirement. A letter to this effect did not solve the problem, and so I had to appeal and appear at a Denver hearing in order to secure an exemption. Had prior owners paid bribe money to the inspectors, and if so, was I expected to do the same? I will never know, but again, what a waste of time!

Hartman Castle, Gunnison, Colorado

Each of the four units in my brick apartment building at 1648 Ogden Street was also unusually large for the area (each over 1,000 square feet), but the building was located north of Colfax Avenue in an area less gentrified than my Cheesman Park buildings south of Colfax. Therefore I decided to sell the 4-plex, and was pleased to find buyers who wanted to convert it into offices, would pay my asking price, and cooperate in a 1031 tax free exchange with a $30,000 note back to me secured by a second deed of trust. I planned to use my $30,000 equity as a down payment on another Cheesman Park apartment building, but I could not find one that met my requirements and time was running out on my 90 day window to complete the tax free exchange. Scanning the income property section of the *Denver Post* one Sunday morning, I saw an intriguing advertisement for "the Hartman Castle." The brick and stone mansion had been completed in 1894 by Alonzo Hartman, a wealthy cattle rancher, reportedly the first white man to establish permanent residence on the Western Slope, who wanted an impressive dwelling for his wife. The mansion had features unusual for that remote part of Colorado: five imported tile fireplaces, custom stain glass windows featuring stylized owls in homage to the great horned owls that nested on the property's ancient cotton-woods, elaborate wood carvings, etc. In *Gaslights & Gingerbread: Colorado's Historic Homes* (1965), Sandra Dallas states that the mansion, which cost an astounding $45,000 to build, blends "Victorian and Western architecture with touches of church elegance" (details and photos at Dallas, pages 40-46).

Intrigued because I am attracted to one-of-a-kind unique, I called "PM," the listing agent. PM gushed about what a great investment the property would be at only $220,000 considering the new airport service from Denver International Airport (DIA), and Gunnison's central location just south of Crested Butte's popular ski resort. A few days later I flew from DIA to Gunnison, and PM showed me the property, which was even more impressive than suggested by PM's property brochure. One mile from Gunnison's downtown, the six acre property included the original Hartman house, "the first frame house in Gunnison" (Dallas, p. 44), which could be used by a caretaker. The prior owners had lived in the original house, and turned the mansion into a gourmet restaurant. The inspection report specifically excluded opinion as to the condition of the restaurant equipment as beyond the expertise of the inspector, but it seemed likely to me that PM was correct in asserting that the equipment alone must have cost almost half the asking price of the property. The house itself was indeed a little "castle" with Victorian and other detail.

On the plane back to DIA, I scribbled numbers and notes about the property and decided to make an offer. My plan was to rent the property to new tenants who would reopen the restaurant and live in the small house—which I concluded was the best use of the property. Restoring the main house to single family use might be feasible in the future, but now would be very expensive to replace the commercial kitchen with a private kitchen. Purchasing the property was more involved than I was used to because it required bank financing and approval of my 1031 exchange note, but all parties cooperated to close the deal for a substantially reduced price of $150,000 just before my 90 day 1031 exchange window expired.

There would have been no time to do a marketing survey, but I thought there was a good chance I could attract a chef and family to move into the small house and reopen the restaurant. I thought wrong. My ads placed in real estate and restaurant publications generated many responses, but they all wanted me to hire them to operate the restaurant. I had no desire to take this alternative course because I knew nothing about the restaurant business and could imagine the many big and petty issues that probably would be involved in such an undertaking. If I could not find someone to take the risks themselves under a blanket rental agreement for the property, my Plan B would be to rent the small house until I could implement Plan A.

With PM's help, an acceptable tenant was found and he soon moved into the small house with rent reduced for maintaining the property. All went well with Plan B. The tenant paid rent on time and I granted rent deductions for interior and exterior painting of the small house beyond provisions already in the lease for maintaining the entire property. The only problem was his call on March 20, 1988 complaining about no heat in the small house. Shades of Silver Plume, the furnace needed replacing rather than simple repair, but I figured the additional investment would add value to my property. The next call I received from the tenant several months later, however, undermined both Plan A and Plan B. The tenant informed me that he was moving out because he had received a notice that reclamation was about to begin on mine tailings in the area.

I could hardly believe it. Mine tailings in the area? A possible ground water threat? Drinking water that might be contaminated at a gourmet restaurant? The potential liability was sobering to say the least. My inspection report did not alert me to this potential problem. Nor had PM who had a professional obligation as a realtor to disclose such information about the property that he knew to be damaging. So too the Gunnison bank that had financed my loan on the property did not disclose any environmental problem. Surely they must have known about the potential problem since they lived and worked in the small town. I called PM about this distressing development and he hemmed and hawed about the mine tailings in the area, not accepting responsibility but clearly worried about his liability to the lawyer to whom he had sold the property. I called the officer at the bank and told him that I would not make any further payments on my loan until this problem was resolved to my satisfaction. The next day PM called from the bank to ask what was needed to resolve the problem to my satisfaction. I told him I would sleep on it and call him in the morning.

That night I considered my options. I would have a case against PM and the bank for non-disclosure ("concealment"), and perhaps against the inspector as well, but as a former litigator I knew that usually only the lawyers win in litigation. Even when a judgment is awarded it can be difficult or even impossible to collect. Even when a monetary award is banked, the time and aggravation take a big toll. Sometimes litigation is the most sensible course, especially when civil rights or other "intangibles" are involved, but such was not the case now. So the next morning I joined a conference call with PM and the bank officer and told them that I would consider it a satisfactory resolution if they marketed and sold the property, this time with full disclosure, for what I had invested. I would be satisfied if I were to remain whole (not absorb a loss) on the property.

The property was listed with an appropriate disclosure and eventually sold, but not for enough to absorb all my loss. Before I decided how to proceed, I received a certified mailing containing a notice of PM's declaration of bankruptcy. I put in a claim to the bankruptcy court, but expected nothing, and that's exactly what I received. What a shame. I sure would like to own the Hartman Castle today if the problem with the mine tailings has been remedied, especially when I look at the photos once again and remember my brief overlap with this small piece of Colorado history.

The Marquette

The 21 unit Marquette apartment building at 1372-78 Downing Street in Denver is the largest building I owned. I purchased a lease-option on the property in March 1982 from SG, a lifetime landlord who had acquired an extensive collection of older Denver apartment buildings over many years. Two years earlier I had contacted SG after researching the ownership of the 8 unit Georgian at 1372-78 Franklin Street, a building I was interested in acquiring because of its attractive Georgian architecture. After several meetings SG agreed to sell the Georgian to me with 90% owner-carry financing at ten percent—a competitive market rate at the time.

After I had established a good track record of timely note payments, one day SG said he no longer was interested in managing so many Denver properties from his Fort Collins home and asked if I would be interested in acquiring additional apartment buildings on the same terms. I expressed interest, but the only other building he offered that I was interested in was the Marquette, a stately Italianate three-building structure at the southeast corner of 14th Avenue and Downing Street. I was a little concerned about an outright purchase because the large original windows appeared drafty and the central heating system, a dated boiler converted from coal to gas, looked like a steam locomotive from the nineteenth century. At the time most Denver apartments included heat as part of the rent and I was afraid that the dated heating system and windows would be too expensive to replace and the consequent gas bills too high to make the building workable for me. Therefore I proposed a lease-purchase agreement whereby I would have responsibility for the Marquette, but not ownership unless I exercised the option to purchase at $460,000 (with similar 90% owner-carry at 10% interest). A joke of course given today's real estate values, but significant enough to barely break even given existing income and expenses of the Marquette at the time. I asked for and received the right to assign my interest at any time so I might share some of the appreciation if I improved the buildings but did not want to exercise the purchase option.

Once the paperwork was signed I persuaded Roy Lutz, my manager at 1436 Gilpin, to move into and manage the Marquette. Roy had proved himself a trustworthy manager and competent handyman, so I was confident that this seasoned property veteran could handle a larger building. Another good tenant at 1436 Gilpin, Jodi Gibson, agreed to take Roy's place as manager of 1436 Gilpin. Among my improvements to the Marquette was painting the decorative ceiling molding in the spacious entry halls gold; thereby bringing the entire hallway to life as if crowned in gold leaf. For a modest investment, the entry halls now created a dramatic "wow" first impression for prospective renters, an important advantage in the depressed Denver rental market at the time. The Marquette soon turned a modest profit for me even given the dated boiler and windows, but Roy tired of management responsibilities and decided to move out of state. About the same time Harris Faberman of CCM Realty in Boulder cold-called one day to ask if I would be willing to sell the Marquette. He did not protest when I said it would take $525,000 to do so and several weeks later we closed at that price, with $50,000 cash and a $75,000 promissory note back to me.

CCM payments to SG and me were made on time for several months until they suddenly stopped. The president of CCM explained that they were underwater on their properties and would have to return the Marquette to SG. As holder of a second deed of trust, the security for my $75,000 note vanished along with the monthly payments. I retained a Denver law firm to protect my interests and liens were placed on several CCM properties in Boulder. When I inspected these run-down houses near the University of Colorado, however, I concluded that I would never be able to collect on the liens and I did not. Nobody ever said that being a landlord was easy; now I had experienced many of the unexpected ways that made it hard.

Selling My Income Property

Many times as I guided these buildings through a depressed Denver rental market I reminded myself that I had to be patient since I was well-positioned for a big windfall when the market turned again. I controlled apartment buildings worth at least $2 million, and my net investment was only about $200,000 plus time expended. But by the late 1980's I had burned out as a landlord and decided to sell all my income property. My tax returns during this period were only audited once; after three hours of careful examination of my detailed records, the IRS secured a deficiency payment of about $150 only because I previously had decided not to take the time necessary to prove mileage and some related costs incurred as part of my property business. When I sold 838 Leyden for $250,000 on February 27, 1997 I retained an adjacent one third of a city lot. The fate of that small piece of dirt makes for another interesting anecdote and is related at pp. 264-268 in Chapter 26. The only other real estate I owned after 1997 was my personal residence in Centennial, Colorado. Therefore I was free to pursue other interests in the time freed from my part-time jobs at PLE and GC.

I thought I had put my landlord/real estate chapter behind me, but then in 2014, when I was in the middle of writing this book, a serendipitous coincidence pulled me back in. At the time I had been debt free since paying off the mortgage on my house at 6048 South Locust Circle in 1998 (Independence Day!), and was enjoying my financial and personal independence. Then both single family houses on my wish list became available at the same time.

One was my dream house five blocks away at 5905 E. Maplewood Avenue where I wanted to retire when my bad back made the stairs of my two story house too difficult to manage, and the other was a property at 6459 E. Maplewood Avenue adjacent to my residence and a key piece of my dream to establish the Make Our Democracy Work Enterprises (MODWE). I had been hoping that the two properties would become available with at least a few years in between so I would have time to adjust before trying to buy the second property. Even though it probably would stretch my resources both personal and financial, I decided to try to purchase both properties.

Entry of Star House

Aerial view of Star House

Star House

Building Sketch and
Dimensions + Plot Plan

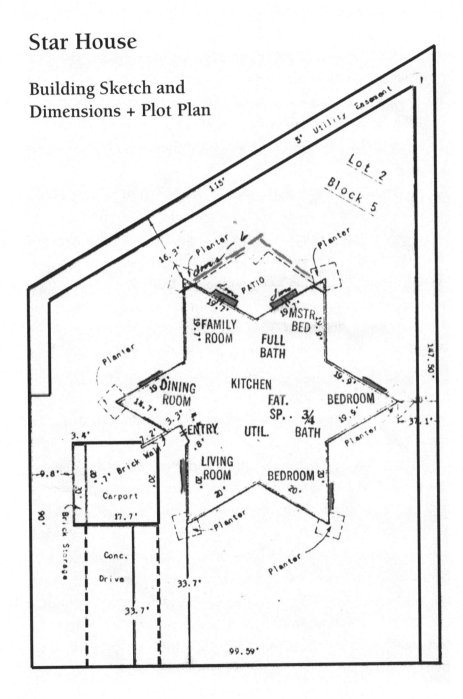

The Star House

Designed by a student of Frank Lloyd Wright, the midcentury modern Star House at 5905 E. Maplewood Avenue is named after the six point architecture radiating from a huge central skylight. The Star House is literally one-of-a-kind; I am not aware of any like it. Part of the story of how I was able to acquire the Star House is told in a special feature of the *Denver Post* (August 22, 2015). The part of the story not told was the difficulty in financing the property.

The executor of the estate told me that seller financing was not an option. When I went to my local bank of over twenty years (located just one block away from the Star House) for advice on where to apply for a mortgage, Bank of the West recommended themselves and said that as a good client for so many years they could offer me conventional 30 year financing at only 3 percent. Then one week before my 30 day contract would expire and after submitting reams of mind-numbing paperwork, they said that their underwriters did not want the Star House in their portfolio because it was too unique! To most investors, unique midcentury modern houses command a premium selling price because so many buyers compete for them.

My case was not helped by a low-ball appraisal that stated the house did not have a mountain view, when in fact the appraiser had somehow overlooked the panoramic mountain view looking across a small park from the back yard (an obvious mistake that I was told would take months to correct). Nor was my case helped by the bank's policy of refusing to count rental income from a first rental house until two years of income could be proved from federal tax returns (how would young investors ever get started in real estate with this requirement?). So after more than twenty years' experience in financing, managing and selling over sixty apartment units, now I did not qualify for a conventional loan for a single family house! The bank certainly had a right to refuse me a mortgage loan but should have done so at the outset before my 30 day contract had almost expired.

Fortunately the sellers agreed to an extension, but not long enough to qualify for an alternative conventional loan with another bank. Therefore I had to arrange for a quick unconventional two year bridge-loan at 9 percent interest. This was three times the original 3 percent conventional rate estimate, but I felt grateful that I was able to secure any loan before my contract expired and I would lose the Star House to sellers who were reconsidering whether to sell the property at all. I think my grey hairs more than doubled in those two months (April-May, 2015) of trying to finance the Star House. But the bottom line was that I succeeded in financing my dream retirement house, even if on unfavorable terms. Yet if my resources at any point prove insufficient to cover expenses on both single family houses, I would sell the Star House before the MODWE House.

The Star House Sold

About two months before my 80th Birthday on June 30, 2023, one of my two tenants at the Star House, a young doctor, informed me that the City of Centennial had delivered a code violation requiring me to remove a dying 30 foot Spruce tree in the front yard. I told him that the tree and yard were dying due to inadequate watering, as proved by the minimal water bills the lease required the tenants to pay. He replied that watering established landscape was not necessary, a claim my tree guy said was nonsense given our desert climate.

This dispute and my age convinced me it was time to sell the

Star House. As a lawyer with extensive real estate experience I did not need a realtor or a typical FSBO (For Sale By Owner) sale involving the numerous realtors and buyers the Star House likely would attract. Therefore I invited a few potential buyers who had expressed an interest in buying the Star House to submit AS IS offers. The winner was Mike Penny, a local realtor who bid $650,000. I consider this a good price since I purchased the Star House for $370,000 eight years earlier, and the AS IS provision saved me over $100,000 in repair and marketing and commissions required in a typical sale. For tax and other reasons I assumed the role of bank by giving Mike a first mortgage loan of $280,000 at 7% interest only payments for six years. For reasons outlined in Chapter 28 I hope the loan (with it's prepayment penalty) can be extended rather than paid off at the end of six years.

Mike plans to turn the Star House into an airbnb short term rental. If you are interested in booking a stay at the Star House, contact Mike at Mike@sbmpventures.com. I am pleased with this outcome as it will enable travelers from around the world to enjoy the unique experience of the Star House. I think the short term rental option is the highest and best use of the Star House. A friend asked if I regretted "leaving so much meat on the bone" since its next sale price is likely to exceed $1 million. The answer is No. I am happy with the return on my investment. Enough is Enough.

The MODWE House

The MODWE House is the key to my dream of establishing a campus for Make Our Democracy Work Enterprises, Inc. This four bedroom property at 6459 E. Maplewood Avenue is adjacent to my residence at 6048 South Locust Circle.

Back of MODWE Center

Front View of MODWE house

Back View of MODWE house

Make Our Democracy Work Enterprises Garden

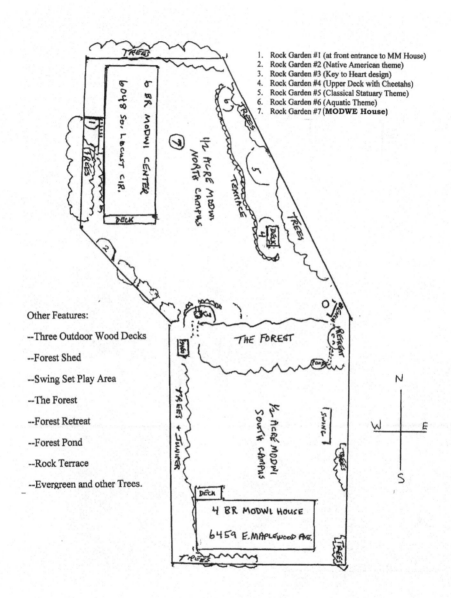

1. Rock Garden #1 (at front entrance to MM House)
2. Rock Garden #2 (Native American theme)
3. Rock Garden #3 (Key to Heart design)
4. Rock Garden #4 (Upper Deck with Cheetahs)
5. Rock Garden #5 (Classical Statuary Theme)
6. Rock Garden #6 (Aquatic Theme)
7. Rock Garden #7 (**MODWE House**)

Other Features:

--Three Outdoor Wood Decks

--Forest Shed

--Swing Set Play Area

--The Forest

--Forest Retreat

--Forest Pond

--Rock Terrace

--Evergreen and other Trees.

Sketch of Make Our Democracy Work Enterprises (MODWE)

When I removed the fence separating the two half-acre properties, I was able to automatically create a contiguous one acre
campus for MODWE in between the two houses. Unlike the
unique Star House, the four bedroom 2,133 square foot house at
6459 E. Maplewood Avenue is cookie-cutter and was a fixer-upper
needing two new bathrooms, new HVAC and extensive renovation. After making 20 percent down-payments on both houses,
the renovation costs stretched my budget to the limits. It did not
matter as I was more interested in the property's half acre lot adjacent to my residence on one-half acre. Now I had a one acre campus to give a physical reality to the conceptual MODWE
framework. Purchase of this MODWE House was also more difficult than it should have been. I had been discussing possible purchase of the house for almost one year after initially approaching
the owner to see if I could just buy the unused "forest" along our
common property line. The day after my agent, Carl Richell negotiated a verbal agreement that was mutually acceptable, the
seller without notice signed a listing agreement and the realtor did
not contact me since in his experience neighbors often express interest but never buy. In Denver's red hot property market, the
house had two full price offers the first day, one of which did not
require bank financing. I immediately contacted the realtor, Bill
Nazzaro, who apologized, and helped put the deal back together
at the last minute. I did not argue about the increased price because I knew that the property was worth more to me than any
other likely buyer. After more brain damage, Wells Fargo offered
a conventional 30 year mortgage at 4.5 percent, and we closed on
May 13, 2015.

On May 13, 2015, I closed on the adjacent property at 6459 E.
Maplewood Avenue for $340,000 plus approximately $35,000 in
renovation and furnishing costs. As this four bedroom MODWE

House also sits on one-half acre, a one acre MODWE campus with secluded wooded area ("the Forest") was created when I removed the fence separating the two properties. (Compare land acquisition at 838 and 830 Leyden as described on pp. 264-268.)

Bill then went way beyond the call of duty and provided valuable assistance in lining up contractors and sharing his lease and related knowledge of renting single family houses. Carl Richell switched hats and completed two new bathrooms and kitchen renovation. His only help was his wife Janet who traded some painting for a grandfather clock and provided instantaneous advice on decorating issues that I had spent days considering. I lucked out when a woman I met at an estate sale, Monica Bourque, agreed to do the interior painting at both houses and then provided her two college sons, Cole and Blake, and also at times her classy husband, Ken, to help complete the houses for furnished executive rental.

Monica then contributed a remarkably professional voice-over for photographer Jeff Morris' photo tours of both the MODWE and Star houses, featured on *YouTube.com*.

COLLECTING

While I do not think it would be accurate to label me a Greedhead, I am definitely materialistic and have filled my big box 4,800 square foot house with an 1,800 square foot finished basement, with books, art, antiques and collectibles. Doing so has proved one of the great pleasures in my life, and I make no apologies for being materialistic. I think my pleasure in hunting and living with material possessions is explained by my impoverished background when I and my family had virtually nothing (detailed in *Volume I of ARR*). I know that I am overcompensating, but don't think I'm hurting anyone in the process.

Darwin First Edition

I planned to devote an entire book to be titled *Metaphors: Serendipitous Collecting* to a history and commentary on my joyful collecting experiences. I did not complete this book but I'll relate one experience here. Of all my materialistic pursuits, finding collectible books was my primary love. My best find was in the summer of 2014 when I was returning from an estate sale where I had purchased eight collectible books for $40. I was in a good mood thinking about my treasures and so stopped on the way back to my house when I saw furniture and other clutter in the driveway of a modest house—a sure sign of a moving sale. Usually I only got out of my 4-Runner at such unadvertised moving sales when I could see books in the driveway. None could be seen, but I felt energized by my prior purchase and decided to look behind the sofa blocking my view. Sure enough, a box of books marked at $2 each. I dug through the cardboard box of books and found four I wanted. As I waited for the seller to give me change from my twenty dollar bill, he suddenly exclaimed, "How did my Darwin book get in that box? It's valuable and I'm not going to sell it for $2."

"How much do you want for it?" I asked.

"Twenty dollars," he said.

I looked at the old book more carefully, wondering if I wanted to pay $20 because I was not sure if it was worth that much. I confirmed that the publication date on the title page was 1859. I do not have a smart phone since I prefer to use the computer in my head, which incorrectly told me that Darwin's *The Origin of Species* was first published about 1850. Certainly many editions of this controversial best-selling book had been published in a decade.

So probably not particularly valuable, but the book was in near-fine condition for its age and so I said, "sold for twenty dollars."

Back home I did some preliminary research, and was surprised to discover that I had a first edition of *The Origin of Species!* A true British first edition in good condition is worth about $180,000. Further research on "points" indicated that my Darwin was a third or fourth issue of the first American edition. I checked *Abebooks.com* for comps (comparables), and found several copies of fourth issue first editions for about $8,500. The comps were for books in good condition; mine was much better than that, and it might be a more desirable third issue of the first edition.

Someday I will take time to research my Darwin further, but the following points indicate that my copy is not a true first. The true first was published in London in 1859 and had only two endorsements on the back of the flyleaf. My copy has four; obviously a later issue. The first four issues do not include a reference to "the Creator" in the concluding paragraph of the book. In an attempt to pacify a Christian England incensed by the secular theory of evolution, including his very religious wife, Darwin added a reference to "the Creator" in all subsequent editions of the book. My copy does not include a reference to "the Creator."

In the United States, Harvard Professor Louis Agassiz established himself as the leading opponent of secular Darwinism, and won widespread popularity with his alternative "Hand-of-God" theory. Each new scientific discovery, no matter how large or convincing, is simply accepted as further evidence of the Hand-of-God.

On October 17, 2015 I made a presentation on book collecting at Academy West; a Denver version of Academy East, both founded by Chris Lane, the owner of the Philadelphia Print Shop and popular appraiser on PBS's Antiques Road Show. In this digital era when traditional books are not part of most people's lives, I welcome opportunities to talk about my experiences in and ideas about book collecting. My presentation used about eight of my books as examples supporting my recommendation for "serendipitous collecting." At the conclusion of my presentation, I related the above story while I passed my Darwin around for examination, and then stated, "You can now say that you have touched a first edition of one of the greatest books ever written!"

WRITING

Since starting my legal career as a staff attorney for the Harvard Center for Law and Education in 1972, I have published about twenty articles in professional journals on equal educational opportunity, including several advocating the civic standard as the primary purpose of public education. See Appendix B.

Manic Writing 2014-15

My first book titled *Metaphors: A Reverse Love Story* (2014) was written under my pseudonym, Steven McMann, as an ironic distraction to the anguish of being jettisoned by Liz, my girlfriend of four years who I had hoped would be a lifetime partner. The concept for *Metaphors* was to write about love and sex late in life; in other words, the prior four years of my life. The book is a reverse love story when compared to the romantic young love story in Erich Segal's *Love Story* (1970) which captured America's heart, and catapulted the obscure Harvard classics professor to fame and fortune. Since Erich had been my Shakespeare tutor at Harvard College, I felt a nostalgic tie to the late author, but when Liz dropped out as co-author of *Metaphors*, the book turned into more of a memoir than a late love story.

Writing a memoir under a pseudonym with most names and places changed proved unnecessary as my pseudonym was soon penetrated. So when my introduction to *A Muse of Fire: A Play Arranged from the Works of Shakespeare* (2014) also started to morph into a lengthy memoir, I decided to write my story as *A Rhodes Retrospective* (2015) under my own name.

Super-Competent Help

I would not have been able to even dream about publishing these books within two years without the help of Ivy Ridlen of Timesavers and Pam McKinnie of Concepts Unlimited who I serendipitously met in February 2014. Both of these super-competent women live up to their corporate names: Ivy saving a great deal of time and expense as my secretary, computer whiz, photographer and all-around assistant; and Pam as the publisher/designer whose magic transforms my writing and sketches into professional form.

One of the most enjoyable parts of writing these books has been my partnership with Pam McKinnie in designing covers for the books. Pam in each case transformed my rough sketches into what I think are exceptional covers which have special meaning for me. My sketch for the *Metaphors* cover outlined a reproduction of the "Silver Pansy" photo surrounded by my books. The concept was directly related to the book's content: a beautiful woman aghast at the piles of books cluttering every room in the house of her bibliophile lover.

So too my sketch for the cover of *A Muse of Fire* and *A Rhodes Retrospective* featured a revision of the cover of the three volume *The Library Shakespeare*, illus. Sir John Gilbert et. al (circa 1900) which I had splurged upon one rainy day in London during my first year at Oxford. The cover is appropriate because *A Rhodes Retrospective* describes how my Harvard College thesis on Shakespeare's Coriolanus affected my life in subsequent years. So too the cover is apt for the companion volume *A Muse of Fire* which is a reprint of my 1966 arrangement of the works of Shakespeare.

Similarly, the cover for *Three Farces* (see photo at p 250) and *Light Works* is a revision of a nineteenth century book from my library—a cover as fanciful and excessive as their contents. All three covers reflect my interest in design. One sub-specialty in my extensive book collection features books with fine graphic design. All the books I have authored include photographs of my three acrylic paintings. See for example, "Players" on page 15 of Three Farces, "Partners in Justice" on page 188 of *Metaphors: A Reverse Love Story* and "Gender Gap" on page 178 of this book. They do not have artistic merit, but I still like them and they serve well as chapter dividers.

Some may argue that the thousands of hours I have spent collecting would have been more productively spent working longer hours on equal educational opportunity or as a lawyer in private practice making large sums that could be donated to various charities, and perhaps that is so. But a large part of the joy in my life, second only to my relationships with several wonderful women, has been in the pursuit, capture and subsequent pleasure of living with my treasures and their related memories.

WHAT WILL MATTER

One hundred years from today
What will it matter

What house you stayed in?
What car you drove?
What club you played in?
What clothes you wore
What goods you trade in?
What job you held?
What church you prayed in?

It's for you, not me, to say
What will matter
One hundred years from today.

Author circa 1969

Chapter 23
DICK CORIOLANE
& GREEDE COLLECTIONS

The supreme end of education is expert discernment in all things—
the power to tell the good from the bad, the genuine from the counter-
feit, and to prefer the good and the genuine to the bad and the
counterfeit.—Samuel Johnson (1709-1784)

(NOTE: Names and places have been changed for this Chapter 23, but otherwise this account is true to my experience to the best of my recollection. MSM)

Interviewing at Greede Collections

Ed Pendleton's PLE collapsed about three years before my fifteen year mortgage would be paid off, at which time I would be financially independent because my other expenses were so modest. So I needed a job for about three years and looked for one nearest my house the old fashioned way, simply by reading the *Denver Post* want ads. I did not contact colleagues or network to find the best position possible in a short time. I was not in the market for a big career move. In fact I did not want to move at all. My house was filling with books and antiques and even a move to downtown Denver would be onerous. The Greede Collections ad in the *Denver Post* was for a General Counsel. What caught my eye was that applications were to be submitted to an office building in Inverness Business Center only about ten miles away from my house, at most a fifteen minute commute. I sent a resume and explanation, and within a few days was invited for an interview with the vice president of Greede Collections, Malynda White, a trim and attractive young blond in expensive blouse and tight skirt. Malynda was skeptical about my credentials which seemed to her to over-qualify me for the position. I explained that I probably could make a lot more money if I pulled up stakes and moved back to Boston where many of my friends and colleagues would want me to join their teams, but I wanted to stay in Colorado and was willing to accept a lower salary in order to do so.

Malynda, "OK, I guess that makes sense. But you also do not have collection experience, and our ad specifically stated we wanted our general counsel to have collection experience."

Merle, "I don't know much about your field, but it is fairly common for lawyers to take on clients in fields they know nothing about. With all due respect, the key factor is not subject matter knowledge, but how to apply legal principles and judgment to new factual situations. Talk to any lawyer in any big law firm and they will tell you that their top litigators often litigate cases with subject matter they knew nothing about a few months before trial. The key is knowing how to work a judge and jury and opposing attorney, not subject matter which one can master sufficiently within a few days or weeks of research. I did not know anything about the oil and gas industry before Ed Pendleton hired me as General Counsel of Pendleton Land and Exploration, but I worked there for ten years, and I think Ed has no regrets about hiring me. By the way, I put Ed down as a reference. Did you have a chance to talk with him?"

Malynda, "No. We think that references are a waste of time. Everyone gets a good recommendation these days. I think it's due to you lawyers who sue at the drop of a hat."

Merle, "I hate litigation. Sometimes it's necessary. But my experience with litigation is that it's usually a lose/lose proposition for everyone involved, except for the lawyers. My legal specialty, by the way, is preventive law, and I practiced that for over ten years in my prior jobs at HCLE, ECS and PLE. Perhaps I can review GC policies and practices and suggest changes that would reduce GC exposure to litigation."

Malynda, "That's an interesting idea. We spend too much time and money on litigation. OK, you've convinced me. I'll recommend to Dick that he should interview you."

Merle, "Dick?"

Malynda, "Richard Coriolane. He's the president and sole owner of GC. He will make the final decision."

When I returned to GC offices a few days later, Richard Coriolane did not smile when I introduced myself. It was not that he was unfriendly; just such a contrast to Ed Pendleton who would have enthusiastically shook my hand with a big smile, asked me if I would like something to drink and made some kind of joke to ease the tension. That clearly was not in Dick Coriolane's DNA. He looked me over with the beginning of a frown on his face.

Dick (motioning for me to take a seat in front of his large executive desk), "So what makes you think you can help Greede Collections?"

Merle, "Well, for a start, as I was telling Ms. White a few days ago, I specialize in preventive law, and if you'll give me a chance, I'll review the policies and practices of Greede Collections and recommend changes that will reduce your exposure to litigation."

Dick, "So you think you know more about my business than I do—the guy who started it from scratch and turned it into a multi-million dollar company? I had heard you Harvard guys think you know everything, but that's laughable."

Merle, "With due respect, Mr. Coriolane, or can I call you Dick?"

Dick, "Mr. Coriolane will do."

Merle, "With all due respect Mr. Coriolane, my education enables me to objectively scrutinize any company in America. Even General Electric and General Motors hire McKinsey & Company to examine their operations. They pay millions for such objective review. You can get me on the cheap. Usually the very persons who are most involved in a company are the ones who cannot see the obvious. We all have blind sides. The difference is some are smart enough to know it, and are open to change. I'm guessing you are one of those."

Dick, "You're guessing, are you? What nerve. You really think you can improve my bottom line?"

Merle, "I can't guarantee it, just as a surgeon cannot guarantee anyone a successful operation. But I have over thirty years of training and experience, and I'm your best bet. Would you rather hire a big firm to examine your company?"

Dick, "I can't believe your balls. Did your rich-ass old man also have big balls?"

Merle, "I never learned anything from my old man who was a deadbeat, abusive drunk who never put any food on the table for me and my six brothers and sisters."

Dick, "Really? Sounds like my background. So how did you manage to become a Harvard lawyer?"

Merle, "It's a long story, but the point is I did, and I'm sure I can help you and your company if you give me a chance."

Dick, "I'm not sure if you're just showering me with bullshit, but I'm going to give you a chance. How much were they paying you at that oil company?"

Merle, "$72,000 a year, but……"

Dick, "I may regret this, but you're hired at $80,000 a year. Can you start tomorrow? What's the matter? I thought you wanted this job?"

Merle, "I do, but I'm worth a lot more given my credentials and experience."

Dick, "And you'll get it if you're half as good as you say you are. And you'll get a lot more than you deserve if you can help me sell Greede Collections. I haven't decided for sure yet, and this is strictly confidential, but can you help me sell my company?"

Merle, "I've sold a lot of real estate, including my own income property. The basic skills are the same. Yes, I can help you sell your company."

Dick, "Well let's stop talking and start doing. Can you start tomorrow at 8 am?"

Merle, "I'll be here."

I walked out of Greede Collections with mixed feelings. I had sealed the deal, but once again my artificially low salary in public service came back to haunt me in private practice. A big competitive salary had never been an important goal, but as a matter of pride and self-esteem I wanted to retire with a six figure income. Most of my peers in private practice were making at least that much, and some, like Prentiss, many multiples more. Will I always get the short end of the salary stick since I took the other road? Well, just a few more years, and I'm out of here, financially independent, free to do whatever I want and salary will be a moot point.

A Bad Situation

The next day I was given a small office at the far end of the second floor next to Ken Nelson, GC's in-house attorney, now my responsibility given my general counsel position. Malynda had told me that Ken served a purpose for a while, but not so much now that GC had grown into a major collection enterprise with over 1,000 employees in seven states. I introduced myself to Ken and told him that I hoped we could be colleagues even though I had been hired as General Counsel. Ken said he was not surprised by my hire and wanted to make the best of a bad situation.

I soon learned what Ken meant by "a bad situation." Later that day when I was studying the federal Fair Debt Collection Practices Act (FDCPA), which governs (micro-manages) collection agencies in incredible detail, I heard Dick shouting at Ken next door. I was shocked. Dick's tirade could be heard throughout the entire second floor. I had never before heard such abusive treatment. I don't know what Ken had done to deserve it. In my view nothing would justify treating an employee that way. I felt sorry for Ken who must have been devastated not only from the public humiliation, but also knowing that I also had heard everything.

As if nothing out of the ordinary had happened, Dick stepped from the front door of Ken's office to mine.

Dick, "How's it going, McClung. You getting settled in?"

Merle, "If you ever yell at me like that, I'm out of here."

Dick, "What?"

Merle, "I said, if you ever yell at me like that, I'm gone."

Dick paused, looked me over once again, as if trying to decide what to do with this unexpected stand by his new general counsel. I waited, my big balls shrinking in the silence. I had just given my new boss the opening to say "you're gone right now. You're fired, now get the hell out of here." Instead he simply said "Fine," and walked away. For a moment I thought I had won this first showdown, but then realized I was so wrong. I had just disclosed a weakness—my thin skin about not being willing to tolerate abuse. Dick had walked away with a valuable piece of information. If he wanted to get rid of me at any time in the future, all he had to do was yell at me. I would be gone, and he would not have to worry about a retaliatory lawsuit, or even unemployment payments. I later observed that this was Dick's standard operating procedure with most employees. Dick rarely fired anyone; he just made working conditions so miserable that they quit. He was on the hook for far fewer unemployment claims than his competitors.

The FDCPA

The next weeks went by quickly as I learned about how the Fair Debt Collection Practices Act (FDCPA) affected GC operations. The federal act had been passed in response to a history of abuse by collection agencies. Observing Dick's treatment of his employees, I can imagine how he treated debtors over the phone. Clearly there was a need for protective legislation, but the FDCPA in my view went too far in micromanaging collection agencies. For example, the FDCPA specified the exact times during the day when a collection agency could call a debtor (one of many FDCPA "bright line" tests). No more midnight or early morning harassment calls. Call one minute too early or too late, and the computerized phone records would record the technical violation. The consequence was an automatic $1,000 penalty; no excuses, even if, as probable, the debtor had suffered no injury which is the first criterion for a viable lawsuit in all other litigation. All the debtor had to do was contact one of the many FDCPA attorneys to be found in every corner of the United States, and the collection agency was on the hook for $1,000 plus attorney fees and costs. The debtor's attorney could simply fill out his standard complaint form and be guaranteed a judgment in his favor. Usually he/she did not have to do even that much work. She would just get on the phone and see how much more than $1,000 the collection agency would pay in order to avoid a lawsuit that it could not win.

The game was not if, but how much the collection agency would have to pay. One of my responsibilities at GC was to manage and settle all actual or prospective litigation.

One of my first cases of this kind came to my desk the first week on the job. A debtor's attorney in northwest Florida called to say that phone records showed a time violation with his debtor client. A quick review indicated the appropriate defense: the call had been made within the permissible hours. I pointed this out to the attorney; he said, "You must be new here." I said I was in my second month as general counsel for GC, but how did he know. "There is a little corner of northwest Florida that is not in the Eastern time zone. I make a good living as a result of this quirk. You would think collection agencies would wise up and place red flags on every account in this part of northwest Florida, and they probably do, but collectors often overlook red flags in the file and make the same assumption about time zone that your collector did in this case. So I'm guaranteed $1000 plus attorney fees and costs; how much more do you want to pay to settle and avoid greater expense of defending an indefensible case in court?" Over time I got to know this attorney very well, as his comment about oversight proved true and therefore I authorized settlements several times. Not much legal training necessary to enjoy a comfortable living filing or threatening to file FDCPA violation cases. This is only one example. The FDCPA is filled with other "bright line" provisions that are a full employment bill for FDCPA debtor attorneys.

Employee Turnover

As mentioned above, Dick's modus operadi was to make life so miserable for employees he wanted to fire that they would just quit. And the collectors on the large open impersonal collection floor quit in revolving door scores, so finding and training replacements was an expensive proposition both in time and dollars. Apparently Dick could still make a good profit, but, given the time and expense involved in training a new collector, he surely could make even more by retaining employees. Like Ed, with partners who rarely became repeat partners, requiring a new search every time, Greede Collections was constantly training new collectors.

One day Dick asked me how my preventive analysis of Greede Collections was going. I said I had already identified several areas warranting change, but none as big as the employee turnover rate. I started to explain why, but Dick abruptly terminated the conversation by saying he had more important things to do. Later I found a small paperback titled something like "10 Most Common Mistakes Bosses Make" which emphasized the win/win returns of treating employees with respect, and attractive wages and benefits. I gave Dick my marked copy of the paperback along with a summary memorandum. Greede Collections clearly failed on eight of the book's ten criteria. So here I was advising the millionaire owner how to run a collection agency after only six months in a company which he had spent most of his life building. Dick never responded to my memo and I assume he found it either offensive or unhelpful—probably both.

I learned a bit of interesting psychology when Dick was considering a 401(k) retirement benefit for GC employees. He asked me to review the proposed benefit, and as usual I prepared a detailed memo concluding that it did not make financial sense, and thinking I had given him some cover for employees who had been requesting same. I discovered how contrarian Dick could be when he promptly approved the program. I noted that I was more likely to get something in the future if I recommended the opposite. I thought, next time I see Dick I'll tell him that I don't want a raise.

Four Day Work Week

The compensation question surfaced sooner than I planned when the Christmas/New Year holidays approached. That year Christmas Day and New Year's Day happened to fall on a weekend. Along with all other GC employees, I assumed that Dick would designate the following Monday as a work-free day, as most companies across America did. To everyone's surprise he did not, and a great deal of resentment followed Malynda's posting of a notice to the effect that Monday would be a working day like any other Monday at GC. The notice stated that GC understood that many would be tempted to claim a sick day or request a vacation day to be with their families on a traditional long weekend, but none would be granted. Everyone was expected to report for a full day of work as usual. I could not believe the notice was not a joke. I immediately took a copy of the notice to Malynda.

Merle, "Malynda, what's up with this 'Scrooge Notice.' It's a joke, right?"

Malynda, "No it's not. I feel terrible. I tried to argue Dick out of it, but he is not going to change his mind."

Merle, "Perhaps I can make a stronger argument than you?"

Malynda, "I would advise against it. I am closer to Dick than anyone in this company, much closer. If he won't listen to me, he won't listen to anyone. You'll only make the situation worse by confronting him."

I was so pissed off that I decided on the spot to ask Dick for a raise in the form of a four-day work week, using arguments that worked with Ed Pendleton ten years earlier at PLE. I resolved to quit if Dick did not accept my proposal, but I thought there was a good chance he would, especially since my workload at GC was heavy—in no small part due to the crises which Dick inadvertently caused by his heavy-handed micromanagement. Long story short, I told Dick that I would quit if he did not accept my proposal. I stated the truth: his Scrooge holiday decision had convinced me that I should not place a high value on my job at his company and I could always find alternative work given my credentials. Dick huffed and puffed, but did not blow the house down. After venting to remind me who was boss, he agreed to my four-day Monday through Thursday work-week proposal, saying he might soon need my help in selling GC.

A few months later Dick handed me a cell phone to use for GC business. This was a first for me since I as a single guy with few outside obligations had never felt a need for a cell phone, but had often wondered whether I should buy one just for use in case of an emergency. I made a trial call at home that evening to make sure it worked, when it occurred to me that I had just negotiated a four-day work week in order to have more time to pursue my other interests. Now I was holding a 24-7 leash which could negate a substantial part of my newly negotiated freedom. Therefore I resolved never to use it. Weeks later Dick asked me why, I told him, and, somewhat annoyed, he said he would give the cell phone to someone in the company who would use it.

Settling FDCPA Claims

The lawsuits and threats of lawsuits against various GC corporations flooded into GC on a daily basis. Most were minor in the sense of total dollar amount involved, but these also triggered Dick's rage. I had never thought about it much before because I assumed the federal law, as in civil rights cases, was designed to protect the weak against the strong and I had little natural sympathy for collection agencies. All lawsuits or threats against GC angered Dick, but I noticed the smaller claims sent him into a rage more than most. I realized that the same was true of me as well since so many of the minor cases seemed clearly extortive in taking advantage of the FDCPA's bias against the collection agencies, especially with the "bright light" provisions which did not permit a defense. While they bothered me, they did not enrage me, so one day I proposed to Dick that he give me settlement authority up to $5,000 on all cases. I knew that Dick, the classic micro-manager, would resist giving up any power, but I explained that dealing with these cases interfered with other GC business that only he could deal with. Given the FDCPA bias, most of these cases settled for about the same amount anyway—in fact many cost GC much more because of Dick's angry involvement. It would be more cost efficient with less brain damage to him, I explained, to let me dispose of these cases as I saw fit.

To reinforce my argument, I told Dick that it hurt me almost as much as him to pay out extortive settlements, even if small amounts. "I know you know that I am frugal when it comes to finances," I emphasized. Dick did know because when he reviewed my expense claims after business trips, as he did so carefully with all employee claims, he could find little to fault with mine. Observing his practice of carefully reviewing each claim which gave him a basis to challenge and intimidate employees, I submitted "preventive" claims, often not bothering to submit reimbursement claims for meals and other petty items. Curious, one day he asked me why I had not claimed reimbursement for any meals on a business trip. I told him the truth, "I was busy and just grabbed sandwiches at fast food places. The amounts were small and so not worth the hassle of keeping receipts and submitting claims—and then dealing with you about the details." One time Dick asked me how I had managed to get to a GC meeting in the Boston metro area without hotel, taxi or rental car expense. Again, the simple truth, "I had no expense to speak of because I stayed at a friend's house and borrowed her car for the meeting. I filled her tank with gas, but the amount was not enough to bother claiming."

Dick thought for a few moments about my $5,000 proposal, then said, "OK, settlement authority to $5,000, but I reserve the right to reverse any settlement you make." He never did, and I think GC saved a bundle as a result, especially if Dick's enhanced ability to focus on bigger issues is factored into the equation.

Rocky Road

Nevertheless, our attorney-client relationship was never smooth. One day after a disagreement when I thought Dick was being unreasonable, I just got up and walked out of his office. Later Dick confronted me demanding to know why I had slammed his door on my way out. I said I did not realize that I had done so, but perhaps I had since I had been upset that he was being "such a dick." Dick paused as if trying to decide once again whether or not to fire me on the spot, and then laughed and said, "You were being a dick yourself, you know." In spite of our conflicts, I knew that I was performing a valuable service to Dick and GC generally. But I did not know that Dick knew it until one day (7/1/97) after I had negotiated a favorable settlement in a major lawsuit against GC with potential for significant financial loss and bad publicity, Malynda confided in me that Dick had afterwards told her, "Merle is the best thing that has ever happened to this company."

Wow! Lawyers do not often get compliments in the normal course of their business. Lawyers are expected to "grease the wheels" of commerce so everything goes smoothly. So when it does, congratulations or other compliments are not usually given or expected. Lawyers are well paid for their time, and that should be sufficient. But of course dollars alone are rarely sufficient, and a compliment goes a long way. In this case with GC, given our uneasy relationship, Dick's compliment was especially appreciated— even if he had not given it directly. Perhaps he wouldn't have voiced the compliment had he known it would make its way to me. Or perhaps he knew. I will never know, but whatever the motivation, I chose to believe it was intended since an indirect compliment was probably the best I or anyone could ever expect from Dick.

Selling Greede Collections

What could I expect from Dick? When first hired he had strongly implied that I would be rewarded handsomely if I helped him sell GC. One day Dick came into my office, closed the door, and announced that the time had come to sell the company. He wanted me to lead the effort—in strict confidence because it would be disruptive if other employees found out. The exception of course would be Malynda, GC's controller (chief financial officer) Mack Thompson, and others on a need-to-know basis. No realtor or other agent would be involved since I could serve that function as part of my "honcho" assignment.

In addition to my normal responsibilities, I worked to honcho the sale by talking confidentially with Mack and others high in the GC pecking order to prepare written statements on various aspects of GC operations. I prepared a "to-the-best-of-my-knowledge" summary of GC's legal exposure, including a summary of the status of pending and prospective lawsuits against GC and best-guess estimates for eventual settlement payments. As the other statements poured in, I placed them all in a large black "GC Due Diligence" binder. The one report that troubled me was Mack's financial statement. When I did my line-by-line, number-by-number, review of his report it seemed too "optimistic," and I did not want a buyer challenging us later over statements and numbers perceived as misleading. Mack eventually convinced me that his financial report was consistent with Generally Accepted Accounting Principles (GAAP), and so it became the key part of our due diligence binder.

When I gave my final due diligence binder to Dick, he asked if it was necessary to share all that data with prospective buyers. I replied that it may not be necessary, but given the possibility of subsequent legal action against GC, it was better to error on the side of providing more than required, especially since I could see no harm in GC providing same. Dick nodded and said I would be very happy with the bonus he would give me if we were successful in selling GC.

Over the next several months Dick quietly contacted several collection companies about a possible sale. One expressed serious interest. MCM based in Los Angeles was one of the largest collection companies in the United States, and had purchased several of its smaller competitors in an "economy-of-scale" expansion program. We shared our due diligence binder with MCM, and when several discussions with its VP level executives went well, a meeting was set for MCM president "BT" and a few of his sidekicks to discuss purchase and sale terms and conditions with Dick at GC. The meeting went well, and the parties agreed to take the next step by preparing a Purchase and Sale Agreement. When BT asked us to call a cab for return to Denver International Airport (DIA) where the MCM corporate jet was waiting, Dick volunteered his

Ford Explorer and my services. On the way to DIA BT asked me what it was like to work for "such an unusual character as Dick." The tone of the question seemed a bit snide, and I surprised myself by coming to Dick's defense. "Dick may be a little rough around the edges, but he started with nothing, educated himself in the school of hard knocks and built GC into a multi-million dollar corporation. How many in this truck can say the same?" I was not unaware that defending my boss would make me look loyal in the eyes of the MCM executives crowded into the Explorer. I dropped them off at DIA, and headed back to GC just as a violent thunderstorm stopped most traffic on Pena Boulevard. I was one who kept trucking, but the going was slow and treacherous as huge cascades of rain mixed with sleet and hail crashed into the windshield. Then the cell phone in the Explorer started to ring. I ignored it because I knew I had to pay full attention to driving. The phone kept ringing and ringing, and I knew that it was Dick wanting a report on MCM comments prior to drop-off. It would be unsafe to stop on the side of the freeway in the storm's afternoon darkness, and unsafe as well to have a cell phone conversation while driving, especially since I did not own a cell phone and would surely fumble with the various keys involved. The phone kept ringing all the way back to GC which Dick had earlier left. I parked his Explorer in the GC parking lot and drove home in my Toyota 4-Runner. I could only imagine Dick's fury. He was not used to being ignored, especially by one of his underlings.

The next day I was relieved that Dick did not say anything about the phone calls. Within days our downtown attorneys approved a draft P&S Agreement to share with MCM. After several revisions by both sides, a meeting in Los Angeles was set to finalize the P&S Agreement with a $42 million price.

I joined Dick, Malynda and Mack for a commercial flight to

LA and we arrived on time at MCM's impressive office building. We waited nervously while Dick and BT talked behind closed doors. After what seemed an eternity, they emerged to announce that the P&S Agreement had been signed, sealed and delivered. Cheers, applause and relief. At the in-house MCM lunch round table hosted by the president of MCM to celebrate the signed Purchase and Sale Agreement, BT explained that he had left more on the table for GC than necessary because his philosophy was to "play nice in the sandbox"—not because he was a good guy, but because in his experience doing so almost always proved "win-win" down the road. I looked over at Dick and Malynda to see their reaction as I knew they took the opposite approach in their dealings. Then BT turned to me and asked several questions about my background. As a result he learned more about me in four minutes than Dick had in four years as my boss. I was impressed that BT was confident enough to focus attention on an underling at the table, but also gratified that Dick had learned some very positive things about my history which the MCM president obviously found impressive.

Promises

In the rental car on the way back to LAX and the plane back to Denver, Dick, Malynda, Mack and I were all somewhat giddy about the signed contract. I think somehow none of us believed the sale would ever happen—at least at that high a sales price. We laughed, reviewed the various characters involved and some of the funny and tense moments prior to signing and I congratulated Dick on securing multi-millionaire status with one stroke of the pen. Dick shocked Mack and me when he responded, "You both will be millionaires too if this deal actually closes." Mack and I looked at each other in shock; we had speculated on how big our bonus might be if GC actually sold, but our speculation was in the six figure range. Wall Street traders may expect million dollar plus bonuses at year end, but Mack and I had never dreamed of numbers at that level. "And if the sale goes through," Dick continued, "you two will help me start a new company to invest and multiply the proceeds. After so many years fighting to meet payroll and keep GC afloat, now we won't have to worry about capital. We are going to have so much more fun than we did as collectors. And I didn't mind signing the Non-Compete Agreement because I have no intention of staying in the collection business. We now have bigger fish to fry." Needless to say, our trip back to Denver was joyful.

Four months later after MCM had completed their due diligence, the sale closed on schedule when Mack confirmed that $42 million had been electronically deposited to Dick's account. Part of the informal agreement was that Mack and I would stay on for a few months to assure a smooth transition for MCM. Dick also had agreed to stay on for a few months, and one day called me into his office. With a big smile on his face, he thanked me for the key role I had played in the sale of GC to MCM and handed me an envelope, indicating I should open it. I did, and found a check written out to me—for $10,000. Now I had not been given a $10,000 bonus in any job before—in fact I had never been given any bonus. In other circumstances I would have been delighted with a $10,000 bonus, but Dick immediately detected my look of disappointment. "I know I promised you more, but our downtown lawyers told me that I could only give you $10,000 tax free." I was tempted to reply that whether the bonus was tax free or not was irrelevant, but realized it was a moot point. Dick had decided. Had he never raised my expectations, I too would have been pleased.

Burning Bridges

Then the few months assisting MCM's transition stretched into many, Dick did not follow up with plans to transition Mack and me to a new Dick company, and Mack and I seemed to be in limbo, knowing that MCM would eventually install its own people regardless of how competent our temporary transition work. Since Dick was not initiating the discussion, one day I asked him when I would be joining him to start the new Dick Company. As if expecting the question, Dick immediately replied, "You will be better off where you are." What? Did I hear that right? I would be better off staying with MCM—a company certain to let me go when they installed their hand-picked replacement? I certainly would be worse off than before, but since he controlled my professional future, only Dick knew whether I would be better off staying put, waiting for the inevitable axe. I was stunned and as usual said nothing in response. Had I responded instinctively, I would have burned my bridges with Dick and any hope of a future with his new company.

While I bided my time assisting with the MCM transition, I continued my general counsel work as before, settling debtor attorney complaints and a ton of the additional legal work inherent in transferring Dick's eight offshoot collection corporations around the country into MCM's stable. One day Dick surprised me during a phone conversation with a request to do him "a favor." "Of course, what is it?" The "it" was to convince MCM to accept Dick's version of a minor dispute that had arisen in interpretation of the Purchase and Sale Agreement. The issue had not been resolved before the close, and several times I had argued Dick's position with MCM. Now Dick wanted me to do so again.

Merle, "I'm sorry Dick, but I can't do that. I don't work for you anymore. My obligation now is to represent my new client, MCM."

Dick, "But you told me before that you thought we had the stronger argument."

Merle, "That's irrelevant. My duty now is to argue the other side."

Dick, "But no one will ever know. And I know that you know that we have the stronger argument anyway. I don't see a problem."

Merle, "Sorry Dick, but I do."

Dick (shouting into the phone), "After all I have done for you, I can't believe (obscenities deleted)."

One time before, I had terminated a conversation with Dick midsentence by getting up and walking out of his office. I instinctively did the same by hanging up the phone. I had no regret, but I knew that I had terminated our relationship as well as the conversation. Dick was not used to being contradicted by his underlings. His immediate fury at me might subside, but not the resentment. I had burned my bridges.

In the months and years that followed I often wondered if Dick's request during that last phone call had been a test of my loyalty. Dick certainly understood that he was placing me in an impossible situation when asking me to represent his views with my new employer. What an affirmation of power and control if he had been able to convince me to represent his rather than my new employer's interests. "I will not do it lest I surcease to honor my own truth...." Dick did not know my history with Coriolanus, but surely he knew me well enough to know that I would never do so. Therefore it could not have been a simple test of loyalty. More likely, I conclude, as with his practice of provoking other employees to quit so he did not have to fire them, Dick finally had the satisfaction of provoking me to hang up, and thus in effect fire my-self from our relationship. And additional satisfaction in not hav-ing to feel any guilt about not keeping his promises to make me a millionaire and continue my employment as general counsel in his new company? The psychology of it all is too complex for me to understand, and so I will never know. But one fact is not debat-able. After I hung up on Dick, we never talked again.

A few months later, Mack and I and almost all other employees except the collectors working the phone banks were given our ter-mination notices. Most immediately filed unemployment claims but I did not consider it for more than a minute. The law was de-signed as a safety net, and although legally entitled, I did not need it. I did not need to go through the cumbersome paperwork and embarrassing meetings necessary to qualify for nominal temporary support when surely my credentials would enable me to secure al-ternative employment within a few weeks if I wanted.

Retrospective

It is now twelve years since Dick had broken his verbal promise to make me and Mack millionaires with huge bonuses when GC was sold. I guess I never really expected otherwise, but like with Ed before, the reason for my missing a big payday continued to haunt my memories of both men. So I decided to include chapters on both self-made men and their companies. I was afraid that Ed, now in his 80's, might have succumbed to Alzheimer's or some other memory depleting disease common to old age. I knew im-mediately such was not the case when Ed answered the phone. We had not spoken since he and Bev attended a party that Pam and I had given almost twenty years earlier, but as with so many male relationships, Ed and I picked up where we had left off, soon joking and trying to out-insult each other at key points in the conversation. Ed was as charming and lively as ever and quickly agreed to my request for an interview to help summarize my experience with him, in particular his view of why our Shamrock contract with Dave Snyder did not close.

When I tried to arrange a similar meeting with Dick, his secretary asked me to hold, returned a few minutes later to say that Dick was very busy, but I could call back another time. I said perhaps it would be easier just to send an e-mail outlining the purpose of a meeting. She gave me his e-mail address; it was a discontinued one. With apologies when I called back, she gave me another e-mail address. My e-mail message to Dick:

> "Hi Dick, A voice from your past. Andrea gave me your e-mail address when I called this morning asking for an appointment with you.
>
> I turned 70 last year with Afib and chronic pain from an unsuccessful spinal fusion surgery in December 2012 that still requires pain medication. This potent combination led me to conclude that if I was going to write my memoirs, I should do so sooner rather than later.
>
> I have finished about 90 percent of the book, and have an assistant, editor and printer lined up to complete the project. I am now writing a chapter about my experience as General Counsel to Pendleton Land and Exploration, Inc. (Ed Pendleton, President) and Greede Collections, Inc. (Dick Coriolane, President).
>
> My plan is to compare you and Ed as entrepreneurs who started with very little, but through hard work each built a company worth millions. I think you and

Ed share many characteristics, but also are unlike in many ways.

Since my memoirs of course focus on me, I also plan to describe missing "big paydays" with both you and Ed. At first I was just going to write from my point of view, but then realized that it would be more interesting to include your views as well. I have an appointment to discuss these matters with Ed tomorrow (Tues.) morning, and hope you can spare an hour to do so as well.

I could meet you at your office, or elsewhere for coffee or a beer at your convenience. Hope you are well and enjoying life.

Please advise. Thanks."

There was no response. I considered calling Dick's secretary again to ask if Dick had received my e-mail and then decided it was obvious that he did not want to meet with me. I was disappointed not only because now the story I tell does not include Dick's version, but also because I think a face-to-face meeting may have underscored his basic humanity and complex mix of positive and negative characteristics. As with Ed, doing so probably would prevent me from labeling Dick a Greedhead. It is not easy to label someone a Greedhead when you know that person well. So this Chapter 23 morphed into the story of a Greedhead—my one-sided view of a stereotypical "greed is good" capitalist. Dick might acknowledge the label as a compliment. One day when asked, he explained to me that his choice of Greede Collections as corporate name, and 303.290.6666 (four sixes a biblical reference to the Devil as a phone number) was a deliberate attempt to instill fear in debtors and admiration in creditors, but also reflected his belief that greed is good in making our free market economy work (versus making our democracy work).

Bottom line: I achieved financial independence without cashing in on my two big paydays. First with Ed Pendleton and then with Dick Coriolane. It is counterproductive to obsess about what could've been (see poem on following page), but even after so many years it is still hard to forget. I need to remind myself from time to time that "enough is enough."

WHAT MIGHT HAVE BEEN

Would've, Could've, Should've.

We've all heard the refrain.

In job, in love, in all,

It's like a ball and chain.

Who knows what might have been?

Yet we can ascertain,

Your life can't begin again

Driving yourself insane

With Would've, Should've refrain.

Partners in Justice, by Author

Chapter 24
MY FAILURE WITH
THE CIVIC STANDARD

*The primary purpose of public education is to prepare students to
participate effectively as citizens in our constitutional democracy.*
—Merle McClung

After my work as general counsel to Greede Collections came
to an abrupt conclusion at age 55 in 1998 as related in the
previous chapter, I decided it was time to retire—at least retire
from desk jobs working another person's schedule. I reviewed my
finances and determined that indeed I could afford to go forward
without a paycheck. I was not a multimillionaire or anywhere
close to one percent status like many of my peers, but even a conservative estimate of my net worth put the figure well beyond one
million dollars. Given my modest needs as a single guy with no
debt and no children to support, I had achieved my secondary goal
of financial independence.

McEdlaw, LLC

What now? I certainly did not want to retire to the golf
course—or, in my case, the tennis court even though I still enjoyed
the sport. I knew what I did not want: a traditional desk job and
someone else's schedule and requirements. In the next chapter of
my life it was clear to me that I did not want to be scheduled. My
enthusiasm for any project in later years almost always had been
undercut by the realization that I had to be at a certain place at a
certain time. I had paid my dues. From now on to the extent pos-

sible, I thought, I will schedule myself, and do so sparingly. Once again, man plans, God laughs, as I was reminded several years later when my health began to decline and I was scheduled to the hilt with endless tests and doctor appointments and all the wait time those inevitably involve in our health care system.

What, I asked myself, really gives me satisfaction in life? The questions and answers were almost the same as I had confronted over thirty years earlier when I pondered offers from Morrison Foerster and Marian Wright Edelman. It became clear to me that what had given me the greatest satisfaction had been my hard work on education law issues—and now I had the luxury of doing so on my own time. I could start an education law consulting business and only take business that interested me. And if I were careful and disciplined, I could do so on my own schedule.

Therefore, with the help of colleagues at Holland & Hart in Denver, I incorporated McEdlaw, LLC on March 18, 2002 as an education law consulting company—not very impressive since it would be run out of my home office as a sole proprietorship with not even a secretary as an employee. I then informed some colleagues in the education law field of my new situation and waited for work that never materialized. I considered advertising my services to various state departments of education but decided against doing so as it would cast too wide a net. While waiting for clients with needs that coincided with my interests, one day I wondered whether anyone had advanced the kind of civic standard that I had advocated for so many years—the seminal primary purpose issue necessary to resolve before any of the classic educational issues could be intelligently decided.

I *Google*-researched the subject and was surprised to discover that no one had done so. All I could find were unhelpful references to the importance of civic education and developing good citizens as an important purpose for public education. Most such did not even attempt to argue as I did that informed citizenship should be the primary purpose of public education. Surely some scholars had published about primary purposes in public education, even if their work could not be picked up by *Google*. So I ordered dozens of books from nearby Koelbel Library over the next year in an attempt to find within them some careful discussion about the primary purpose of public education. Again, I was surprised to find so little.

The Civic Standard

The best work I found on the subject was by Amy Gutmann, then a professor at Princeton, now in 2016 the president of the University of Pennsylvania. Her book, *Democratic Education*, is superb but it does not posit a civic standard based on the specific language of the United States Constitution, but rather a democratic standard based on historical educational and political theory. Anyone can challenge that kind of analysis; my thought was that it would be much more difficult to challenge a proposed primary purpose that is rooted in the U.S. Constitution itself, especially if it incorporated the long history of judicial interpretation, as is the case with the civic standard. So it seemed like no one had advanced the ball. In fact, it seemed like no one even considered it important to do so. Well, I still did, and therefore resolved to research and publish an article to that effect. Since no one was beating down my door for education law services, I had the time.

I thought about applying for a grant from the Department of Education or one of the many foundations interested in public education to help defray costs, but the time and effort and restrictions that seemed inevitable with this approach also seemed formidable. So on my own dime I researched the issue and revised several drafts, until I was satisfied enough to submit a final manuscript to *Kappan* magazine—the gold standard at the time for reaching a broad audience of academics and education practitioners. "Public School Purpose: The Civic Standard" was published as *Kappan* fastback 503 in October 2002. To my surprise, my work did not generate as much response as any of my earlier articles on education law. So I published other articles on the civic standard with not much more success. The civic standard did not get any traction even when the Privatizers of public education effectively advanced their charter schools, performance pay, vouchers and related "reforms" which assumed an alternative primary purpose of competing in the global economy. For a summary of Diane Ravitch's courageous work challenging the Privatizers, see Chapter 4 of *Volume I of ARR.*

My inability to convince the powers that be, and the powerless who could make a difference that the civic standard could be a useful tool to help save public education from the Privatizers has been the biggest failure of my life. I have devoted over twenty years of my life on my own dime to do so and I am no closer now to achieving my goal than when I started, if actual difference is the measure. I haven't even been able to start a serious conversation about the topic apart from small groups of friends and colleagues who are predisposed to giving me the benefit of doubt.

I am now in the last chapter of my life and resolve to not go out with a whimper. It will be difficult since it goes against the grain, but I will change character and become a shameless self-promoter in order to get the civic standard recognized as a viable concept. I will also stop being a Mr. Nice Guy. Being passive and quiet in the back row will no longer be my role. I will stop playing nice in the sandbox and this chapter marks the beginning of that change. I will name names and let the chips fall where they may.

Anyone who has read this far in *A Rhodes Retrospective* will agree that I have led a charmed life, even though it did not start very well. When anyone asks about my childhood I simply say, "I was one of seven children supported by a divorced mother who worked as a medical records clerk in a small town hospital. Do the math, and you get the picture." I have endless details about how an impoverished childhood can cause damage to an individual but I tend not to relate them as I don't want anyone's sympathy. Also I don't want others to look down on me as a poor white boy. I just want to compete on equal terms, just as do most African-Americans and other minorities in the United States.

White poor outnumber all U.S. minorities, and if poor whites and poor minorities organized around their common low socio-economic status (SES), they as a group would be a formidable political and economic force. One regret I have at age 72 is that I have spent most of my life concealing my low SES origins rather than using them as a tool to help others like me rise above their circumstances. Actually, not concealing so much as rarely disclosing, except to a few close friends. I would not mislead if asked but I was not proactive in disclosing SES and it rarely came up on its own.

Recently courts have used class (SES) rather than race as a standard in assessing illegal discrimination against various classes, following the Supreme Court's 2014 opinion in *Schuette v. Coalition to Defend Affirmative Action*, overturning the University of Michigan's affirmative action plan based on race. Many criticize the court's decision given the pervasive effects of racial discrimination in our country, and they make a strong case. Yet I think years may have been wasted by focusing on race rather than SES. In personal terms, I couldn't help lead the SES fight and at the same time not be proactive about my low SES origins. In other words, I did not trade off my impoverished origins as that would be a form of self-promotion considered a character flaw in southwestern Minnesota. I had a choice, and in retrospect I made the wrong one. I succeeded so well in limited disclosure that most people saw me as a privileged white elitist; not surprising after my resume started to fill with the elite credentials of Harvard College, Oxford University and Harvard Law School.

My dilemma in extent of disclosure of my low SES origins reminds me of the complex contradictions of Coriolanus' refusal to show his wounds to the crowd as a matter of pride. It is demeaning to do so, especially when the crowd already knows about his military achievements. I adopted a similar stance in rarely disclosing either my low SES origins or my elite credentials. It was not that I did not take pride in both, but rather that I preferred that they be disclosed by others, as self-disclosure would be seen as self-promoting. This approach had always worked to my advantage in basketball. No one could accuse me of self-promotion, a passive stance was easier and the impact was greater if not self-generated.

The problem is that this approach did not work well for me in the real world after basketball. In Colorado, unlike Harvard's Cambridge, I was not known sufficiently for anyone to raise my background or credentials for me. No one knew or cared, especially after I left public service for private practice as general counsel with two closely-held corporations in Colorado. In these years in private practice it did not make a difference as lawyers usually work behind the scenes to maximize their contribution to their clients. So at first I was flattered when the president of the second corporation asked me to hang my diplomas on my office wall as impressive for his business associates and clients. Then I realized that by doing so I left myself open to "showing off" if and when anyone entered my office. Fortunately, most important business meetings were held in the conference room or the president's office, so very few stepped foot into my office.

When I returned to public service education law in 2002, I discovered the difficulty of re-entering a competitive non-profit world, especially for a sole entrepreneur with no university affiliation and an education world with only a vague recollection of my earlier work in the field. I thought this would change after my self-funded research and writings about the civic standard were published. I was wrong, as detailed in this chapter about my failure with the civic standard.

Poster Boy?

As I turn 72 in bad health, a new perspective convinces me that with such credentials I could have and should have made more of a difference for my SES group. I could have been the perfect low SES "Poster Boy" to promote the civic standard. My childhood was difficult as one of seven children supported by a divorced mother working a low-paying job. She placed a high value on education and taught us to respect our public education teachers who could help raise our low SES. See "Learning" poem on page 37 of *Volume I of ARR*. I benefited greatly from my small town public education, and now I had developed the civic standard as a tool which I thought could help Diane Ravitch and her supporters save public education from the Privatizers. In my Walter Mitty dreams I fantasized the headline: "LOCAL POOR PUBLIC EDUCATION PRODUCT PAYS IT FORWARD BY PROMOTING CIVIC STANDARD AS TOOL TO HELP SAVE PUBLIC EDUCATION: Focus Shifts to Preparing Citizens rather than Global Competitors."

I realize that there are reasons why I would not have been an ideal poster boy for the Goodheads and the civic standard. My story gives some validity to the Horatio Alger myth that in the United States everyone can "pull themselves up by their own boot-straps" (a physical impossibility) because all it takes is initiative, persistence, hard work and pluck. Many of the Privatizers' reform programs in education are premised on this myth: for example strict disciplinary programs implying that what the poor need are more grit and determination. Only a small percentage like me can be allowed to succeed, at the price that our stories then can be used to justify the current political and economic system. The few like me who succeed by these measures thus help validate the status quo which in turn perpetuates racial, gender, class and other barriers.

In my case I benefited from my skill with the basketball since athletic ability and skill (especially in the "manly" sports like football, basketball and hockey) are valued by the rich white men who control the political and economic gateways to success. Would the gates have opened for me if my ability and skill had been in art or music? I can't do anything about these arbitrary inequities, other than to acknowledge them and point out that the civic standard calls for effective participation by all students in school activities, not just the athletes, class officers and other "winners." I admit that I did not do more to help others because I was too proud to trade on my low SES status, but on the other hand I did not kick down the ladder I had climbed and did not succumb to the Greed-head values of money and power. I declined the opportunity to follow the traditional legal path to wealth and power when offered a position with a big prestigious law firm. With the confidence provided by my Harvard and Rhodes credentials I chose a public service career, albeit a somewhat lofty one at the Harvard Center for Law and Education and then the Education Commission of the States. When I later accepted general counsel positions at two privately-held corporations, in both cases after one year proving my value to the corporation, I negotiated shorter work weeks at the same salary in lieu of customary raises, explaining that time was more valuable to me than money. Perhaps I could and should have done more with my free time for the low SES class from which I came.

It is too late now—or is it? Despite declining health, I still have my legal skills, a passion for the civic standard and hopefully a few more good years. Perhaps my story can still be leveraged to promote the civic standard. So far I have been a colossal failure with the civic standard and do not know why. Two main explanations are (1) the civic standard is not viable because (fill in the blank), or (2) I have failed in promoting the civic standard sufficiently for it to be seriously considered by those who matter (Goodheads at high levels and their counterparts and other citizens at the grass roots level).

The second explanation is more likely since the civic standard seems to me so obviously better for our country than our current global business standard. I am like Coriolanus in being "too proud to court the plebeians" vote, thinking my achievements should be sufficient to win the day without the humiliation of parading my battlefield scars in the public square. Like Coriolanus, I have never needed to blow my own horn as my actions on the hardcourt battlefield spoke for themselves and were reported and praised by others. As such I became passive and never learned the difficult self-promotion skills necessary to succeed in today's Darwinian survival of the fittest world. I am still the naïve high school jock from a small southwestern Minnesota town where self-promotion is considered a character flaw. People deserving respect are the quiet doers (Goodheads) like the traditional Republican Ollie Rekow rather than the fast talking Predatory and Power Pricks (Greedheads) who undermine traditional American values. (See pages 169-72 in Volume I for definitions.) Too late for career advancement and very late in the game of life, I am now discarding old values and shamelessly promoting myself and the civic standard in every way I can think to do so, including this book.

I also realize that for exceptionally skilled Goodheads like Bill Drayton and several others included on my Goodhead list (p. 172 of Volume I), promoting one's cause does not necessitate compromising personal values. If I had the resources and persuasive power, I would try to get Bill to lead a campaign for the civic standard. He combines his intellectual and empathetic strengths with a focused determination to advance his Goodhead causes. Part of his success derives from his fascination with how organizations and people work. So Bill, if you ever need a new challenge and sufficient resources can be found, I have the perfect next challenge for you. Unfortunately for the civic standard, highly proficient and motivated persons like Bill Drayton usually have their own causes to promote.

Some wit once defined Rhodes Scholars as persons with great futures behind them, and that clever comment has haunted me ever since. Rhodes Scholars are an ambitious lot and we want to validate the special status granted by our selection. This creates a heavy burden that few of us would want to discard. Who would not want a burden with such nice benefits? The guiding value for Rhodes Scholars was set by the founder himself when Cecil Rhodes stated that he wanted the beneficiaries of his Trust "to fight the world's fight." Clearly Rhodes was not thinking of the kind of fierce self-interest that characterized his own success as a diamond titan (See Rhodes poem at page 5 of Volume I). He was a Greedhead wanting to be a Goodhead in the world's fight for the greater good. With a history of Greedheads, armed with a Darwinian survival-of-the-fittest free market philosophy, controlling our political and economic systems, American Rhodes Scholars tend to be a conflicted group (if any substantial generalization can be made about such a diverse group). At least I am, as at times I feel the Greedheads' pull to acquire wealth and power and fame almost as much as the Goodheads' push to fight the world's fight. The other line that has haunted me almost as much as the "future behind" quip is William Wordsworth's "getting and spending, we lay waste our powers." Wordsworth is so obviously right that just repeating as if a mantra the powerful economy of his words helps "lead me from temptation" and maintain a Goodhead focus.

I think that most Rhodes Scholars feel like I do that we have a special obligation to serve the public interest rather than self-interest given the rarity of the honor and the history of the coveted prize. I still think of myself primarily as a low SES guy with the common touch but have heard others refer to me as an elitist, and it burns as one of the worst insults I can imagine. Elitists think of themselves as better than others and I do not either in theory or practice. Thinking about this insult, however, I have to ask when someone like me stops being low SES, and becomes elitist by the very fact of having won or achieved coveted credentials.

This is a relevant question not only for those lucky enough to possess a Rhodes Scholarship or impressive Ivy League degree, but also for those with more modest achievements like low SES state and community college graduates who overcome hardship to become the first in their family to earn a college degree. Such graduates get good jobs, make good money and participate as productive citizens in society, and so at some point can no longer claim the "inverse status" of low SES. Similarly, for example, does a low SES graduate of an Ivy League school have a right to claim SES discrimination when denied tenure at a public university? If one had some justification for claiming protected low SES as a high school student, that claim surely disappears at some point as one rises in the system. These questions seem worth examination, even though to some extent SES depends upon the perception of the individual involved rather than others, as in Hamlet's astute observation that "nothing's so except thinking makes it so."

All this discussion about whether and when a person loses low SES is a prelude to my concern about the definition of success and failure in the context of my Rhodes Scholars Class of 1965. I raise the issue because I have been blessed with extremely good fortune ever since my difficult start in life. An impartial observer may say with all the success I have had relative to what others face, I have little reason to complain about a few small or even big failures along the way. I am concerned about this issue because at age 72 I am trying to deal with what I consider the biggest failure of my professional life: my inability to get others to see the validity and potential of the civic standard to steer public education in a better direction for our democracy. My ambitious goal is to get the various communities and the powers that be to focus on one key question: **Can the Civic Standard be a helpful tool to counter the Privatizers' of public education?** I think so, but even if not, would like to engage in a discussion of why not? For example, is the civic standard too complex, too divisive, too specific, too vulnerable, too (fill in the blank)?

The Civic Standard v. The Privatizers

Whenever someone is so sure they are right about their conclusions, like me about the civic standard, some self-examination is in order. The civic standard sounds good in theory, but could it be stood on its' head in practice, and used as a rationalization for a super patriotic authoritarian state at odds with individual liberty? State versus Individual is one of the great dualities with an unfortunate history given fascist and communist regimes in the past. But this possibility would fly in the face of the core values incorporated in "our constitutional democracy," and therefore also incorporated within the exact language of the civic standard. The first example that comes to mind is Justice Robert H. Jackson's inspiring words in *West Virginia Board of Education versus Barnette*, 319 U.S. 624 (1943), overturning a law forcing schoolchildren to salute the flag and say the Pledge of Allegiance to begin each school day: "Freedom to differ is not limited to things that do not matter much. That would be a mere shadow of freedom. The test of its substance is the right to differ as to things that touch the heart of the existing order. If there is any fixed star in our Constitutional constellation, it is that no official, high or petty, can prescribe what shall be orthodox in politics, nationalism, religion, or other matters of opinion or force citizens to confess by word or act their faith therein." A totalitarian state, or state with authoritarian inclinations, is not consistent with the civic standard.

If the answer to my question about whether the civic standard could be used as a helpful tool to counter the Privatizers is Yes, then forward to questions about national versus local control of public education. Since I sought dialogue about the concept, anything, even the weakest version of the civic standard, totally discretionary and totally local would be better than nothing in order to test the concept. Regardless of the specific language of the civic standard, just the general tone of preparing critical thinking citizens rather than global competitors would be a big improvement for public schools. In other words, if educators simply believed that the civic standard represented the true primary purpose of public education, regardless of its formal adoption as policy, the consequent effects would be beneficial.

Ideally the civic standard would be adopted by local boards of education as a unifying national goal, but still open to choice at the local district level as to implementation and experimentation. The civic standard would recognize the proper federal role in (1) promoting a unifying national primary purpose for public education, and (2) enforcing federal civil rights laws. Given these two legitimate roles for the federal government in education, I would recommend adoption of the civic standard at the local board of education level. I would emphasize "the People" more than "the States" language of the Tenth Amendment to the U.S. Constitution: "powers not granted to the federal government by the Constitution, nor prohibited to the States, are reserved to the States or THE PEOPLE" (emphasis added). And I would interpret "the people" to be local boards of education and others at the grass roots level.

The specific language of the civic standard creates a strong presumption against separation of students by race, sex, ability or SES. Some readers may skip past the historical justification for the civic standard and reject it because it has implications they do not like, such as its strong presumption against separation. If one believes that girls should be educated separately from boys, then she/he will reject the civic standard. The civic standard's focus on participating effectively in our democracy requires participatory interaction as much as possible in public schools since it is difficult to learn to participate effectively if one is separated by race, sex, ability, identity or SES.

So too, the civic standard is not for you if you believe that students, teachers and schools should be evaluated primarily by the results of standardized test scores. The specific language of the civic standard requires qualitative as well as quantitative assessment, recognizing the limitations of each.

If *Brown v. Board of Education* (1954) was the first-generation desegregation issue (ongoing), and tracking within schools and classrooms was the second-generation desegregation issue (ongoing), then charter schools and their "choice" counterparts are the third-generation desegregation issue. The "choice" schools, promoted and partially funded by the Privatizers, create another two-tier system of public education: one for the motivated easy-to-teach "creamed" students (including some minorities) for selective schools; and another for all the rest ("losers") who public schools must take regardless of motivation, ability, behavior, handicap, etc. Second class citizenship is contrary to the civic standard. At least traditional private schools buy their own privilege by paying their own way. Charter and other "choice" schools try to have it both ways: considered private for purposes of freeing themselves from onerous public school laws and oversight, but public in demanding equal tax dollars for their privileged alternative.

Helped by the spin of the Privatizers, we like to think we have made good progress in civil rights, pointing to the election of Barack Obama as President. However, today our public schools are MORE segregated sixty years after *Brown v. Board of Education*. According to a study published last year (2014) in the journal *Education and Urban Society*, "Students are more racially segregated in schools today than they were in the late 1960s and prior to the enforcement of court-ordered desegregation...." Charles Blow also writes about increasing cultural segregation: "We are self-sorting, not only along racial lines but also educational and income ones, particularly in the big cities...." (*NY Times*, 4/11/14). Americans are becoming more segregated by choice: the voluntary choice of many to live in separate enclaves in gated or other homogeneous communities where different classes (SES) rarely mix. As Blow notes, it is hard to understand and get along with others if you rarely interact with them.

CIVIL RIGHTS MOVEMENT

Determined not to be mistreated
Rosa Parks rose far more than a fuss
Refusing to be segre-cheated
At the back of a Montgomery bus.

To others who fight segre-cheated
Her brave stand gives impetus
Civil movement not yet completed
Still moving to the front of the bus.

As discussed in Chapters 4 and 10 of Volume I, Americans are losing the socio-economic battle on all fronts. Extreme income inequity has replaced traditional income inequality. Our health care reform (Obamacare) has been built on a broken free enterprise foundation that continues to reward the Greedheads at the expense of patients, and the more rational single payer alternatives are not even a part of the debate. Public school systems are more segregated sixty years after *Brown v. Board of Education* declared separate schools unconstitutional. And our society is increasingly self-segregating. Goodheads are losing on all fronts, and need to regroup and wage a smarter fight. In public education, the civic standard offers a new tool based on an old concept.

I have advocated the civic standard concept for public schools since 1972 when I submitted my third year paper on "Ability Grouping" to Professor Frank Michelman at the Harvard Law School (HLS). The third year paper at HLS is comparable to a thesis in other academic contexts. My third year paper originated as a legal analysis of what courts would and should do when applying traditional legal tools like the due process and the equal protection clauses of the *14th Amendment* to developing second generation desegregation problems. Public schools in the north as well as the south were undercutting the letter and spirit of the Supreme Court's holding (some say dicta) in *Brown v. Board of Education* (1954) that separate is inherently unequal. Many school districts were desegregating their schools under court order, but then re-segregating students within the schools according to ability into separate classes ("tracking").

Ability grouping is most justified in some skill courses in math and science where prerequisites are necessary to understand course content. For example, algebra before calculus, although some argue such prerequisites are unnecessary when weighed against the benefit of integrated classrooms. The practice is most egregious in social studies where, for example, a group of high achieving white students may be engaged by their teacher in a First Amendment discussion on one side of the hallway, while on the other side the same is taking place with low achieving "losers", usually disproportionately low SES students. Tracking creates a two tier education of the "haves" and the "have-nots," similar to the creaming of the easiest-to-teach today by selective charter and other "choice" schools—at the expense of public schools which must take everyone regardless of SES, motivation, ability, behavior or handicap. The civic standard on the other hand, creates a strong presumption that students learn from each other (and "the hidden curriculum"), and therefore the participatory benefits of integrated classes outweigh possible academic benefits. Separation is inherently unequal as emphasized by the Court in *Brown v. Board of Education*. It often comes down to a conflict in whether the primary purpose of public education is seen as academic/economic or democratic/civic. The media and Greedheads usually assume an academic/economic purpose, and are preoccupied with standardized test scores as if such were the only measure that matters.

I did not see how second-generation re-segregation or most other difficult education issues could be resolved without first identifying what is the primary purpose of education. I researched this seminal issue and was surprised to find that the founders did not see an economic or academic purpose as primary. Although their exact words may differ, I summarized as follows the underlying concept of George Washington, and even such fierce political opponents as Thomas Jefferson and John Adams, and several other founders as well: "the primary purpose of education is to prepare students to participate effectively as citizens in our constitutional democracy."

In other words, the primary purpose of education is to help make our democracy work, a goal at least as important now as then. Later I named the concept "the civic standard." I considered the more accurate term "the democratic standard," but concluded that too many would interpret "democratic" in a partisan political sense that would undercut or at least distract from constructive discussion. Today I would opt for "the democratic standard" since those inclined to put a partisan spin on the concept will do so regardless of what it is called.

The civic standard runs counter to two-tiered education of any kind. Heterogeneous education is favored more than economic or academic goals which are legitimate but secondary. In other words, even if the creation of two or more tiers (by race, sex, ability, SES) could be proven to increase market share or standardized test scores (and it has not), the relevant question is what practice best advances the goal of preparing students to participate effectively as citizens in our constitutional democracy? It is not unlikely that the business standard as the primary purpose of public education has produced an oversupply of Greedheads that are a big part of the problem today.

In making the primary goal of public education competition in the global economy, the Bush and Obama administrations have continued to favor profits over the common good and Greedheads over Goodheads. "Greed is good" is the extreme value of some Greedheads, but it should be challenged for the moral depravity it represents. In addition to other problematical effects, global competition contributes to more and more depletion of our natural resources with little consideration for the cost. The free market is good at making widgets, but is not willing to measure the environmental and social costs. Do we need more widgets? Do we want more self-interested Greedheads, or more critical thinking Goodheads who in time could vote the Greedheads and their supporters out and replace them with Goodheads for the common good?

My research showed this was not a dilemma for the founders. This is not a new observation. The rhetoric of citizenship as an important and even primary goal has been adopted ever since the founders advanced the concept. What is new with my proposed civic standard is that it is not some vague concept for rhetorical purposes only, but that each word in the definition has important implications for the content, process and assessment of public education.

Writing Long v. Writing Short

My original plan was to publish some articles in education journals and use the discussion generated by them as the basis to develop more sophisticated arguments for an eventual book about the civic standard. I have enough materials to write several and one book is already more than half written. It expands on every paragraph in my journal publications: more detail on the Founders' view of education; more analysis of more key education decisions by the U.S. Supreme Court and lower courts; more background and discussion of education issues, including the history and politics of George Bush's No Child Left Behind Act (NCLB). And the inexplicable Obama/Duncan expansion of NCLB with their Race to the Top (RttT) criteria continuing to promote "choice" schools, teacher performance pay and competition in a global economy. In my prospective book, I would also provide a more detailed explanation of the civic standard's implications for the content, process and assessment of public education. The task, although difficult, appealed to me since I like to explore in detail and discuss various nuances that are inherent in any complex social issue, including vulnerability to unintended consequences.

Then I had an enlightening discussion with Lee Dembart, an astute observer of contemporary America who I met through Prentiss Willson. Lee convinced me that the task should not be to write longer, but to write shorter, if my goal was to get the civic standard seriously considered. A book at best might win academic awards but the shorter you write, the greater the chance that some person or group in a position to actually influence policy will read and act on it. Write a book about education policy, and it will probably go largely unnoticed. So too with a lengthy scholarly article in a law or education journal. More people will read a *Kappan*-sized article (limited to 3,000 words) than a 20,000 word report. Lee argued that I should reduce my *Kappan* article on "Repurposing Education" to an executive summary if I really wanted it to be read by influential people. Two pages at most, but one page would be better yet. If I could somehow manage to revise it to be "ready for prime time," Lee, how about the one page article submitted and rejected for the *Kappan* authors' blog below. "The influential almost by definition are busy, and rarely read more than one page of policy analysis and recommendations about anything," Lee repeated. Upon reflection, Lee's suggestion sounded exactly right to me, and so my future writings will be shorter rather than longer expositions.

Do you remember the familiar reaction of most students to secondary school teachers who assigned ten, twenty and even thirty page papers? Yes, the more pages, the louder the groans. What most of us didn't know then, before we all became such opinionated windbags, is that it is harder to write short than long. Lee Dembart would agree with Blaise Pascal's comment in a letter to a friend, "I have made this a rather long letter because I haven't had the time to make it short."

Joan Richardson and *Kappan* Magazine

I had hoped my three publications would at least generate some debate on this seminal issue in public education. The limited feedback from my publications, however, was not substantive. Some professors assigned the articles for their classrooms, but for the most part my articles disappeared into the abyss, including "Repurposing Education" which was my best attempt at describing in concise form the important implications of the civic standard for the content, process and assessment of public education. Therefore shortly after "Repurposing Education" was published in May 2013, I was pleased that the editor of the *Kappan* magazine, Joan Richardson (JR), invited me and other authors to contribute to a PDK authors' blog ("Learning at the EDge") because it offered a way to connect with kindred spirits and further discuss issues raised by the article. Therefore on July 16, 2013 I submitted a brief post asking for comment on three questions raised by "Repurposing Education." JR responded by correctly pointing out that my initial submission of about 100 words was too short, incorrectly assumed that *Kappan* blog readers had read my *Kappan* article and I should at least summarize the civic standard in my post. I did so on July 17th, and then, not hearing from JR, on October 3rd added additional commentary within JR's 500 word limit. I reproduce our e-mail exchange here because it allows me to multitask: (1) describe and discuss the civic standard, including the three key questions I had tried to raise in my blog submission, and (2) raise some questions about editorial professionalism.

Here is the revised post I submitted to JR on October 3, 2013 for inclusion in her "Learning at the EDge" authors' blog:

REPURPOSING EDUCATION: THE CIVIC STANDARD
Ground Control: What is your destination?
Pilot: I don't know, but we're making good time.

The economic purpose of getting a job or getting into college in order to get a better job, has evolved into the de facto primary purpose of K-12 (and higher) education. The result has been a dangerous narrowing and privatization of public education. Business models prove to be a poor fit for education problems. In my May 2013 *Kappan* article on "Repurposing Education," I propose an alternative that would serve us better. The civic standard: "The primary purpose of public education is to prepare students to participate effectively as citizens in our constitutional democracy." Each word has important implications for the content, process and assessment of public education. By shifting the emphasis to the critical thinking and empathetic citizens necessary to make our democracy work, I argue that the civic standard will also produce the kind of graduates that employers need in the 21st century.

Recently I was discussing the civic standard with some teachers at a small dinner party when one asked, "Why not let each local school board choose its' own purpose or purposes?" While pausing to formulate a concise response to a question that merited another article, her husband added, "Or keep it simple for all, like education-for-education's-sake?" Relieved, I said education-for-education's-sake sounds good but is so vague that almost anything can be justified and so is not of much use in setting and implementing priorities. So too with alternatives like "educating the whole person" which do not lend themselves to prioritizing among competing claims. Unlike the civic standard, what do such formulations say or imply about the content, process and assessment of public education? About probability/statistics rather than algebra/calculus, heterogeneous versus homogeneous classes or qualitative versus quantitative assessments?

Some friends and colleagues stated that my article did not address other important issues such as:

1. Would adoption of the civic standard necessarily mean more top-down federal control of public education?
2. Should the civic standard be mandatory (enforceable) or simply a guideline (aspirational)?
3. Could the civic standard be a useful tool to help counter the growing privatization of public education?

I think that the civic standard could be useful at any point on the #1 (national←→local) and #2 (mandatory←→discretionary) continuums, but would appreciate comments on these and/or other issues raised by my article.

On January 31, 2014, I sent JR the following e-mail since she had not responded to my July 17th and October 3rd submissions:

Hi Joan,

I just received your e-mail re Call for Manuscripts which states that you have published dozens of submissions to post on your "Learning at the EDge" blog. As you never replied to my last e-mails several months ago about my proposed post for your blog, I'm left in the dark as to why not.

I don't think I've ever had an education law submission rejected in my long ed-law career, and so am curious as to the reason. Is it because my submission is too theoretical for your readers? I find that educators love to discuss issues raised by the civic standard when given the chance. Do I have bad breath?

Don't worry. This is not a nudge to get you to change your mind, and I can find other avenues to dialogue with kindred spirits. I have moved on. But an explanation would be appreciated if you have the time for a quick reply.

Thanks,
Merle

——————— *Original Message* ———————
From: "Richardson, Joan"
To: "Merle McClung"
Subject: Re: Query?
Date: Mon, 3 Feb 2014 16:39:51

Merle,

I'm so sorry to have overlooked your emails. I'm at a loss to explain how I could overlook several emails. And, no bad breath is not the answer!

But I do think you should tackle the blog anew. It's not quite ready for prime time. Instead of just listing the questions that friends and colleagues say you overlooked in your original article, why not use the blog to answer them? No need to point out that readers thought you failed to do this the first time, just tackle the questions more directly. I think that would be a fine way to extend what you originally wrote.

By the way, I liked your ground control/pilot exchange at the beginning. I might have to borrow that for my writing workshops.

Dear Joan,

Thank you very much for responding to my 1/31/14 query. I am relieved to hear that I do not have bad breath.

Your standards are too high for me. I raise the questions precisely because I don't have all the answers and would like to dialogue in the kind of open and unrestricted access necessary to easily exchange thoughts with kindred spirits. I thought that is what blogs are supposed to facilitate, but now realize there must be all kinds. When I am more certain of my views on these tough education issues, I will seek to publish in the traditional way rather than in a blog. We clearly have different objectives, and so I will look elsewhere.

Best,
Merle

JR's response to my inquiry about why she had ignored and then rejected my proposed submission to the *Kappan* author's blog floored me. JR calls her blog "Learning at the EDge," and yet she faults me for raising questions at the edge of my proposed civic standard concept? She wants me to focus on answers rather than questions? That strikes me as anti-intellectual and even authoritarian. I try to give everyone the benefit of doubt; in fact always remind myself to take everything as a compliment even if it might be an insult because life is short, and it is better not to get involved in petty squabbles. However, I read and reread JR's February 3rd response many times over the next few weeks and I could not manage to read them in any way other than snide, smug, officious, demeaning, contemptuous, imperious, unprofessional, censorial— I keep trying to find the right word to capture her response.

Even if my proposed submission was "not ready for prime time" (you be the judge), does an editor not have a responsibility to be civil in responding to her colleagues and inferiors? Whatever happened to the customary, "Thank you for your submission. We regret that it does not meet our needs at this time." Why respond with, in effect, "Your third rewrite of your submission to my blog is still not ready for prime time; why don't you start over using a different organizing principle?"

At the beginning of my legal career several Harvard Law School Professors gave me A's in their courses, including Professor Archibald Cox, former Solicitor General of the United States and Special Watergate Prosecutor, who praised my analytical writing in words shamelessly quoted in Chapter 7 of Volume I. Now with over forty years of experience, including scores of published articles, my submission is not good enough for JR's blog? I know that my body is failing after seventy years, but I am not willing to accept that my mind is as well.

What did I do to someone I have never met to invite such a condescending response? Why is she jerking me around? Does JR really believe that the purpose of the *Kappan* authors' blog is to answer difficult education questions (within her 500 word limit) rather than offer a forum in which to discuss them? Why criticize me for raising follow-up questions on a complex education issue when her *Kappan* limit for my article was 3,000 words. I would love to be so accomplished that in 3,000 words I could propose a novel education concept, discuss it and then answer several possible follow up questions that might legitimately be raised, but I don't think that has ever been done in the history of education, regardless of the number of words allotted.

So what is JR's real reason for rejecting my proposed post? My God,... sorry, My Joan, it's only a 500 word blog submission; it's not like a more formal submission for a typical *Kappan* article. I submitted my first proposed post on July 16, 2013, a second on July 17 (unanswered), a third on October 3 (again unanswered), and it is now more than six months later (February 3, 2014), and you want me to revise it once again in hopes that this time it will meet your criteria for being ready for prime time?

This reminds me of the delay in publication of my "Repurposing Education" article. On December 2011 JR accepted that article for publication in *Kappan* Magazine. Then I waited and waited for weeks and weeks and then months and months before the article was finally published in the May 2013 issue. What strange irony in our new world of instant communication that it takes *Kappan* Magazine eighteen months to publish an article? In that time, most articles dealing with contemporary issues need to be rewritten several times just to keep up with developments in the real world. For example, the Occupy Wall Street commentary in my article written summer 2011, submitted in October and accepted in December 2011, was a hot national topic for the media at the time; eighteen months later when "Repurposing Education" was finally published, Occupy Wall Street was rarely mentioned on TV and had receded from the front pages to an infrequent reference buried somewhere as a footnote to old news. As I list all these problems with my PDK experience, I turn Hotspur and make a resolution. Never say never, but I will never again submit an article for publication in the *Kappan* Magazine.

So this response raises two additional questions: (1) does the JR response, including delays and non-responses, constitute abuse of editorial authority? and (2) will this book, publishing the follow up questions rejected for the *Kappan* authors' blog, elicit some response to my question about civic standard viability? I was thinking about creating a Civic Standard website/blog for ongoing commentary when JR invited me and others to post on her *Kappan* authors' blog. This seemed a better alternative at the time since her blog was already set up with ties to PDK membership. Now that my participation on the *Kappan* authors' blog will never happen, I have created a new website/blog *MakeOurDemocracy Work.com* with a section on education. So readers are invited to submit posts and join the discussion at *MakeOurDemocracy Work.com*.

Since JR's last suggestion that I once again rewrite my submission for her blog comes more than six months after my initial submission, I consider it a rejection. JR's e-mail rejections come near the end of my legal career. I never expected to be given a gold watch upon retirement, but how about a little respect, or at least common courtesy?

JR's e-mail rejections also come at a time when I am especially irritable and cranky since spinal fusion surgery on December 20, 2012 was unsuccessful and as I write this in May 2014 I still need the tramadol pain medication prescribed after the surgery. The tramadol is only partly effective, and I live in pain almost 24/7. My doctors will not prescribe the stronger new FDA approved medication until proven safe and non-addictive. Is addiction to a pain killer worse than continued pain for a seventy year old man who also has unfixable Afib? So I am in no mood to suffer insult with grace and good will. This is the absolute lowest point in my career. I could better handle my physical deterioration and back pain than the implied insult to my intelligence and writing ability. Once again I compare myself to Prentiss Willson.

Prentiss Willson

My good friend Prentiss and I are much alike, graduating from Harvard Law School about the same time with many career options. The main difference is that Prentiss has a better hook shot and sharper elbows, as proven many times on the Miles College faculty basketball team on which we both played while teaching at that small black college in Birmingham, Alabama in the late sixties. I see Prentiss as my alter persona since after we left Miles College and graduated from Harvard Law School, we stopped at the proverbial fork in the road. One led to a lucrative career in a big prestigious San Francisco law firm (Morrison & Foerster); the other to a low-pay but stimulating public service career. We both had attractive offers from MoFo; Prentiss accepted and I took the other path. Often when the less traveled public service path seems more onerous than necessary, I wonder what my life would have been like if I had made the same choice as Prentiss. Today is one of those times as I know that Prentiss bills his clients $750 an hour to get the benefit of his expertise. I have just spent twelve years of my life at my own expense researching and publishing about the civic standard which conceivably might help save public education from the Privatizers, and I can't give my expertise away free of charge to this editor.

I try to imagine all the reasons which might justify JR's rejection of my submissions and none seem plausible. To be sure, the *Kappan* magazine used to be the standard bearer in the field for elementary and secondary education and educators of all ages and PhD candidates still compete to get published in the *Kappan* as a prize to parade before their employers and tenure committees. It can't be easy when so many fawn and depend on your decisions for their career advancement. Publishing for a fourth time with PDK has no added value for me other than to make contact with

Merle McClung and Prentiss Willson

some kindred spirits and discuss some important issues relating to the civic standard. Perhaps JR was just having a bad day and I just happened to e-mail her at the wrong time, and so her smug response was not an example of systematic abuse of power. If so, she should be forgiven—but not by me. As editor, JR has the right to reject submissions she thinks are not ready for prime time. As a PDK author I have the right to question her judgments.

So Joan, if you are reading this and just dying to tell your side of the story, how about doing so in 500 words or less in the place you have given yourself in your *Kappan* authors' blog—editor's prerogative, or does some other PDK official have to approve your posts? If so, perhaps it would be easier for you to set the record straight in one of your monthly editor's columns. Better yet, why not devote an entire issue of the *Kappan* to doing so, as the civic standard could use the publicity. Even better yet, feel free to post your response on my new website/blog: *MakeOurDemocracy Work.com*. There is no word limit and I will publish your post even if it is "not ready for prime time." And you are guaranteed instantaneous publication on my blog; no need to wait for months and months to share your views.

I am sure some readers are thinking "why all the fuss about a trivial dispute about a trivial issue by trivial people?" Shades of Puck in *A Mid-Summer Night's Dream*: "Lord, what fools these mortals be!" So too the classic answer to the question of why are academic politics so vicious: because the stakes are so low. Surely a valid point, but since more than twelve years of my life have been devoted to research and writing about these issues, JR's arbitrary rejection of my blog submission raises questions about my competence, her judgment and more important, the viability of the civic standard.

Trivial disputes are not limited to trivial people. In his fascinating book *Naturalist* (1994), Edward O. Wilson in a chapter called "The Molecular Wars," describes his conflicts with James Watson, co-discoverer of the structure of DNA (as depicted in *The Double Helix*), including over office space at Harvard. You think my little tiff with JR is excessive? The mild-mannered evolutionary biologist, who opened up a larger world for all of us via his study of ants, describes Watson as "the Caligula of biology" (p.219). It happens.

Clarification: my 1/31/14 e-mail to JR stated that "I don't think I've ever had an education law submission rejected in my long ed-law career." Not true. While I have published over twenty articles in legal and education journals, including a seminal article in the *Fordham Law Review* (1979), an early version of the civic standard that I submitted to the *Harvard Education Review* in 2002 was rejected. This started a pattern of my failure with the civic standard but was not as disturbing as being rejected by JR for a mere blog twelve years later.

I think it important to public education generally, as well as to me personally, to discuss and try to answer this one key question: **Can The Civic Standard be a helpful tool in countering the Privatizers' attack on public education?**

I have found it surprisingly difficult to get anyone to even address this question in general terms much less discuss it in a meaningful way. After my "Repurposing Education" article was finally published in May 2013, I hoped for and expected some substantive feedback because the article represents the best I have been able to do to summarize the civic standard and its implications. But it was like the article had fallen into an abyss. As mentioned earlier, no substantive responses were received. Some professors used the article as a discussion piece in their classrooms, but there was no consideration at the city, state or national levels where it could conceivably make a difference.

Justice Stephen Breyer

In an unsuccessful attempt to bridge this gap, I audaciously handed copies of my article to U.S. Supreme Court Justice Stephen Breyer and former Justice Sandra Day O'Connor. Here's how it happened. On June 29, 2013 my girlfriend and I accepted a Harvard Club invitation to attend a live taping of the *Aaron Harber Show* with the two Justices in Aspen. The topic included *Making Our Democracy Work*, the title of Justice Breyer's 2010 book. In college and law school I rarely joined other students around the podium after lectures to interact with professors, but I screwed up my courage this time and handed each a copy of my *Kappan* article.

I explained to Justice Breyer that I thought the article fit in well with his book. In *Making Our Democracy Work*, Justice Breyer, a Clinton appointee, states that the book's title is his guiding judicial philosophy in deciding cases on the Supreme Court. "The Constitution's most basic objective is the creation of a single nation," a goal it advances "by creating political institutions strong enough to permit the 'people' to govern themselves." In addition to the general concept, Justice Breyer argues that a focus on purpose and consequence rather than "originalism" should be the key to judicial determinations. The language of purpose and consequence is also a match for my treatment of the civic standard.

Indeed, Prentiss Willson sent me the following about a KQED Public Radio program aired on 2/20/11: "If you haven't already read Justice Breyer's new book you may want to listen to this. About half way through he tells a cute story about a conference he, Justices Kennedy and O'Connor attended where the question was what about the Constitution should be taught? The lawyers were suggesting freedom of speech, privacy, etc. and he said that all three justices had exactly the same reaction: all were important but the central importance of the Constitution was the pursuit of democracy. And that meant an informed and active, participating citizenry. Sound familiar?"

Justice Sandra Day O'Connor

So too I thought that Justice O'Connors' work on civic education was an essential, but not sufficient part of the civic standard, and suggested she might find it interesting to consider how the article outlined further implications. Justice O'Connors' good work with the content and promotion of civic education can be followed on her *iCivics.org* web site. Several years earlier in 2008 I had sent Justice O'Connor a letter:

"Re: Civic Education Project
Dear Justice O'Connor:
With most public schools preoccupied by NCLB requirements, it is refreshing to read about your Civic Education Project in the April 9th issue of *Education Week*.

As summarized in the enclosed PDK fastback "Public School Purpose: The Civic Standard" (2002), I think that the civic standard has important implications for the process and assessment as well as the content of public education. Have you given any thought to expanding your Civic Education Project to include process and assessment implications for teachers and policy makers?"

My question was designed to underscore that content recommendations calling for more civic education for students is a fairly modest and conservative undertaking focusing on changing students, whereas the process and assessment issues of the civic standard also calls on schools to make systematic changes.

Since simply publishing an article that I presumptuously consider important did not work, I stepped into my new self-promoting role and forwarded links to the article to the four people in the field I most respect: Diane Ravitch, Deborah Meier, Harry R. Lewis, and Michael A. Rebell ("The Big Four").

Diane Ravitch

Diane Ravitch is the leading figure trying to save public education from the Privatizers. She has published two important books particularly relevant to the Privatization movement. The first is *The Death and Life of the Great American School System: How Testing and Choice are Undermining Education* (2010). Her current best-selling book *The Reign of Error: The Hoax of the Privatization Movement and the Danger to America's Public Schools* (2013) is must reading for anyone concerned about what is happening to public education today. See chapter 4 of *Volume I of ARR* summarizing her important work, including "Diane Ravitch's Blog" revealing "the common core" initiators to be the Privatizers and DOE rather than the states (top down rather than bottom up reform). Her recently formed organization (*www.campaignforpubliceducation .org*) is the best hope today for organizing the professionals, parents and all other stakeholders necessary to contest a standardized testing regime which narrows the curriculum. And which trains our children to compete in the global economy rather than participate as citizens in our democracy. Diane is particularly despised by the Privatizers and many in government and foundation circles not only because she publicly changed her mind about these issues, but then had the audacity to launch a national reform movement in response.

Deborah Meier

Deborah Meier at one time was the progressive voice in *Education Week's* "Bridging Differences," engaging in spirited dialogue with the conservative Ravitch before Diane's conversion. While Amy Gutmann has written the best academic exposition of *Democratic Education* in her 1999 book of same name (compared to the civic standard in my 2002 PDK Fastback 503), Deborah Meier has spent her entire career advocating and implementing hands-on democratic approaches and values in public education. She founded and led the Mission Hill School in Boston and Central Park East Schools. Her many publications including *The Power of Their Ideas* (1995) and *In Schools We Trust* (2002) discuss this experience. Considered the founder of the small schools movement, no one in public education today can offer more enlightened and experienced counsel on democratic (civic standard) education than Deborah. In my opinion, she is among the most worthy recipients of the MacArthur genius grant. Deb generously sent me e-mail congratulations and encouragement after reading my *Education Week* article (12/3/08).

After several e-mail exchanges on related issues, on 11/29/09 I wrote her: "You probably are too busy to do so, but I would appreciate your critique of "The Civic Standard" (*EdWeek*, 12/2/08). We need to provide a viable alternative to the narrow business model (primary purpose as preparing students to compete in a global economy), but frequently advanced alternatives like "educating the whole person," "education for education's sake" and "intellectual development" are so vague and general as to justify almost everything and thus provide little guidance. So too multiple purposes (like the Seven Cardinal Principles of the 1918 Commission) which are politically expedient, but do not provide guidance to prioritize among competing goals.

On the other hand, it seems to me that the strength of the civic standard as the primary purpose of public education is that it provides a legal, historical and political rationale/basis for a more democratic model. But is it too complex, or are the democratic implications such as non-segregated participation and critical thinking too difficult for our times?"

Harry R. Lewis

Harry R. Lewis is the former Dean of Harvard College who challenged Harvard President Larry Summers for leading Harvard in the wrong direction. In *Excellence without a Soul: How a Great University Forgot Education* (2006), Harry explains how Harvard was losing its primary educational mission of preparing students for civil society in its competitive pursuit of faculty and grants. From the dustjacket of the book: "while striving to be unsurpassed in the quality of its faculty and students, Harvard has forgotten that the fundamental purpose of undergraduate education is to turn young people into adults who will take responsibility for society." Not the most sensitive expression of Harvard's mission, but Lewis' book raises questions about the primary purpose of higher education without getting specific about the concept. In my recent pushy role, I tried to encourage Harry to develop a civic standard for higher education, comparable to the civic standard I promote for K-12 public education. Since he has not yet done so, this is another of my Cass Sunstein nudges.

Michael A. Rebell

Michael Rebell is my Harvard College '65 classmate who has devoted his entire legal career to advocating for equal educational opportunity for disadvantaged school children. His many publications include *The Right to Comprehensive Educational Opportunity*, 47 *Harvard Civil Rights-Civil Liberties Law Review* 49 (2012). Michael was the intellectual and driving force representing low SES New York City school children in their successful "adequacy" litigation to guarantee more equitable funding among New York school districts. *Campaign for Fiscal Equity v. State of New York* raised the seminal questions about the primary purpose of K-12 public education. I am particularly interested in the case because it centered on interpretation of a similar civic standard in New York law, and Justice DeGrasse's opinions discuss the standard's implications in helpful detail. Given his extensive experience on related education issues, I think Michael is one of the best positioned lawyers in the United States to analyze and comment on my proposed civic standard.

Google their names to learn more about the impressive careers and extensive publications of The Big Four. These leaders in education are my role models. Therefore I was disappointed that three of the four had nothing to say about the seminal issues my *Kappan* article raised for public education. Only one made a brief substantive comment and I was surprised that the other three all said that they could not read my article because it was behind a $5 paywall! This is true, I swear to Joan. Since I had spent so many years of self-funded research and publication on a novel concept that might be important in their work, I was surprised and dismayed that my article was not worth even the $5 that PDK charges non-members to read the article. But determined to elicit some substantive responses from leaders I respect, I swallowed my pride and sent each paper-copies of the article by snail mail and waited for responses. Again, none materialized.

So then the question as to why? Am I considered some kind of wing-nut outsider after so many years in private practice? Do they shake their heads and wonder why I am still trying to convince everyone that the civic standard is important when it is so (fill in the blank) as to be a waste of time to even discuss?

Prentiss, being the good friend that he is, has a more palatable answer. "Today almost everyone is so busy with their own agendas that they simply do not have the time to respond, especially the big names you tried to reach. If they acknowledge reading your article, they will feel obligated to make some substantive comments and that takes more time that they do not have. And if you then respond to their comments, as is likely, they will feel obligated to spend even more time they can't spare. So it's not that they don't respect you; it's that they respect you so much that they don't want to dismiss you with superficial comments. Best not to respond at all."

Prentiss is probably right. I should interpret the silence as a compliment and move on, but I'm in my new aggressive self-promoting role in order to advance what I believe to be an important concept so this anecdote is a way to call them out and force the issue. This is me not playing nice in the sandbox. If I had the resources, I would invite The Big Four to an expense-paid Rocky Mountain Summit at Aspen or Vail to discuss the key civic standard question posed above. Perhaps a carrot or two to incentivize is in order? A briefcase full of recently legal Colorado cannabis for all to share might do the trick, and have the further advantages of warming up a possibly reticent group, and alleviating my (and Diane's) now chronic back pain. A pot party with "edibles" just might be the answer.

Or going one step further, I could submit a proposal to all the usual suspect foundations and even to the U.S. Department of Education (DOE) headed by Arne Duncan (a former Harvard basketball player), asking for funding for a Rocky Mountain High Conference focused on the civic standard question, with The Big Four and little me making a panel of five for the traditional conference format of presentation and exchange of ideas. I don't have the organizational energy to do so, especially since most of the foundations and the DOE are too busy funding and encouraging the Privatizers. But if any younger motivated reader is so inclined to take the civic standard baton, I will provide whatever support my aging body and mind can.

There are many possible reasons why the answer to my civic standard question could or even should be a resounding No. The Civic Standard may be too divisive, too specific, too idealistic, too vulnerable, too (fill in the blank) to be a useful tool against the Privatizers. If so, perhaps it could be revised to be more viable. Or the discussion might lead to the development of other tools that would be more effective in countering the Privatizers. We need more effective tools, as supporters of public education are losing the battle with every passing year. We are headed towards training more and more of our charges to promote our economic interests in a global economy rather than preparing them to participate more effectively in our democracy.

Arguably there are bigger issues facing our country. Closing the gap between the one percenters and the rest of us as discussed in Chapter 10 of *Volume I of ARR* is one, and requires the more difficult fundamental changes in theory and practice. The education reform contemplated by the civic standard is incremental, since it incorporates our core values and already is accepted as rhetorically correct by most. We just need to translate the rhetoric into practice; not by any means easy, but an incremental rather than fundamental change.

I am forced to admit that in this most important task of my professional career, I have failed, and am not likely to change that harsh reality before I reach the finish line. But I will not quit. Perhaps my new website/blog *MakeOurDemocracyWork.com* and the related Make Our Democracy Work Enterprises ("MODWE") (discussed in Chapter 28) will help turn the tide. It could happen. "Diane Ravitch's Blog" now gets an enormous number of hits, and has paved the way to her *www.campaignforpubliceducation.org*—which is the best hope so far for common sense prevailing in K-12 public education.

So in the end I decide I will not quit. I will continue self-promoting in my new role; escaping my prior Coriolanus mode where others naturally come to you—which works when you are a star in sports (Bill Bradley), education (Diane Ravitch), or politics (Elizabeth Warren), but not for lesser lights like me. I refuse to accept failure and am determined to push and shout my message until I no longer can. Even then there still may be hope for the civic standard as some public education advocate in the future may see promise in changed times more open to the concept. If not, perhaps it will be resurrected when some member of my extended family sometime in the future wonders: why was Merle McClung so preoccupied with the civic standard?

EXPERT TEASE

Don't you think it's time we all recognized
That we have become far too specialized?
In football, kicker and punter are two
And neither can block or tackle for you
As that is someone else's job to do.

If your car spews excess carbon emissions
Don't ask a mechanic who does transmissions.
The dentist specializing in root canal
Will not have skills to fill your teeth too well.
Professors of medieval poetry
Can't help you with romantic hyperbole
Much less with modern forms of irony.

The lawyer who will help you make your will
Will not try to draft your prenuptial
Thus refers you to others with that skill
And if not paid on time, all of them will
Have another lawyer still, collect the bill.

You're at the wrong end of the anatomy
Taking your headache to podiatry
Or tonsillitis to proctology

The logical end of this trend is clear
Doctors who treat the right, but not left ear.

Oh where is the modern Renaissance man
And the woman for all seasons who can
Comprehend, repair, heal and do it all
Even write a poem and throw a ball?

Yet if my heart ever needs surgery
Please send a surgeon immediately
Specializing in cardiology.
Thus this critique of modern expertise
Incorporates its share of special tease.

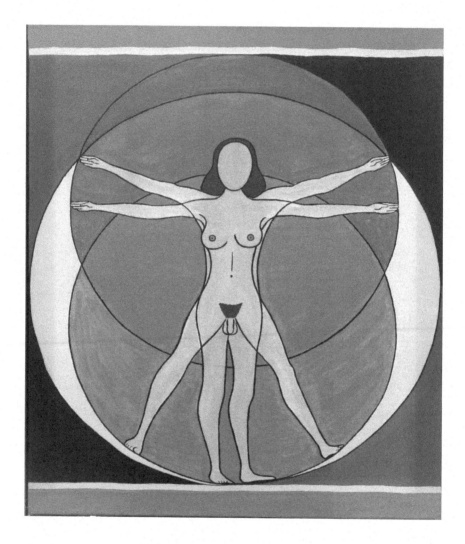

Gender Gap, by Merle McClung

Chapter 25
HEALTH ISSUES

The money ain't in the cure; it's in the medicine —Chris Rock

M y birth certificate states that I was born to Ernest and Martha McClung in Clara City, Minnesota on June 30, 1943. So I was a World War II baby, and Ernest was exempt from the draft as a farmer necessary for the food needed for the war effort. I almost died before my first year. When old enough to notice, I asked my mother about the eight inch vertical scar under my left armpit. Blood poisoning, my mother explained, and the country doctor said I might not survive the surgery. Later I wondered why blood poisoning required such an incision, but it seemed a moot point. I was alive and focused on surviving, one of what would become seven children after my mother moved the family to 523 North 5th Street in the nearby city of Montevideo (population about 5,000).

The most painful moment in my life occurred when I was about seven years old. My older brother David and younger brother Vernon and I would frequently play a game we invented by throwing a ball against the recessed front side of the house above the porch. One day in the rush to catch the rebounding ball one of my brothers pushed me and I fell head first onto one of the eight inch iron stakes that had been inserted into the corners of the lot which connected rope in a futile attempt to keep us off the grass-seeded dirt in front of the house. The stake tore through my upper right lip and broke off about half of the front tooth behind the lip. Screaming in pain I ran the six or seven blocks to the Montevideo hospital where my mother worked as a medical records clerk. The accident left a scar over my right upper lip, encouraging me in later years to grow a moustache for cover.

Except for the usual minor injuries of an athletic kid, I was healthy and avoided the hospital until I needed oral surgery for gum disease caused by that childhood injury. I spent three nights at age 22 recovering in an English hospital where my expenses as an Oxford student were covered by UK universal health care. No paperwork to speak of and the nurses were quite wonderful. For about the next 30 years regular participation in basketball and tennis kept me out of hospitals and even away from doctors until a kidney stone ended the run in 1992. I thought I was keeping my body in fit shape by playing pick-up basketball games with younger guys instead of eating lunch on most days—until my body told me to stop at age 52. Only then did I realize that I had been staying in shape at the expense of breaking down my joints.

Hip Pain

When my "chronic" bilateral hip pain started to interfere with my sleep, I made an appointment with my primary care physician (hereafter "Primary Physician #1" to preserve his privacy). (I had many PCPs before him, but he is #1 for purposes of this memoir). On May 31, 1988 Primary Physician #1 diagnosed the source of my hip pain as "mild rheumatoid arthritis" based on a physical examination, hip x-rays and blood test results. That was the beginning of over twenty years of misdiagnosis of my hip pain. Primary Physician #1 prescribed continued exercise and ibuprofen as needed. I did not question the diagnosis since I thought the science of blood testing yielded definitive results.

Osteoarthritis

My hip pain continued but successive Primary Care Physicians examined my hip x-rays and concluded my arthritic hips were not serious enough to warrant different treatment. Keep exercising they advised, and take ibuprofen as needed. My hip pain gradually grew worse until I asked Primary Physician #6 for a referral to an arthritis specialist at Denver Arthritis Clinic near Rose Hospital in Denver. On February 9, 2000 the specialist took the form of Dr. HK—a six foot tall brunette so stunning that I instantly forgot my hip pain in favor of a relationship fantasy, enhanced when she asked me if I had a brother in northern Iowa. Distracted by my fantasy I realized that I had been gawking at her without answering her question, and so joked that as far as I knew I did not have an Iowa brother unless my mother had engaged in some extracurricular activities no one knew about. Why do you ask? Laughing at my bad joke, she replied, "I did a double take when I first saw you because you are a dead ringer for my high school boyfriend." "Probably just some other incredibly handsome six foot six guy," I joked as she asked to see my left hand, and my fantasy continued while she gently held my wrist with her left hand and with her right hand probed each finger. My first thought was if Dr. HK had been attracted to someone who looked like my twin, why not now with me, especially if the old embers still burned. My second thought, after realizing that Dr. HK was probably happily married with children, was perhaps my lifelong fantasy about having a long lost biological father rather than the deadbeat I grew up with, was true. Montevideo, Minnesota in southwestern Minnesota is only a short drive from Iowa's northern border, after all. Could it be?

Then I heard a shocking statement from somewhere outside my fantasy, "Mr. McClung, you do not have rheumatoid arthritis." I was stunned and asked her "Are you sure I don't have rheumatoid arthritis? I have been treated for rheumatoid arthritis for the past ten years!" "I'm almost positive that you have osteoarthritis," she replied, "but let's take some x-rays to be sure."

As I continued my wonderful fantasy about all the delightful nights HK and I would enjoy together in the future, the x-rays were taken and processed. "The x-rays confirm you have osteoarthritis. See these dark spots next to your pelvic bone? That is a clear sign of osteoarthritis. But it is not severe enough for me to recommend surgery." "What do you recommend," I asked, hoping that she would say something like "many years in my bed." No such luck, as she replied, "Continued exercise, and ibuprofen as needed." Not only was my fantasy deflated but I was beginning to think I was a wimp for complaining so much about my hip pain. My related symptom, the sporadic severe pain which occasionally shot down my right hip to behind my right knee Dr. HK concluded was probably bursitis, but did not require any different treatment unless it became a recurrent problem.

Dr. HK's report dated February 9, 2000, included the following:

"CHIEF COMPLAINT: Lateral Hip Pain.

HISTORY OF PRESENT ILLNESS: The patient is a 57-year-old Caucasian gentleman who is a lawyer. He was diagnosed as having rheumatoid arthritis 10 years ago, at which time he had a low-titer rheumatoid factor according to his report. He reports joint pain dating to age 20, when he had lateral hip pain in the cold, damp weather of Britain. Over the years, he has had intermittent lateral hip pain which occurs after vigorous exercise such as basketball and is nocturnal when he is not using his hot waterbed to sleep on. He has not ever had pain or swelling in the wrists, MCP or PIP joints, or any other region. He has reported trouble sleeping through the night due to hip pain when he does not sleep on his waterbed and reports that he needs to get up in the middle of the night to exercise for a few moments and loosen his hip so he can return to sleep. He denies low back or anterior groin pain and he denies morning stiffness. He does not have hip pain when he gets up in the morning.

The last hip x-rays were apparently done 10 years ago. Advil has been used for hip pain and works dramatically— 400 mg prior to a bike ride or playing basketball which helps significantly.

* * * *

The patient denies a history of plantar fasciitis, low back pain, uveitis and psoriasis. He did have blood in the stool and a flexible sigmoidoscopy and colonoscopy showed benign polyps and hemorrhoids there. He does not have diarrhea.

PAST MEDICAL HISTORY: 1) Benign prostatic hypertrophy. 2) Sinusitis. 3) History of "rheumatoid arthritis." 4) Cholecystectomy, 1998.

MEDICATIONS: Include Advil and multivitamin.

FAMILY HISTORY: Mother died of colon cancer. There is no family history of inflammatory arthritis or any form of arthritis for that matter.

SOCIAL HISTORY: The patient is a single lawyer who grew up in a small town in Minnesota. He does not smoke and drinks alcohol only occasionally. He very much enjoys sports and misses these activities.

REVIEW OF SYSTEMS: Essentially unremarkable. He has gained about 30 lbs over 60 months due to less physical activity. His connective tissue review of systems is negative. His general review of systems is positive for nocturia, occasional dyspnea and sensitivity to the cold. He has occasional blood in the stool which is attributable to polyps and hemorrhoids.

PHYSICAL EXAM: On physical examination today, the patient was a pleasant, tall gentleman in no distress. Height was 6'6" by our measurement, weight 298 lbs. and blood pressure 138/74. Head and neck exam was normal, cardiac, lung and abdominal exams were normal. Joint exam showed no synovitis or pain in any joint. Hip range of motion showed internal rotation to be 40 degrees, external rotation 35 degrees with no pain. Both trochanteric bursae were palpated and were non-tender. The low back was non-tender along with the sacroiliac joints. Schober's test increased from 10 to 15 cm with forward flexion and chest expansion was 5 cm, both of which are normal.

ASSESSMENT: I suspect this gentleman has trochanteric bursitis which is brought on by his sports activities, is intermittent and resolves quickly with Advil and rest. Other possibilities are early hip osteoarthritis or degenerative arthritis of the back with referral to the lateral hip. Sacroiliitis is a possibility, considering his morning stiffness, but the patient has no other features of spondyloarthropathy.

PLAN: 1) X-rays of hip, low back and sacroliliac joints. 2) Review x-rays with patient. 3) Regular use of an NSAID would be quite appropriate....

Addendum: X-rays of the lumbar spine showed some mild facet osteoarthritis in the lower spine. There was some mild medial joint space loss in both hips. There was no evidence of sacroiliitis.

Results were discussed with patient and x-rays were reviewed with him. I believe that his lateral hip pain is a combination of all 3 processes, namely some mild osteoarthritis of the hip, some facet osteoarthritis of the back and likely intermittent trochanteric bursitis brought on by impressive exercise such as basketball.

Recommendations would be to maintain weight as low as possible to decrease stress on the joints and to use Advil on a regular basis. Complete blood count, SGOT and creatinine should be checked every 6 months while on this drug…. Pamphlets were given to the patient on osteoarthritis, exercise and NSAIDs. He will come back on an as-needed basis."

Reading Dr. HK's report today (11/25/15) differs from my first reading as now I note her indications of possible lower lumbar problems as the source of my hip pain. Walking out of Dr. HK's office that day, however, my focus was on her surprising immediate diagnosis of osteoarthritis rather than rheumatoid arthritis, the consequent relief that perhaps my pain now could be better managed as a result of a correct diagnosis and disgust that I had suffered through ten years of incorrect diagnosis and related treatment. I shared Dr. HK's report with Primary Physician #6, and he recommended "Exercise and ibuprofen as needed" unless my hip pain got worse.

Miles College Reunions

I continued to exercise, mainly at my new favorite sport, tennis, for several years, but gradually my hip pain did grow worse and therefore my tennis exercise less. In May of 2007 Prentiss Willson invited our former Miles College faculty basketball team to a long weekend of pampered vacation at an Exclusive Resorts marble McMansion near Puerto Vallarta, Mexico. One day was set aside for a walking excursion through downtown Puerto Vallarta, but I opted for a bench by the ocean to watch the parade of humanity on the beach because I knew I could not endure the consequent hip pain. Prentiss had arranged to treat our group to lunch at the splendid Hacienda Del Angel, a fine restaurant located in an old mission. The problem for me was that the restaurant was high above the port and I had great difficulty climbing the series of steps leading up to the restaurant. I made it after resting several times but was embarrassed and disgusted that I was so limited in front of friends who I used to dominate in basketball and tennis (just kidding, guys). I wanted to get my life back and started to seriously consider hip replacement surgery, even though in my case it would probably mean two operations since my hip pain was equally severe in both hips ("bilateral").

Atrial Fibrillation

My aging body was further underscored the following year (2008) when I turned 65 and the physical examination recommended by my Medicare package disclosed that my heart was in atrial fibrillation. Since the A-fib had never caused any pain, this deterioration was a complete surprise. I figured that it might have been the cause of the chronic fatigue I had been experiencing for several years which the docs could not explain. Now I needed a cardiologist. Dr. Roger Damle prescribed several tests and treatments, including cardioversion, but concluded my Afib was unfixable because my heart did not recover normal rhythm even for a few seconds. He immediately put me on a warfarin blood thinning schedule with diet restrictions and frequent visits to test my INR. This dependent regimen was very frustrating, so I was relieved a few years later when Dr. Damle recommended the expensive but liberating Xarelto as an alternative to warfarin.

Xarelto indeed was liberarting, but after several weeks caused urinary bleeding, as did the alternative Eliquis recommended by Dr. Damle. With both these blood thinners, my urinary bleeding stopped a few days after stopping them. Although denying that Xarelto and Eliquis caused my urinary bleeding, Dr. Damle recommended a Watchman heart surgery designed to reduce the risk of blood clots. Given my traumatic experiences with the medical establishment, I declined. So too when Dr. Cohen agreed with the urologist's lithotripsy recommendation that would break the cluster of kidney stones into shards to expel (YIKES!), I delined.

Denny's Troubadour Defense

About two years later a scenario similar to the one in Puerto Vallarta materialized when Liz and I walked Jeff and Ann Zorn the several blocks from a Picasso exhibit at a fine art museum to their nearby home in San Francisco. I had to sit on doorsteps to rest about every block or so. The pain and embarrassment of my handicap was relieved because we were still laughing about the analogy between Picasso's troubadour painting and Denny Reigle's bullfighter "troubadour" defense while playing for our Miles College faculty basketball team. Not so funny was the fact that I was gradually restricting all my physical activities, including the essential one of walking, thereby gaining weight which further aggravated my back pain. I was losing my life and needed to do whatever was necessary to get it back. So I decided to bite the bullet and get my hips replaced. I had resisted this step ever since reading about standard hip operations whereby the surgeon literally cuts off your leg at the hip with a saw! A molded glass or metallic cap is then positioned over the sawn end of the leg before being positioned into the hip joint. This seemed so crude to me, almost like civil war surgery, and with advances in stem cell therapy it seemed likely that within a few short years sawing off the leg rather than growing new stem cells would appear barbaric. I questioned several Greenwood Athletic Club members who had undergone hip replacements and about half reported that it was not an especially difficult recovery after the first few days; the other half reported a lengthy and difficult and only partial recovery. Double hip replacement obviously was not going to be an easy decision.

Prentiss & Janice Wedding

In August 2012 Prentiss Willson invited Liz and me to attend his wedding with college sweetheart, Janice Rude. He would pay for our room in the elegant old Huntington Hotel in Pasadena. The story of Prentiss and Janice's love affair is simply amazing.

During his sophomore year at Occidental College in Pasadena, California, Prentiss became engaged to a junior, Janice Rude. Their wedding announcement stated: "No date has been set for the wedding." However, her father disapproved and cut off Janice's tuition and other support until she stopped seeing Prentiss and eventually was successful in forcing them apart. Fifty years later in August of 2012 at ages 69 and 70 the "date was finally set." More than one person at their wedding voiced words to the effect: "most romantic wedding ever." And given the ages of the bride and groom this was a group that had been to a lot of weddings! The unlikely romantic story of their early and late love is told at

(1) www.huffingtonpost.com/2013/01/07/janice-rude-prentiss, and

(2) www.oxy.edu/magazine/winter-2013/long-engagement, and

(3) https://www.youtube.com/watch3v=AhKiM17DE6E.

Friends speculate about who will play Prentiss and Janice in the Hollywood version of their story. Today they are enjoying semi-retirement; Prentiss with a national reputation as "the Michael Jordan of state tax law," and Janice as a 2012 inductee into the U. S. Diving Hall of Fame for her work at Duraflex International where she put her chemistry degree to work improving its diving boards.

My "Dive"

Liz and I took a taxi from the airport to the Huntington Hotel, arriving about 3:00 pm, two hours before the pre-wedding dinner for about thirty special guests. My hips were hurting and I needed a nap to recover from the trip so Liz left ahead of me to find Prentiss and Janice. About an hour later I joined them and several other guests who had begun to congregate in the outdoor reception area of the Huntington Hotel's Terrace Restaurant before dinner. Hotel staff circulated among the guests generously refilling wine glasses amidst growing excitement as we could see the long white linen-covered dinner table set up adjacent to terrace steps leading down into a romantic garden. I rarely have an alcoholic drink of any kind and so instead the waiter brought me a diet coke in a wine glass.

The usual clinking of wine glasses quieted the group for Prentiss' welcome and request that all take their pre-assigned seats at the table. I started to walk between the table and the terrace steps looking for my place card on the elegantly appointed table. As I stepped around two guests who were standing by their place at the table, my left foot came down in thin air and I tumbled down a flight of concrete steps to the garden landing below. In falling I managed to turn sideways and keep my wine glass upright as instinctively I did not want to break the glass. A guest later told me that I would have broken my wrist if I had used my right hand to break my fall. I fell on my right side and the shattered wine glass cut into my right hand and arm. I must have blacked out for a few seconds because the next thing I was aware of was a beautiful lady standing over me and calling for help while other guests circled the scene. The waiter who had brought my diet coke assisted with bandages to stop my bleeding. Some guests suggested I go to the emergency room for x-rays, but I said my injuries looked worse than they felt and I would be OK.

I took my seat at the table between Janice and her lovely Goodhead lawyer daughter and started to joke in an attempt to deflect attention back to the bride and groom. It worked as Prentiss cleverly announced that he would only give me a 5.6 on my "dive." The Olympic diving judge sitting nearby disagreed, saying "a 5.0 at best." I protested saying that I deserved at least a 7.5 on style points alone and several laughing guests agreed. The diving jokes were appropriate as several of the wedding guests were on the Board of Directors for Duraflex International, Janice's family diving board business. The concerned waiter returned with additional bandages and asked if I wanted to go to the hospital. Again I declined because I felt more embarrassed than hurt. Fortunately the meal proceeded with repartee and laughter as the focus shifted back to Prentiss and Janice. After the dinner a young couple asked me if I was OK, and said that I should sue the hotel for placing the table too close to the terrace, saying, "It was an accident wait-ing to happen." I thanked them for their concern, but said I was really OK, and I did not want to spoil my friends' wedding mem-ories with the inevitable ill-will inherent in litigation.

In the middle of the night I awoke in severe pain on my right side. Liz said I should at least go to the hospital for x-rays since I had probably broken some ribs but I once again declined as I knew that nothing could be done for broken, fractured or bruised ribs. The only treatment was time—and pain pills. The wedding that Sunday morning was in another romantic setting in a beautiful Occidental College building on campus where Prentiss and Janice had first met and fallen in love. After both shared touching mem-ories and traded personal vows, Dan Nowell, the original "Balloon Boy" who is Prentiss's friend and "life partner," declared them Hus-band and Wife. One guest shouted, "Prentiss, what took you so long?" and Prentiss immediately quipped, "I was stupid!" A burst of laughter, as most of the guests obviously agreed. More laughter during each of the toasts that followed, including those by Lee Dembart and me.

Lee Dembart

As the guests lingered around the wedding tables, I found an alcove where I could sit down and rest my hurting arthritic hips and bruised ribs. Lee soon joined me saying that he too could not stand for long. As Lee recounted his story of horrific back and other pain that had not been mitigated much by years of surgery and other treatment, we started to share stories about our mutual passion for book collecting. Unlike me, Lee could say that he had read every book in his collection, or at least intended to do so. Years later I was impressed when he remembered my anecdote about passing on a gigantic facsimile of the *Gutenberg Bible* at a library book sale because the $750 price was too much—a copy of which he possessed and never regretted paying $2,000. Lee and I had met before because Prentiss was sure our book collecting would be a bond, and it was—along with our respective "organ recitals." Lee wrote a delightful biographical piece as a law student about his prior work for the *New York Times* which Prentiss shares with his friends to this day.

Back home in Denver, PCP #6 agreed that I probably had broken, fractured or bruised ribs, but the only treatment was pain medication and rest—usually about eight to ten weeks. And he was correct as my painful ribs continued for about ten weeks while I gained weight and restricted my exercise to walking in the pool at Lifetime Fitness. My hip pain continued unabated and grew worse. PCP #6 said that my Pasadena fall had probably aggravated my hip pain. In fact my hip pain became so severe that I could only walk a few yards before I had to sit down and rest. I was losing my life—at least an important part which made it enjoyable.

Another Misdiagnosis

My hip pain became so constant and severe that I asked Primary Physician #6 to authorize a consultation with an orthopedic surgeon. I was convinced that I would need hip replacement surgery—in fact, double hip replacement as my hip pain was so obviously bilateral. Long story short, Dr. Robert L. Thomas, Center for Orthopedics near Littleton Adventist Hospital, examined my gait and leg motion, and ordered additional x-rays. To my surprise he told me that the x-rays showed moderate hip arthritis, but not severe enough to warrant hip replacement. To my even greater surprise, he said that he thought that my hip pain was referred pain from serious spinal problems. What? I have been treated for years now for arthritic hips and my pain is actually referred pain from an arthritic back? Dr. Thomas showed me lower lumbar dark spots, observable on the x-ray because he had asked the technician to make sure the x-ray included my lower spine as well as hips. Dr. Thomas said that he was almost positive my hip pain was primarily caused by my arthritic spine, and so he would order an MRI and recommend a subsequent visit with a rehabilitation clinic.

Dr. Thomas' report dated October 10, 2012 included:

PHYSICAL EXAMINATION: A pleasant male in no distress. He gets up from a sitting position with a mild amount of difficulty. His gait is somewhat antalgic. He has severe varus deformity to both knees with visible osteophytes. His knees, however, are non-tender to palpation.

DIAGNOSTIC DATA: X-rays, AP pelvis and lateral, both hips, demonstrate osteophyte formation off the lateral aspects of both acetabula. Joint spaces, however, are well maintained. Femoral heads are spherical. Impression: Mild to moderate degenerative arthritis, bilateral hips.

Lumbar spine AP lateral spot view demonstrates marked sclerosis in the facet joints from L4 to S1. He has grade 1 spondylolisthesis of L4-5. Impression: Marked lumbar spondylosis with grade 1 L5-S1 spondylolisthesis.

IMPRESSION: Bilateral hip pain in a 69-year-old male. This hip pain is likely referred from the facet disease in the lumbar spine. The arthritic change in his hips is, from an x-ray standpoint, mild and there is no provocation of pain during his physical examination. Asymptomatic degenerative arthritis, bilateral knees.

Dr. Thomas' plan was to refer me to a rehabilitation clinic for treatment of the lumbar spine through nonsurgical means, but I reminded Dr. Thomas that I had over twenty years of doctors telling me to exercise and take ibuprofen as needed, during which time my hip pain had gradually increased and at age 69 I did not want to delay any longer if a surgical fix was feasible.

Once again I walked out of a medical specialist's office stunned at a new and different diagnosis. Also, I was almost giddy. I had gone to Dr. Thomas thinking that two surgeries (one for each hip) would be necessary; now, if he was right, perhaps only one back surgery would suffice. In my mind, the problem now was that as Dr. Thomas indicated, the surgeon would probably recommend physical therapy—in other words, "Exercise, and take ibuprofen as needed." I did not want more years or even months of the same "exercise and ibuprofen" routine; I was getting older, worse and wanted a fix. Again, long story short, when I finally arranged to see Surgeon Specialist #1, I told him about my doubt that continued exercise and ibuprofen would work. When I read the MRI report I was shocked to read that my entire spine seemed riddled with serious problems:

INVISION SALLY JOBE

MRI OF THE LUMBAR SPINE WITHOUT INTRA-VENOUS CONTRAST

EXAM DATE AND TIME: 10/19/2012 5:00 PM

INDICATION: Back pain

TECHNIQUE: Multiplanar, multi-sequence MRI of the lumbar spine was performed.

COMPARISON: None.

FINDINGS:

VERTEBRAE AND CONUS: There is mild grade I anterolisthesis of L4-5. Alignment is otherwise normal. Bone marrow demonstrates no concerning abnormality. Paraspinous soft tissues demonstrates no concerning abnormality with a T2 hyperintense lesion of left kidney present, likely a cyst. The tip of the conus medullaris is normal in position and configuration at L1-2.

L5-S1: Posterior disc margin is normal. There is a severe bilateral facet arthropathy. There is no spinal canal stenosis or subarticular zone narrowing. There is mild to moderate right neural foraminal narrowing. There is mild left neural foraminal narrowing.

L4-5: There is uncovering of disc material with a central annular tear. There is severe bilateral facet arthropathy. There is epidural fat posteriorly. There is mild spinal canal stenosis. There is no significant subarticular zone narrowing. There is mild to moderate bilateral neural foraminal narrowing.

L3-4: There is a concentric disc bulge with small foraminal protrusions. There is bilateral fact arthropathy. There is epidural fat posteriorly. There is mild spinal canal stenosis. There is no significant subarticular zone narrowing. There is mild-to-moderate bilateral neural foraminal narrowing.

L2-3: There is a concentric disc bulge. There is severe facet arthropathy. There is epidural fat posteriorly. There is mild-to-moderate spinal canal stenosis. There is minimal subarticular zone narrowing without evidence of impingement of descending nerve roots. There is no neural foraminal narrowing.

L1-2: There is a minimal disc bulge. There is bilateral mild facet arthropathy. There is no spinal canal stenosis or subarticular zone narrowing. There is no neural foraminal narrowing.

IMPRESSION:

1. Multilevel degenerative changes of the lumbar spine as well as prominent epidural fat posteriorly combines to result in mild-to-moderate spinal canal stenosis at L2-3 and lesser stenosis at other levels. There is no evidence of significant stenosis to cause nerve impingement. Multilevel neural foraminal narrowing also present, as described in detail above which is mostly due to severe facet arthropathy.

THIS DOCUMENT HAS BEEN ELECTRONICALLY SIGNED:

APPLETON SCUTCHFIELD

Failed Spinal Fusion

Specialist Surgeon #1 showed Liz and me the MRI on a color monitor, indicating that the worst problems with my back were at L4-5 (the most common area causing back pain) and concluded that a spinal fusion would probably eliminate most of my hip pain. He emphasized that one risk was that a L4-5 spinal fusion might just transfer the back stress to L3-4, but said that there was a 90 percent success rate with this kind of spinal fusion surgery. Ninety percent was immensely encouraging. I liked those odds. I would have opted for surgery even if told the odds were 50-50. Sure the recovery would be long and painful, but a few months of pain after so many years of pain seemed like a "no brainer." When I asked Liz, my girlfriend of almost four years who agreed to join me for the consultation, what she thought of Specialist Surgeon #1, she said, "If I had to have back surgery, I would want him to do it."

Sensing hope replacing skepticism and pain, I signed up for spinal fusion surgery at the earliest possible date: December 20, 2012.

During the various pre-surgery routines, I emphasized to several medical assistants and doctors that I did not want anyone to remove my catheter after surgery because urine blockage had been my biggest problem after an earlier successful hemorrhoid surgery. The Percocet that relieved my pain after that surgery also caused plumbing problems and I had to return to the hospital to be catheterized and sent home with a catheter in place for several days while my body recovered.

When I awoke from the spinal fusion surgery, Liz said that Surgeon Specialist #1 had told her the operation went well, and I was also pleased to see that my catheter had not been removed. I successfully completed a short walk around the hospital corridors and the next morning was surprised that I could urinate on my own. The catheter was removed and my Florence Nightingale took me to her upscale house in Denver for further recovery. Liz's en suite bathroom had been remodeled to include a double-sized shower and I felt incredibly spoiled by her home cooking and looking after my every need. I joked that my recovery might take a very long time; little did I know that I would not recover as the spinal fusion made my pain much worse. Man plans, God laughs.

Plumbing Problems

The problems started on December 23rd when I could not urinate. I remember that after taking an oxycontin pain pill I felt like I was floating above the bed—a sublime feeling of well-being. So this is what it is like to be high, I thought, having declined drugs all of my life. But then when I felt the urge to urinate, I could not do so. I drove Liz almost crazy with my determination to urinate—

standing over the toilet and then the bathroom sink in continuous unsuccessful attempts while Liz repeated many times that we should go the ER at nearby Rose Hospital. I kept refusing, saying I felt just on the edge of being able to urinate and surely I would be able to do so soon.

In the meantime, I called all my medical contacts at the hospitals, Primary Physician #6 offices and even local pharmacies to ask if I could purchase a self-catheter. Almost everyone had left for the Christmas holiday, and the few unlucky youngsters who got stuck working the Christmas Eve shift said they did not know if self-catheters were available. So finally about 5 pm on Christmas Eve I agreed to let Liz drive me to the ER at Rose Hospital where a nurse inserted a catheter and relieved my incredible bladder pain. The nurse commented that the quantity of urine drained from my bladder surely must be a record high.

I left Rose Hospital prematurely relieved because the entire scenario repeated itself on New Year's Eve. This time the Rose ER nurse sent me home with a catheter and urine bag attached to my leg with instructions to see a urologist as soon as possible. The shock of seeing the ER bills was almost as great as the one I experienced when the urologist's assistant removed my catheter the following Monday and casually showed me how to self-catheterize with one of the several self-catheters she gave me to take home. What the fuck? For a few dollars for self-catheters I could have avoided almost a week of great pain and co-pay expense for two ER visits! Liz was as disgusted as I at the absurdity of the situation. To add insult to injury, Rose Hospital subsequently re-billed me with threatening letters for co-pay for one of the visits when I distinctly remembered paying both times with my credit card; apparently in the holiday chaos one of my signed authorizations had been lost because when I had recovered enough to find and review my Visa statements several weeks later I too could only find one Rose debit.

Physical Therapy

My problems with spinal fusion recovery were not over. I went to four of eight physical therapy (PT) sessions approved by my United AARP Medicare Complete Secure Horizons insurance. The half hour sessions started with ten minutes of back massage which I told Liz were not nearly as effective as were her good hands. Then twenty minutes of PT exercises that seemed to me inadequate. Friends at Lifetime Fitness told me that they too found their PT not to be worth the $40 per session co-pay. I made the mistake of telling Liz this fact when I decided not to get a new PT trainer after my PT trainer quit her job after (but not because of) four sessions with me. I continued to do the PT exercises on my own at Lifetime Fitness but Liz got upset with me because she thought I should have completed the eight sessions.

Liz's annoyance with me increased when a friend of hers who worked as an assisted living care specialist told her that many elderly patients neglected their PT and so never made full recoveries. Liz became convinced that I was avoiding the pain of PT when in fact I was doing my PT exercises and more at Lifetime Fitness. She assumed that I was trying to save the copay cost of the four PT sessions. Now I admit that I am frugal and did not think the $40 co-pay was well spent, but I am not stupid and would not jeopardize a five figure surgery and recovery over a mere $160 of co-payments.

At one point a concerned Liz took smart phone pictures of the back of my calves which had been toned and muscular before the spinal fusion. I was shocked to see that the tone and muscle had disappeared and resolved to work more religiously on my physical therapy.

To prove to Liz and myself that I was not shirking, I added "robots" (weight resisting machines) to my PT at Lifetime Fitness. I went from ten minutes on the stationary bike to about two minutes on each of ten robots, plus two exercises that Liz devised for me. The simplest of these was rising a few inches on my toes at the edge of a stair for ten reps—but it proved one of the hardest for me to do. I was careful not to push too hard and backed off accordingly during the thirty minute routine. Then I would walk and eventually swim (back and side strokes) for thirty minutes in the indoor swimming pool where my back was happy with the weight displacement caused by water therapy.

I continued this routine every other day (since my body needed a day in between to recover) for several weeks. My upper body strength increased substantially and I started to recover my shoulder and arm strength, but my back pain persisted. So I cut out the robots and reduced my workouts to the PT exercises plus twenty minutes each on the stationary bike and in the pool. Still my back pain persisted. I called Specialist Surgeon #1's office requesting a postoperative visit with him since I had not seen him since the day he had showed me my MRI and explained his proposed plan for a spinal fusion. I was told that he was not available but I could speak to his PA. She was very empathetic but did not seem qualified to do a postoperative evaluation. But she gave me a prescription for tramadol which she said was a pain killer somewhere in between the strong oxycontin (which I had stopped taking because it caused urinary stoppage) and Advil. The tramadol helped cut about 50 percent of my back pain and the PA refilled the prescription one time. When I called back for a second refill of tramadol the front desk coldly told me that they would no longer approve such and all further requests for pain medication should be made to my primary physician.

I thought that response was rather abrupt, but what bothered me more at the time was that I had not been able to see Specialist Surgeon #1 for a postoperative review (something that my friend Doug Bury was afforded without asking after his successful L4-5 spinal fusion at another hospital). I got the feeling that Specialist Surgeon #1 did not want to see me because his "90% successful spinal fusion surgery" clearly had been unsuccessful in my case. Perhaps the fact that I was a lawyer had something to do with it but I had no intention of suing or even blaming Specialist Surgeon #1. He did not promise me a successful outcome and I did not expect a guarantee. Not even the most competent lawyers win all their cases. I just wanted to talk with him about my specific outcome and his recommendation going forward. My suspicion seemed confirmed when his office did not call to arrange for the one year x-ray evaluation as promised at the outset. I waited for almost two months expecting a call; then I called and an x-ray was taken with a subsequent report that everything was OK but still I was not able to talk personally with Specialist Surgeon #1. So I never saw him again after our first meeting.

As reported on page 217, almost two years later Dr. Melamed examined a new MRI and concluded that the two screws in the back half of the metallic cage had not fused. Another surprise as I had been told that the follow-up x-rays a year after my L4-5 spinal fusion surgery had proved normal. Why, if half of the fusion had not fused? Had I been the victim of some kind of cover-up to protect Specialist Surgeon #1's reputation? Or was it simply too early one year later to see that the back half of the fusion had not fused? And was this failure to fuse the cause of my intensified back pain for the next three years?

In the three years between back surgeries I tried everything I could think of to find relief. My super-fit friend Jordan at Lifetime Fitness, who regularly swam laps to prepare for grueling long distance bike races, kept telling me that I should go to "Amy" who had miraculously helped him and another LTF swimmer with their serious back pain. So I called the office of Dr. Amy Valenta to get her assessment of my back issues and was told that I needed a referral from my primary physician before an appointment could be set. I had no primary physician because PCP #6 was on some kind of leave, but his boss Dr. RF provided the referral after his assistant confirmed that my AARP United Health Care insurance would cover Dr. Valenta's treatments. I set up an appointment for about three weeks in the future; an appointment that never happened because Dr. RF's office called a few days later to say that while my insurance covered Dr. Valenta, it turned out that she was "in a different insurance pod" that was not covered. Would Dr. Valenta have been successful where all others had failed? I'll never know.

My exercise routine at Lifetime Fitness was boring and so occasionally I persuaded Liz to hit some tennis balls with me. I love the feeling of hitting a tennis ball cleanly off the racket and seeing it fly fast and hard into the other court. Now I couldn't move in any direction without pain but I could stand at the net and deflect balls back to Liz at the baseline. Since bending over to pick up a tennis ball was agony, we worked out a routine where I had a metal caddy full of balls next to me at the net and would use all of them before using the caddy to recover them. I rationalized that this routine was good for Liz's game as well as she got more balls to hit in one of our practices than she would get in several sets of tennis. The main difference between average and professional tennis players (actually, in any sport or endeavor, as Malcolm Gladwell would argue) is not power but control and consistency, and our determined practice hitting hundreds of balls was just the ticket. But Liz must have been aware that she was now playing tennis with a different person—an old man who could not move more than a step in any direction.

I continued my alternate day routine at Lifetime Fitness for several months in the hope that my back would eventually recover. It did not. In fact, it got worse. Before my spinal fusion surgery I was managing my back pain with over-the-counter Aleve; afterwards the Aleve was inadequate and I needed the prescription pain medication tramadol. Before my surgery, I could walk about twice as far before fatigue and back pain would force me to sit down and recover. Four months after surgery I could barely do one block, and as of today (12/13/15) less than a half block. I had to face the fact that either Specialist Surgeon #1 had a different definition of successful surgery (I left the hospital breathing?) or I was one of the unlucky ten percent. After years of good luck I finally had drawn a bad card.

Liz Leaves

And then I drew another bad card when Liz without explanation, walked out of my life after four enjoyable years together—a big blow because I was hoping she would be my lifelong partner. I was hurt and troubled by Liz's leaving and also by her apparent inability to explain why. My phone calls and e-mails went unanswered for months before she called to apologize. She could not formulate a reason for leaving, but it was obvious to me that she could not deal with my new status as a handicapped senior. I was on a downhill slide; she was fourteen years younger than me and still had prime years left to live. She had done more than her part as Florence Nightingale after my surgery, but she had not signed up for long-term disability.

For months after Liz left me I was devastated and confused. Perhaps she had concluded that I was not trying hard enough to recover. I had assured her that I was pushing myself as hard as I could, and if I didn't show it, it was because I retain my Minnesota stoicism with a lifetime of experience in toughing out pain without complaint. It may have been the wrong message to deliver. Perhaps it was worse in her eyes if I was not getting any better and there was no likely fix. I do not know, because Liz avoided giving me a reason for her departure, but she did not need to. I knew when I looked in the mirror one morning and did not recognize the face looking back at me. It was an old man's face. I was shocked. I retrieved a photo we had taken a year earlier at Redstone Inn after the televised Aaron Harber Show in Aspen with Justices Breyer and O'Connor. In the photo I have a relaxed smile, my face is full and healthy looking and I do not look older than Liz, much less fourteen years older. Now when I compare the face in the mirror with the one in the photo, I see clearly that I have aged more in one year than in the prior ten. My hair is still full with only traces of grey, but my face is hollowed out around the eyes and below the cheek bones and I see wrinkles when I grimace or smile. I now look like what I am—an old man. One year of continued back pain and the medications to control it, have sucked a great deal of life out of me. I wouldn't want to stay with me, so why would Liz? I had thought that at our advanced ages when we met (she 53 and I 67) that we were in the same age boat. Now however I realize that the age difference had been magnified rather than minimized. At seventy my activities are limited. At age 56 Liz is still in her late prime and has many good years before she reaches my reduced condition. She did not sign up for this. "So run, Liz, run. I would do the same. I miss you, but I do not blame you. I wish you would have had the courage to explain why you were leaving rather than just suddenly dropping out of my life without explanation. I know that it probably was that I was rapidly and unexpectedly becoming an old man, but I could not help but wonder if it was for any of a hundred other reasons you might have dumped me—reasons that hopefully I could do something about."

A sympathetic and wise female friend told me that she thought that Liz left as she did and did not return calls because she was not ready to have that conversation with me yet. In other words, the silence was because Liz loved me too much, not too little. This explanation is easier to accept than any of the other hundred that I wondered about, so I'm going with it. It's positive, and keeps open the possibility that with time Liz will be able to have that conversation with me.

So to the continued pain in my back I have to deal with the added pain in my heart and head. This is obviously a low point in my life, and if you read Chapter 25 about my unfortunate experience with the *Kappan* editor, you will realize that it felt like a triple blow: physical (back), mental (Liz) and career (rejected post). I don't relate this for sympathy. Almost no one likes to be the object of sympathy. How demeaning. How patronizing sympathy can be. I relate the triple blow as fact to explain why this clearly is the lowest point in my life.

With my back pain seeming to get worse, I went back to Primary Physician #6 on September 9 (2014). He said that I should consult with Dr. William Choi or another neurosurgeon about a possible laminectomy (cutting away nerve compressing facets on my spine), and he ordered an EMG as a precondition to determine if I had nerve damage. Another appointment was scheduled for the EMG technician. The old EMG machine looked like a dinosaur around all the other shiny new medical equipment, and the lengthy procedure was surprisingly unpleasant but disclosed that I had only mild edema around my ankles and some neuropathy in my feet. I expected the next step to be a referral to Dr. Choi for a possible laminectomy. I had sworn I would never have another back surgery again but now I was even more desperate and therefore reconsidering. Before discussing a possible laminectomy with Dr. Choi, I decided to explore alternatives so that I could make an informed choice about how to proceed.

Acupuncture and Chiropractic

One morning soon thereafter I read a *Denver Post* flyer about the success Dr. Carly Carney had with her low impact chiropractic treatments, and based on an initial interview with her, signed a reduced-price contract for $3,800 for a twelve week program at Thriveology. I was told that insurance would not cover the treatments. The first treatment with one of Dr. Carney's assistants was a disaster; she did not know how to deal with a back as bad as mine and I walked out of Thriveology in greater pain than before. I went home and typed up a notice of termination of my contract explaining my decision. Dr. Carney apologized and volunteered to refund my payment immediately but suggested that I try a tailor-made program where she personally would practice her chiropractic and her husband, Mark, his electric acupuncture specialty on my back. Carly and Mark were sure that they could cure my back problems without invasive surgery and said they would refund my payment if I was not satisfied with the outcome after a ten week trial period. Long story short, they tried and their treatment alleviated my back pain somewhat but only about fifty percent for about three hours each time. Since this relief was about the same as I experienced by taking one tramadol pain pill, there was no point in continuing after about 20 treatments in 10 weeks, and the Carneys refunded my payment as promised. I am sure their program works well for some patients but I think my back problems are too severe for their services.

Upon hearing about my experience with chiropractic and acupuncture, Primary Physician #6 introduced me to a chiropractor who had an experimental treatment with "a decompression table." Dr. Paul Burns, Chiropractor #2, examined my x-rays and showed me where my spine was compressed at the L3-4 level just above my L4-5 spinal fusion. He recommended an eight week program combined with steroid injections by a pain doctor. The latter would be partly covered by my insurance as before, but his decompression program was not and would cost a discounted $2,800.

Primary Physician #6

I seriously considered Dr. Burns' proposal, but then the new pain doctor who replaced Dr. Schwettmann did not return several of my phone call messages. Primary Physician #6 was less than enthusiastic about his personal back treatment by Chiropractor #2 and I decided I could not waste more time on such a problematic approach. I needed to discuss a possible laminectomy with Dr. Choi. Also I wanted to follow up with my brother, Mark, in Berlin to determine whether German stem cell therapy might be a better option than surgery, but two docs later informed me that stem cells would not help with my stenosis, which was the primary reason I could not walk very far. I still wanted to get all options in front of me so I could make an intelligent decision on how to proceed, but then inexplicably Primary Physician #6, who had earlier recommended referral to a neurosurgeon for a possible laminectomy, did not forward my medical records as requested to Doctor Choi or to Charité Hospital in Berlin. When I requested same for the third time in writing and the second in person, he said, "We should take it one step at a time." First, he said, I should have an EMG. I was shocked. Only a few weeks earlier I had undergone the unpleasant EMG exam at his request, and reviewed with him the results which showed some nerve damage (neuropathy in feet). I repeated my request that he forward my records to Dr. Choi and to Charité Hospital in Berlin so I could evaluate my options. Primary Physician #6, who several months before had recommended I see Dr. Choi about a possible laminectomy, replied, "It's your pain talking; let's take this one step at a time." My pain talking? See pp. 255-257 discussing how demeaning and dehumanizing such a comment is. I don't know the cause of this weird turnabout but perhaps it is a natural consequence of being on a medical/insurance treadmill requiring too many patients per doc. Over many years with Primary Physician #6 I knew he was very bright and a Goodhead as well, but I think he got caught up in a treadmill of twenty minute appointments and relied on his brilliance to compensate for hurried decisions. Whatever the reason, this strange reversal, combined with the fact that my ordinary tramadol refill prescriptions were getting screwed up by his office on a regular basis caused me to look for a new Primary Physician. I e-mailed Primary Physician #6 an explanation for why after so many years I had decided to find a new primary care physician. After some research, I found Dr. Philip Cohen who now is my Primary Physician #7.

PCP #7: Dr. Philip Cohen

Dr. Philip Cohen was one of three primary care physicians (PCPs) that a United Health Care representative told me were qualified for their plan and practiced close to my residence. I was confident I had found the right doctor to treat me. A new employee of Senior Care of Colorado located at 399 West Hampden just west of Swedish Hospital in Denver, Dr. Cohen told me that he had negotiated a three day work week with Senior Care because he wanted more time to himself and his daughter now that he was 68 years old. I told him I could understand because I had also negotiated three day work weeks to allow more time to pursue my private interests. A second reason, Dr. Cohen, explained was that as an internist he wanted to pay more attention to each of his patients. He was tired of the twenty-minute assembly line care given in most medical settings and wanted to spend a full hour with each of his patients if needed. His whole focus was on listening and trying to figure out what his patient clients wanted. This reinforced my positive impression of Dr. Cohen. I briefly summarized my experience with my prior PCP who seemed not to listen to patient concerns.

Encouraged, as Dr. Cohen reviewed my records on the monitor in front of him, I explained that I had set up a website to discuss our upside-down health care system. I boldly stated that I thought that our health care system built on a free enterprise model was self-defeating because it provided incentives for all the stakeholders to compete against each other rather than collaborate to serve the patients' best interests. To my surprise Dr. Cohen agreed, adding that in his long career as an internist he was disgusted with the way so many promising young docs entered the system with the best of intentions, but then got seduced by the many easy ways to make money as a doctor. Soon he said, most become businessmen rather than doctors. I indeed had found the right Goodhead doctor who hopefully would focus on my needs.

I told Dr. Cohen that his comments on *MakeOurDemocracy Work.com* would be very helpful, but would other docs or administrators get upset with him if he blogged frankly about our health care system? "Hell no, I'm 68 years old and I don't give a damn what they might think." Super! I hope Dr. Cohen finds time to contribute his experience and expertise on my website.

Overpriced Prescription Drugs

Dr. Cohen even gave me his personal e-mail to use as needed, and I used it about a week later to complain that the tramadol prescription which his office had given to my King Soopers Pharmacy now cost $180 rather than the usual $4. Dr. Cohen's assistant, Margarita, called the next day to say I should call her instead of e-mailing Dr. Cohen about problems in the future. She confirmed that I wanted 50 mg tablets instead of 100 mg tablets and when I asked, she did not know what different prescriptions cost. If helping docs fill prescriptions is her job, she should know. Patients know the difference between $4 for 50 mg rather than $180 for 100 mg tablets, and so too should the docs when they prescribe drugs. I presumptuously sent an e-mail to Dr. Cohen stating that he should know the cost of the drugs he prescribes and to his credit, Dr. Cohen apologized and agreed.

I am not really surprised at this differential pricing of prescription drugs. Americans face a similar problem every day when their prescriptions cost much more than their Canadian counterparts. Canada has a single payer health care system that is rationalized and can negotiate for better pricing; Americans have a free enterprise free-for-all where the pharmaceutical companies and their

Greedheads extract the most the market will bear—and more.

One particularly egregious example made headlines in September 2015 when Martin Shkreli, head of Turling Pharmaceuticals, bought and then raised the price of a 62 year old generic drug (Daraprim) from $13.50 a pill to $750—an astounding 5,400 percent increase. In the public spotlight that followed when the *New York Times* reported on the scandal, Martin Shkreli, a former hedge fund manager turned drug company entrepreneur, became Greedhead Exhibit A. Some Greedheads were quick to argue that Shkreli's action was the exception and should not be used as an excuse to tarnish the entire pharmaceutical industry. Really? See "Price Gouging in Health Care is the Rule, Not the Exception," Jared Ball (*Real News Network*).

Robert Borosage, Campaign for America's Future (12/10/15) writes: "Wealthy pharmaceutical companies have never had it so good—earning record profits while dodging taxes....Pfizer alone has more than $140 billion in untaxed profits stashed offshore." Tax dodging schemes are tempting to many U.S. companies due to corporate tax laws which need revision, but tax "inversion" schemes sometimes can be reversed by public opinion. Compare, for example, Walgreen's recent "inversion" plan which was jettisoned when President Obama called it unpatriotic and public outcry led to a quick reversal by Walgreens. For details, see the Politics/Business section of *www.MakeOurDemocracyWork.com*.

Aggravating unregulated prescription drug pricing is the common practice of pharmaceutical companies paying docs to push their pills and some docs accepting paid tax deductible jaunts to Hawaii and other vacation destinations to speak at pharmaceutical conventions. This questionable practice is so commonplace that many Americans figure it's just how our system works and nothing can be done about it. Many if not most patients almost expect their docs to be business men more concerned about their bottom line than them. Sure, pharmaceutical companies need to charge more to finance their research for better products, but are their incredible profits justified by any reasonable measure? How much of their profits actually go for research rather than big boats and other toys? See page 244 about the documented extraordinary waste in the U.S. health care system and the ColoradoCare Initiative 20 to try to minimize such waste.

Friends' Recommendations

I read somewhere that most Americans will suffer serious back pain at some point in their lives. The affliction is so pervasive that it is not surprising that countless remedies have been developed to respond to the need. You can take your pick of scores of back braces, heating wraps, vibrating machines, lotions and ointments and of course professionals who offer chiropractic, acupuncture, decompression and other services. Many actually work to alleviate back pain, so it should not be surprising that many well-meaning friends recommend docs and treatments that work for them. In fact, so many that now I don't want to hear about any more of them. Each takes considerable time and usually expense to pursue and so far none that I have tried have worked for me. Back pain is highly individualized.

A case in point: last year a friend recommended ozone (oxygen) injections as an alternative to the usual steroid injections (two sets of steroid injections at Porter Hospital by Dr. Rick Schwettmann had worked, but only for about six weeks each), saying that they had cured her back pain when nothing else had. Since I respected her and her story was so compelling, I identified a local doctor who specialized in ozone treatments. Like chiro, acupuncture, decompression and marijuana, and other promising remedies, ozone treatments are not covered by insurance and I was shocked at Dr. Jonathon Singer's $880 charge for the first of several treatments. Dr. Singer's diagnosis of "neurogenic claudication" and focus on ligaments rather than muscles sounded convincing, but his ozone and prolozone injections did not help more than taking my tramadol medication. Therefore I discontinued the treatments, notwithstanding his protest (as with the PTs stretching my back on their decompression X-Machine, which had been highly recommended by another friend) that I had not given the treatments a chance to work. How much time and expense are justified in seeking alternative treatments when your pain continues unabated?

Dr. Choi

So moving forward on my perilous journey through the best health care system in the world, on December 2, 2014 I called to make an appointment with Dr. William Choi, reputedly one of the best neurosurgeons in the United States. After being put on hold and leaving endless messages on machines to get an appointment with some specialists (and often not getting a return call), I was impressed that his secretary answered my call the first time I tried. I summarized my history of failed spinal fusion and asked for the earliest possible appointment with Dr. Choi to discuss whether he could help me. "Yes, I can give you an appointment with Dr. Choi for January 15." "But that's six weeks from now," I protested, "I'm in pain every day, can't you get me in earlier? Perhaps you could call me if you get a last minute cancellation?" No, I must wait six weeks just to get an appointment to talk with a specialist. Does it take longer in Canada and Europe where they have single payer systems?

Dr. Choi's assistant was very efficient. "You need to have your primary physician forward all medical records, including MRI—not the electronic version but the actual physical disc." So I e-mailed my request to Primary Physician #6, noting prior failures to forward my records and emphasizing the importance of compliance with my request. When I called Dr. Choi's office a week before my appointment I was not surprised to be told that my records had not been received. Fortunately there was time to correct the omission.

Finally January 15 arrived and my friends Liz and Nash joined me for support. We started by looking at my MRI in brilliant color on the modern screen with Marshon Jones, Dr. Choi's assistant, and joked as he prepared his report for Dr. Choi. It took much longer than seemed necessary and at one point Marshon asked me if I had any more to relate about my back pain history. "I've given it to you in a nutshell in order to be concise." Marshon said, "That's OK, keep talking." I realized why when Dr. Choi finally arrived looking stressed, complaining about the traffic on Arapahoe Road from the airport. He was almost one hour late to the appointment I have been waiting on for six weeks! It was now clear that Marshon had been stalling to cover for him. Exasperated, I told Dr. Choi "I've been waiting six weeks to see you; I hope you don't shortchange me on time." Dr. Choi, very cool and professional, ignored my comment and immediately pointed out a fracture at L3 and also fatty buildup around my L3 facets which were compressing into my spine and related nerves.

What? I have a fracture at L3? No wonder I have severe back pain. Did the 'dive" at the wedding cause the fracture, and I couldn't pinpoint the source of my pain because I focused instead on my fractured rib pain? It seemed likely, but, if so, why had I not been told about this before? Did my L3-4 fracture not show

up on prior x-rays? By now I was no longer surprised by misdiag-
noses and related screw-ups in the best heath care system in the
world. In fact, I did not want to get into a blame-game. I wanted
to move forward and finally get a fix so I could get my life back.

So I was encouraged when Dr. Choi said that he thought he
could get rid of most of my back pain by cementing the L3-4 fracture ("rhyoplasty"?)—as well as a laminectomy. Both procedures
he explained, to my great relief, were less invasive than my prior
spinal fusion. But he now needed to get better x-rays to make sure
my spinal fusion was stable before he could proceed. "But you
have a June 2014 MRI in front of you! Doesn't that indicate how
stable my spinal fusion is?" "Yes," Dr. Choi responded, "but I want
a more detailed look at your spinal fusion, and so need additional
x-rays." I groaned impatiently because this additional imaging
meant more delay before I can get my back fixed.

I impatiently waited for February 11 when I was scheduled to
return to Dr. Choi for his opinion about whether my spinal fusion
was stable enough for the less invasive procedures. February 11
finally arrived, and Dr. Choi confidently stated that the x rays confirmed his earlier diagnosis and the need to go forward with the
proposed surgery. When Dr. Choi said he was not certified to do
the cementing procedure, I responded that my preference was to
have both procedures done at the same time so I would not have
two operations from which to recover and asked if he could recommend a surgeon who could do both. Dr. Choi understood my
concern and recommended Dr. Itay Melamed, a former colleague,
who was certified to do both procedures.

Dr. Melamed

On February 15, 2015 I had the first of several meetings with Dr. Melamed. My good friend Nash joined me. Nash is a very smart and perceptive observer and I value his opinion because often I miss important information in complex medical discussions. Dr. Melamed said he could not form an opinion based on the recent Touchstone x-rays and my June 2014 MRI so a new MRI would be required. Also, bone density and blood tests. Groan—more delays.

Dr. Melamed's assistant arranged for me to go to a different location with a newer and larger imaging machine after I explained to her how claustrophobic I had found the prior MRI procedure. This time I needed an IV insert for "a contrast MRI," but the imagining assistant could not find an acceptable vein in my arm and so inserted the IV into my right wrist. The new imaging machine was larger but still after what seemed an excessively long time I felt claustrophobic and started to sweat profusely. I tried to hold on, but could not, and finally pressed the alarm monitor the assistant had given me in case of a problem. She was very annoyed with me because she said now that she had stopped the MRI machine the whole procedure would have to be started again from the beginning. Then I noticed that blood was soaking into the right side of my best exercise suit—which the assistant was quick to point out was my fault since apparently caused by bumping my wrist into the inside of the narrow MRI machine, thereby displacing the IV. She applied some bandages and asked if I wanted to return another day to complete the MRI. No way, one trip was enough.

My disposition did not improve when Dr. Melamed reviewed the MRI results and recommended further PT rather than surgery. The fracture at L3-4 appeared to have healed on its own, he explained and additional physical therapy might alleviate the need for a laminectomy. He also said that the imaging showed that the back two of four screws from my prior L4-5 spinal fusion had not fused. Stunned, I asked if that was the cause of my increased back pain. Another surprise: Dr. Melamed replied that the fact that two of the four screws had not fused into my vertebrae was a good thing because it meant my back was not as inflexible as it would have been if completely fused. It was hard to focus on this new "fact" because I was so disappointed that Dr. Melamed was recommending even more PT.

What to do now that one surgeon recommended surgery, but not the second? I decided to get a third specialist opinion to break the tie. My brilliant Harvard College '65 classmate, Dr. Curt Freed, referred me to Dr. Stephen Shogan at Rose Hospital, but when I called I was told that he was on sabbatical with no date given for return. Another friend, Dr. Arlen Meyer, recommended Dr. Peter Witt at CU Medical Center, but his office told me that Dr. Witt would not take my AARP United Health Care medical insurance and at earliest could see me in about six weeks if I left a $500 deposit and paid for all treatments thereafter by credit card within 30 days. Primary Physician #7 referred me to a neurosurgeon at the Colorado Brain & Spine Institute who, it turned out, had left for Texas many months earlier.

Since it was proving so difficult just to identify and get an appointment for a third expert opinion, I decided to go forward as recommended by Dr. Melamed: additional PT and a step by step program with Pain Specialist #2 who would use a series of steroid injections to determine which vertebrae was the source of most of my pain. I overlooked Pain Specialist #2's gruff bedside manner with me and his assistant (and one mishap when his injection needle slipped and hit my sciatic nerve, causing incredible pain and need for their help in standing up and eventually staggering out of the office) because the first few steroid injections did alleviate most of my back pain, especially when injected at L3-4. When the effects wore off in about six weeks and I called for the next steroid injection in the program, I was told that Pain Specialist #2 no longer worked there and had left no forwarding number or address.

My frustrating journey through the best health care system in the world seemed endless, and my back pain and reduced mobility gradually worsened. When I realized I had been finding excuses to miss my regular workout at Lifetime Fitness (even though I had scaled it down to thirty minutes a visit swimming since nothing hurts in the pool given weight displacement), because the walk from the LTF parking lot to the locker room tested my limits, in the summer of 2015 I finally swallowed my pride and applied for a handicapped sticker to attach to the windshield of my car. I had always felt sorry for those who needed handicapped parking spaces; now the right to take advantage of them myself made a big difference in my everyday life.

Dr. Choi v. Dr. Melamed

The PT program that Dr. Melamed and I agreed upon proved unhelpful. After several long trips to a facility near Parker for PT treatment with an "X" machine to stretch backs (which had worked wonders for my friend Randy Merhar's bad back), I concluded that they did not relieve my back pain any more than taking a tramadol pill. Same story repeating itself. When I reported my decision to Dr. Melamed, he recommended finding a new pain specialist and trying a new PT program. I repeated my earlier comments about almost three years of different PT programs and nonsurgical alternatives and my preference for L3-4 back surgery. Dr. Melamed said he would perform the L3-4 laminectomy but recommended in any case that I start with a new pain doctor and also try Dr. Jones' rehab therapy—inconveniently located on the northwest side of Denver. I carefully considered Dr. Melamed's recommendation once again, but then decided that after three painful years of trying to find an alternative to surgery, I now was sure that I wanted Dr. Choi to perform the surgery if he still was willing to do so.

I did not advance the medical ball throughout the rest of the spring and summer of 2015 because my two dream houses became available at the same time and I was totally absorbed in the stressful task of contracting, financing and renovating both at the same time (see Chapter 28 for details). The effort clearly took a toll as on August 6th I fell seriously ill with blood reappearing in my urine once again. My fingers would shake so much that I could not type an e-mail or key a phone number. Thinking I might have Parkinson's, I suffered through the weekend because I wanted to get Dr. Cohen's opinion on how to proceed. On Monday morning Dr. Cohen was not available and another doc advised that I go immediately to ER as that is probably what Dr. Cohen would advise anyway. I was fortunate that the ER wing of Swedish Hospital was not busy that early on a Monday morning. I was given an IV almost immediately by a nurse who assured me that my trembling fingers were simply "senior tremors" rather than the more serious Parkinson's disease. Within 30 minutes Dr. David E. Rosenberg said his review of my labs indicated cystitis, a kidney infection warranting the antibiotic Ciprofloxacin ("Cipro").

Within a week the Cipro worked to clear blood from my urine, but my aging body did not recover nearly as soon as when younger. The kidney infection had knocked me for a loop. I was weak and tired and had lost my appetite, eating nothing the first few days, and very little for several days thereafter. In that time I lost 24 pounds, proving once again that weight depends more upon diet than exercise (at least for me). I was grateful to God, Chance or whatever, when I recovered to my prior health without the scary "senior tremors," with only back pain with which to deal. Well, not quite, as one of my lower front teeth fell out on September 3rd, and David Roderick DDS responded with a root canal and crown for $3,000 (who has dental insurance these days?).

After almost three years of trying to alleviate my back pain through PT, steroid injections, ozone and prolozone injections, X-machine, chiropractic, acupuncture and many home remedies, it was time to take the risk that this time back surgery would give me back my life. If there was a reasonable chance that I could stand and walk again for more than four or five minutes, I had to take the risk. So I left a voice mail with Dr. Choi's office on October 22 (2015) asking if he could schedule me for his recommended laminectomy. The call back stated that I needed to make an appointment with Dr. Choi. So once again the earliest appointment was several weeks away: November 19, 2015. Finally November 19th arrived. Dr. Choi examined my contrast MRI and reaffirmed his January 2015 opinion that most of my pain would be alleviated by a L3-4 laminectomy because spinal compression was pushing facets against my nerves at that location. But he said he would also need to perform "a fusion extension" because he was not convinced that my fracture at L3-4 had healed sufficiently to support the laminectomy without reinforcement, especially since only half of my initial L4-5 fusion had fused. I related Dr. Melamed's comment that I was fortunate that two of the four screws attaching the metal cage had not fused because now my back was more flexible; Dr. Choi looked at me in disbelief, but said nothing. Obviously, Dr. Choi and Dr. Melamed practiced a different kind of medicine, and interpreted the same facts very differently.

Second Back Surgery

So once again I faced the question of which expert opinion to rely upon in a decision that could alter my life dramatically for better or worse. After brief consideration, I decided to go with Dr. Choi's opinion because it was reinforced by the opinions of Primary Physician #6, Dr. Burns and Pain Specialist #2. Nevertheless it was disappointing to hear that my failed first fusion, combined with Dr. Choi's doubt that the L3-4 fracture had sufficiently healed, meant that additional screws would be inserted into my back and recovery would be longer and more difficult than a typical laminectomy. A three day hospitalization was projected. But having come this far, I was not going to let a few months of additional recovery or pain change my mind.

On November 30th Dr. Cohen conducted the customary pre-op physical examination to confirm that I was fit for the prospective back surgery. All seemed to go well, and I was pleased that the scales showed I had not regained any of the 24 pounds lost from reduced appetite a few months earlier recovering from my kidney infection. Dr. Cohen said all signs looked good and approved my pre-op examination, "subject to labs." On December 7th Margarita called to say the lab work showed that blood had reappeared in my urine, and Dr. Cohen would not approve my surgery until I was cleared by a urologist. I almost panicked because getting an appointment with my urologist on short notice was unlikely, but fortunately another patient cancelled for the next day and I was the beneficiary (otherwise I was told the first available appointment would be after the New Year!).

Pre-Surgery Urology

Dr. A, my urologist, ordered a CT scan of my abdomen and conducted a cystoscopy to make sure that the blood in my urine was not caused by a cancerous tumor. I was a bit surprised to see that my insurance co-pay for the cystoscopy was $345. I can afford to absorb this kind of unexpected expense, but those who live payday-to-payday probably could not. Fortunately the cystoscopy did not reveal any tumors, and Dr. A concluded that the blood in my urine probably was caused by a combination of my 4X size enlarged prostate and my Xarelto blood thinner. A CT scan with contrast also proved negative, and so another hurdle, hopefully the last before surgery, was cleared.

Bladder Blockage Again

Wishful thinking! At the outset of his examination on 12/8/15, I explained to Dr. A that the last time I had been in his office was after two ER visits to Rose Hospital when I had painful post-operative urine blockage. At that earlier 2012 follow-up visit when his office opened on Monday morning, I said, continuing to relate my earlier experience with urine blockage (pp. 207-208), including the sympathetic nurse who gave me a sample self-catheter kit to take home with me. Grateful that I now had a backup plan if the situation re-occurred, I placed the self-catheter kit in my linen closet and forgot about them until today (12/8/15) when I returned home for a repeat performance. I could only manage a few painful dribbles of reddish urine at a time—not enough to evacuate the two quarts of liquid (half orange juice and half water) I drank after the exam per instructions. Now that liquid was building up in my blocked bladder, I stopped drinking liquid and read the post-procedure cytoscopy instructions. A painful burning sensation while discharging pinkish urination was to be expected for a few days, but immediately below it I read contradictory instructions to call the clinic if I had trouble urinating or pain during urination. I had all of the above. What to do? It was about 9 pm in the evening and the clinic certainly was closed. I would have to go to the ER once again for a simple catheter but decided to try the self-catheterization kit first. The instructions inside the unopened "Bard Dispoz-A-Bag Leg Bag with Flip-Flo Drainage Valve" were given in ridiculously tiny print, but were easy to follow once I found my magnifying glass. Several pieces in the kit fit together in a logical way. I applied some E-Z Lubricating Jelly from an unopened tube and prepared for relief. But the inserted catheter did not result in any urine flow even though I had pushed the catheter tube almost to the hilt. I even tried to "prime the pump" by sucking on one end of the catheter like many do to draw gas from a car. Nothing. Perhaps the catheter was too old even though unopened. I had been about to ask Dr. A for replacement ones earlier when discussing self-catheterization. He had paused as if to offer but before I could ask, he proceeded to explain several pieces of CYA paperwork that I needed to sign. Anyway, now I pulled the catheter out and sucked again. No air flow even though I could see the small opening at the other end of the catheter. Defeated, I tossed the catheter and returned to customary urination that now would not flow. Only a few painful dribbles. If I repeated this scores of times during the evening and smoked a joint, would it be enough to provide relief until morning?

Here I was eager to get to my December 15 surgery, and now I had painful urine blockage even before surgery. I cursed, and played a Leonard Cohen CD as a distraction. Then it struck me that if my diagnosed 4X enlarged prostate (4 times normal size) could block my urethra, perhaps the other half of my plumbing could do so as well. Perhaps my enlarged prostate had combined with my constipation to block urine flow. They occupy the same neighborhood, after all. Since starting tramadol to alleviate my back pain I often needed to give myself enemas for recurring constipation. I had read somewhere that pain medication can cause constipation as well as urinary problems. Within five minutes, the enema did its thing and suddenly I could urinate as usual. As I type this about 11:30 pm on 12/8/15 I am feeling incredible relief. I am so grateful that I can relieve myself, even if the burning painful sensation persists while I do so. Am I just fooling myself like tramadol, which tricks the mind into thinking there is less pain? As with the tramadol, I don't care about the psychology of pain relief as long as I feel less pain.

The relief did not last for long. About midnight everything started to hurt more than usual: my hips, my back, painful bloody urination and now my head felt like an overinflated basketball. I started to sweat and felt nauseous. I swallowed another Aleve, put on a Mary Chapin Carpenter CD and tried to force myself to sleep. Before I drift off it hits me (my pain talking?) that I now feel much worse than when I went into the urology clinic for various tests that morning. I had been managing my pain as usual. I had no urinary pain then but after my pre-op visit, in addition to a rare headache, I now was experiencing painful urine blockage except for a small burning discharge that had turned a deep red color. The expensive and invasive cystoscopy which did not find any tumors, obviously had caused major trauma to my system. Of course if it had uncovered a cancerous tumor, I would have been grateful for early discovery but when Dr. Cohen reviewed my prior case of urinary blood, he said that I shouldn't worry as he was pretty sure it was not cancer because the lab work did not show the usual indicators for such. If Dr. Cohen could reach this conclusion simply by reading my lab reports, was the invasive cystoscopy necessary? Dr. A had ordered the cystoscopy and CT scan almost casually— as if it were no big deal. At the time I had signed the CYA paperwork as a matter of course; was this extensive testing another form of CYA, or worse, profit driven? Whatever the reason, I had suffered almost six miserable hours in the aftermath. How would I, with no medical training, know except by consulting other experts? My fate, like almost all patients, is in the hands of the experts and ultimately we almost have to defer to their expertise. Our health care system conceivably can be changed by united action by patients, but we are all dependent upon the expertise of the docs regardless of system. With these dark thoughts in my head I drifted off to sleep. The next day I felt very weak and could hardly complete my 30 minute swim. The required pre-op tests obviously had taken a toll on my aging body.

Second Spinal Fusion Scheduled

At the time I wrote the first draft of this chapter, I was scheduled for an "extended fusion and a laminectomy" with Dr. Choi at Castle Rock Adventist Hospital on December 15, 2015. I felt especially thankful that finally a remedy for my back pain and/or restricted mobility might be at hand.

A winter snow storm hit Colorado on December 14, 2015, the day before my scheduled surgery with Dr. Choi. My assistant Ivy Ridlen called to say she could not drive me to the hospital the next morning as planned because the forecast was for continued snow, and she was afraid to drive on icy, snow-covered roads. After waiting so long to schedule the surgery and knowing re-scheduling would delay surgery for many weeks given the medical protocols involved, I decided not to postpone even if I had to drive myself to the hospital. Fortunately my friend Herb McBride generously agreed to drive me, and we arrived at the hospital on time at 5 am after a difficult drive on I-25.

When I awoke from surgery, Dr. Choi's assistant told me that the operation had gone well, but in the following weeks it became apparent that the operation had not reduced my back pain. At our post-op meeting on February 4, 2006, Dr. Choi seemed confused and clearly did not remember me as a patient. He said he would send me a copy of the operative report from the hospital. After some difficulty in obtaining the hospital operative report, I noted its summary contradicted Dr. Choi's version of the operation.

****

My March 15, 2016 letter to Dr. Choi picks up the narrative:

March 15, 2016

William Won-Slk Choi, MD
Precision Spine Center
6825 So. Galena St., #314
Centennial, CO 80111

Dear Dr. Choi:

I have just received the Castle Rock Adventist Hospital operative report you promised me at our post-op meeting on February 4, 2016. The report indicates you did work on my prior L4-5 fusion, and also "L2-3 and L3-4 Laminotomy."

Contrary to the operative report, these procedures were NOT discussed or proposed at my pre-op meeting with you on November 19, 2015—at which time you stated you would do an "extended fusion" to L3-4 and L2-3 (explaining that the extended fusion included laminectomies).

My first question, of course, is why? Given the time and expense involved in the surgery, I think I am entitled to an explanation.

My second question is what do you advise going forward?

At our post-op meeting I told you that about one-half of my back pain was gone since the December 15 surgery, but my original level of pain has returned since about mid-February. Earlier steroid injections resulted in eliminating almost all of my back pain for about eight weeks each treatment (but treatments are limited), so the surgery has proven much less successful. Just as important, I still cannot walk or stand for more than about 4-5 minutes without needing to sit down because my back gives out.

I continue to do my PT exercises and also swim for thirty minutes on alternate days at Lifetime Fitness, but the exercise does not seem to help with my back pain or ability to walk or stand, and I still need to take my tramadol pain medication. You did not guarantee a successful outcome, but do my two failed surgeries mean that I will not be able to get my prior life back, or is there hope for improvement with further interventions?

I think you have good intentions given your impressive Mongolian program, and I still have hope that you will prove to be "the hero of my bad back story." Please advise.

Sincerely,
Merle McClung

****

May 19, 2016

Dear Dr. Choi,

I am very disappointed that you have not found a few minutes to respond to my letter of March 15, 2016 (over two months ago) asking for an explanation of why you did the "bandaid" L4-5 screws and "laminotomy" rather than the "extended fusion (including laminectomies)" we agreed upon at our November 19, 2015 pre-op meeting. I agreed to these procedures because laminectomies were also recommended by three other doctors (Yudez, Melamed, Burns) who stated that imaging indicated that facets at L3-4 were causing pain by compressing on my spinal nerves.

Your failure to provide an explanation seems to me equivalent to your not taking a few minutes to review my file before our February 5, 2016 post-op meeting when you did not remember the surgery you performed. When I asked where the L-3 & L-4 hardware for the extended fusion was that did not appear on the X-Rays we were viewing, you seemed confused and excused yourself, returning about ten minutes later to say you had performed L4-5 screw replacement and L3-4 and L2-3 laminotomies. When I asked why, you said you would provide a copy of the Castle Rock Adventist Hospital operative report, and left the room.

When I asked Amber for the operative report, she said it would have to be ordered from the hospital, and she would do so. Two weeks later the report was not forthcoming, so I called again, and Amber said she would follow up and send me the report. Over four weeks after the initial promise and request, when I called again and was referred to your office manager, she told me that I needed to sign a medical release in order to release my medical records to myself (which I did even though I protested that such should not be necessary).

Obviously it appeared to me that you and/or your office were hoping I would forget about my request for the operative report. Finally about six weeks after my initial request I received a copy of the operative report—which falsely stated that we had discussed the "band-aid" procedures (saying nothing about the agreed upon extended fusion/laminectomies). I told you about my book *A Rhodes Retrospective Vol II* completed a day before surgery on December 15, 2015, which details my account of the three years leading to the surgery and a contemporaneous account of your proposed "extended fusion" surgery.

The above facts prior to and after the December 15 surgery make me wonder if you also were confused the morning of the surgery about what surgery to perform, and then later took steps to cover-up. From my point of view, the above facts indicate you are trying to hide something, especially since it would seem so easy to take a few minutes and provide an explanation. Surely you can do so given the time and expense of my unsuccessful surgery. I waited three years for this second back operation, the hospital billed $97,000 for the two day stay ($20,000 approved by my United Medicare insurance), plus whatever you billed for your role. Surely I am entitled to a satisfactory explanation about what happened. I may be only one of scores of forgettable patients you operate on, but for me your surgery and its results are something that I live with every day, every hour and every minute, since my back and hip pain continues as before. Am I supposed to forget about my experience with you, find a new neurosurgeon, and start all over?

I am a lawyer who does not like the aggravation and expense of litigation, but if you do not provide a satisfactory explanation, I will take appropriate legal action.

Sincerely,
Merle McClung

****

The following is a summary of a phone conversation between Dr. Choi and myself from May 25, 2016 at about 9 pm:

Dr. Choi said he had tried to call before (and could produce a phone record if I didn't believe him), and so was surprised to receive my letter. He said he wanted to explain my surgery, but I said I was at the end of a very long day, was very tired, and wanted his explanation in writing so I could review it with a friend when I was not tired. He said he would do so, but asked if he could also explain now on the phone. I said OK but I was very tired and not able to carry on a meaningful discussion.

Dr. Choi started by saying that he had explained his surgery to my family after my operation. I said he must be thinking of a different operation and patient because I had no family or friends with me at the hospital (Herb McBride dropped me off in a snowstorm at Castle Rock Adventist Hospital, and picked me up two days later). Dr. Choi then backtracked, saying he could not remember since he has performed so many surgeries he can't remember all of them, but his practice is to talk to family after surgery. His assistant Marshon Jones visited me the morning after surgery, and when I asked about the surgery, he said he did not have any details, and I would have to ask Dr. Choi at the post-op meeting.

Continuing, Dr. Choi said that he was concerned because he

had never been sued before because he has a good reputation with his surgeries and his patients. I replied that I chose him for my surgery because I had been told that he was one of the best neurosurgeons in the country. Dr. Choi sad "thank you," as if I still thought so. He said that in my case I had loose screws in my prior fusion, so in his judgment it was important to replace them. But he knew about loose screws before surgery at the pre-op meeting (see ARR with my contemporaneous summary of screws that had not fused during original L4-5 surgery), and did not mention at any time that he would replace them. Instead he said he would do an extended fusion (with laminectomies) to L3-4 (as my contemporaneous summary in ARR shows). He mentioned the risk involved given the extensive arthritis in my spine (but imaging showed this from our first meeting, so was not a surprise he discovered during surgery). At no time during his call did Dr. Choi say why he did not do the extended fusion with laminectomies as agreed at our pre-op meeting. He made it sound like we had agreed to screw replacement surgery (never discussed at any point!).

He asked me if I understood better now, and I repeated that I was too tired to absorb everything he was saying, and wanted it in writing to review with a friend. Dr. Choi once again said he would put his explanation in writing and mail to me. He ended the conversation by saying that he would be happy to continue to treat me if I would schedule an appointment. He said his records showed that I only consulted him once after surgery (as if I were at fault for the lack of communication rather than his absence at the first follow-up with Marshon Jones, and his failure to follow-up with me or my letter after the post-op meeting with him.) I told him I would have been happy to continue with him after the first letter I wrote asking for an explanation, but not now since I had lost confidence in him after having to write a threatening letter in order to get a response.

In sum, Dr. Choi's explanation sounds more like a self-serving cover-up than a satisfactory explanation of why he performed X rather than Y as agreed, but I'll withhold judgment until I read his follow-up explanation in writing. Perhaps his written explanation will be satisfactory.

****

Related thoughts regarding Dr. Choi's "Greedhead" tendencies (opposed to his Goodhead Mongolian project):

1. When Dr. Choi said he needed current imaging, his office recommended Touchstone Imaging. I said that I had used Sally Jobe in the past, and preferred to continue with that company because it was more convenient for me. I was told that Dr. Choi prefers Touchstone because their imaging is better. I said OK, but wondered at the time if Touchstone was better because Dr. Choi had some kind of financial interest in Touchstone.

2. After my post-op meeting with Dr. Choi, when I asked for a list of recommended PT providers to choose from (as had been provided by Dr. Prawl's office after my first back surgery), I was told that there was no such list, and the PT provider recommended by Dr. Choi was Vernon (details on business card Dr. Choi's office gave me). Vernon is in the same building as Choi, and again I wondered if Dr. Choi had some kind of financial interest in Vernon PT. I did not use Vernon because it was inconvenient being on the North side of I-25 near congested Arapahoe Road (and also because I already had the PT exercises from prior surgery which I continued on my own at Lifetime Fitness in addition to swimming.

3. A related issue involved the pain specialist referred by Dr. Itay Melamed who worked in Dr. Choi's office—Dr. Hall. As mentioned in my book ARR II, Dr. Hall was often quite rude in communicating with me and his assistant (and one time made no apology after his injection needle slipped and painfully hit my sciatic nerve during treatment). During my first meeting with Dr. Hall to discuss the steroid injection program to be coordinated with Dr. Melamed (didn't happen, and when I asked about coordinating with Dr. Melamed, he said he was now in charge of my pain program!), he was annoyed that I had not stopped my Xarelto prior to the visit because he could not bill my insurance company if he did not do injections that day. I did not know I needed to stop my Xarelto, but in any case was surprised that Dr. Hall would so blatantly express his concern for his pocketbook in front of a patient. I continued with his steroid treatments because they did alleviate my back pain for about six weeks each time, but then when I called to schedule a subsequent injection, I was told that Dr. Hall no longer worked in Dr. Choi's office. I stated I was surprised that I had not been given notice of his departure (apparently Dr. Choi's responsibility since Hall worked for him), and asked for Dr. Hall's new address. Dr. Choi's office said they did not have a new address for Dr. Hall, but they would soon hire a new pain specialist for the office. When I later told Dr. Choi that I had not received notice of Dr. Hall's departure, he said nothing in response (as if it had nothing to do with him).

In retrospect, a pattern of concern about maximizing dollars more than patient needs by Dr. Choi's office emerges. See also my e-mails complaining about delays in providing the operative report, and his office manager's rude and unnecessary demand to sign a release to myself.

After discussing my concerns with Dr. Cohen and a few others, I decided that it was not worth the time and brain damage a lawsuit would entail. Even if I won, my bad back would remain, and monetary damages have never been my goal in dealing with our profit-driven health care establishment.

ColoradoCare

The Health Care section of my website is focused on ways to make our health care system work better. Although I am convinced that a single payer system would serve citizens much better than Obamacare which is built upon a broken free enterprise model, and ironically underscores problems inherent in "the best health care system in the world," I am equally convinced that Goodhead doctors within our broken system manage to provide treatment that is among the best in the world. A single payer system may be possible for our grandchildren if Goodhead citizens can agree to focus on such dramatic change. In the meantime, there are many incremental steps that seem feasible in a shorter term. One such is Initiative 20 in Colorado which would have provided universal health care for all Colorado citizens. A booklet titled "Colorado-Care: How It Would Work" (June 2015) by Ivan J. Miller outlines the proposed reform. Of particular note is the pie chart on "Waste in U.S. Health Care System" and the graph on "Growth of Physicians and Administrators" at page 18, and the following related commentary:

"The Institute of Medicine estimates that on a national basis, 27% of health care expenditures, $765 billion in 2012, are unnecessary and avoidable (Institute of Medicine, 2013)."

"Between 1970 and 2010, the number of U.S. physicians has increased about 200% while the number of administrators has increased about 3,300% (Himmelstein & Woolhandler, 2012). Administrative complexity continues to grow with the Affordable Care Act. The Administrative complexity is not only wasteful, but also can impair efficient treatment. The largest savings in ColoradoCare comes from eliminating this unnecessary expense."

The beneficiaries of such unnecessary health care expense of course will combine their powerful forces to preserve the status quo. While not an easy task by any means, single payer health care systems are politically possible in many states and should be encouraged. Perhaps some states could even come up with better alternatives that one day may pave the way to a national universal health care system in the United States worthy of the title "the best health care system in the world."

REUNION 1998

Come to Denver, Vern again instigate,

Reunion in August of ninety-eight

Life is short, and it has been far too long,

Let's do it before this Century is gone.

Randy drove two family in S.U.V.

Mark's in Vern's Merc and plane from Germany.

They kept coming until there were fifteen,

Shocking us out of our normal routine.

First a picnic hike in Mount Falcon Park,

But as our group started to disembark,

Anticipating her cooking rib meal,

Mellie wouldn't let Dave toss his banana peel.

Art told Doorisa to finish university

Before getting her MRS degree.

Ryan and Taylor danced round and round

While all sang along to Mark's guitar sound.

Flip then belted out the Titanic theme

For us and the girl of Jon's parents' dream

In bikini, she flipped in-line skates for free,
Charmed by young boy's song and audacity.

Played tennis, softball and even hoops
When HORSE winners chose players for two groups.
The Colorado sun burned her too much,
But Angie showed a nice basketball touch.

Trash talk Marked team led by Jordan,
But good guys on Emily's team won
When Em passed to Vern for winning shot.
Jor-Adam played well, but we were too hot.

Since it's harder to cook than to pay,
Merle ordered in a Chinese buffet.
Vern egged on Dan's soft-spoken repertory,
Igniting his unity candle story.

While Dave scored lowest on the golf course,
Bruised Patty limped by to tell of her horse.
So Dave dodged another lecture from hell
About smoke coating lungs and teeth as well.
After cooking Sooper spaghetti meals,
Wives formed two teams to uncover good deals.

Viv led one group to new Park Meadows mall,
While Sylvia's team planned Antique Row haul.

Saw younger selves on Otto's video,
Soundless film saved ears from trumpet trio.
Saw Vern give Barry's butt a cuff or slap,
Audrey and Underbrick sitting on lap.

We laughed through family adversity
In Monte Five-Twenty and Six-Oh Three.
Who was that boy in lace and fringe dress,
Spitting tangerine seeds, and making a mess?

Singing cowboys hit a humorous note,
Won a bike and ride on first prize float.
Was that the bike Mark rode eyes shut to see
How far he could go before hitting a tree?

Mavis so cute in her birthday outfit,
Sylv rolling on floor in a laughing fit.
Parents, grandparents, aunts and uncles too,
Our family around us as we grew.
Their future was us, most have left us now,
But we manage to carry on somehow,

And seeing your kids one understands
The future is still in very good hands.

Kudos to Mellie, Viv, Jeanie and Jan
For putting up with the males of our clan.
Let's end with Missing Moberg's taped tune:
All come to Sara's wedding next June.

THE TIM & FANNY SHOW

DOCTOR SPERM

THREE FARCES

WHITE COLLAR TIME

BY MERLE McCLUNG

Chapter 26

CHOICE & CHANCE

Education belongs pre-eminently to the church…neutral or lay schools from which religion is excluded are contrary to the fundamental principles of education. —Pope Pius XI

CHOICE

This memoir began twenty-five chapters ago with the disclosure that it is being written because I am experiencing serious health issues at age seventy. Therefore it should not be surprising that I am very interested in end-of-life discussions and laws. As underscored throughout by direct statement and various illustrations, I have lived a charmed life. The seventy years summed up in the prior chapters have been an unexpectedly wonderful journey and I feel like I have once again won the national lottery. Am I being too ungrateful to want and even demand that the end of my life be under my control?

The Individual's Right to Choose

I don't want anyone else to make life and death decisions about my life or death, especially doctors or Greedheads. Many if not most of them argue that the United States has the best health care system in the world. It is the best—for them, but not for patients. I keep emphasizing that our free enterprise health system creates a perverse system of incentives because it is worth repeating. Consider end-of-life care in our country where most of a patient's net worth often is consumed by health care that most would not want because of the expense and/or prolonged misery of their final days. The person most affected, the patient, has little to say even if he/she has executed a written agreement with specific instructions. The docs and hospitals have little incentive to let patients decide about their lives. First, the Greedhead docs and hospitals maximize their profit by keeping patients alive as long as possible. Even the Goodhead docs and hospitals cannot afford to take the risk of lawsuits if they have not ordered the most extensive tests, regardless of cost. The Hippocratic Oath, they argue, requires them to do no less. I think that is a misinterpretation of the Hippocratic Oath ("first, do no harm") because of the harm caused by prolonging life unnecessarily, especially when the patient has executed a written document to the contrary about his/her own preference about when and how to die. Indeed, *Wikipedia* cites a 2000 survey which found that 60 of 122 U.S. medical schools used the original or modified Declaration of Geneva, Oath of Maimonides, or other revisions that are less restrictive and thus more in keeping with modern thought. But since the alternative interpretation is so pervasive, Goodheads everywhere should join forces to change the law to take docs off the hook on patient choice so they do not need to fear lawsuits by Greedhead family members.

Months after she was diagnosed with terminal brain cancer at age 29, beautiful newlywed Brittany Maynard chose to end her life on November 2, 2014 pursuant to Oregon's Death with Dignity Act. Her decision sparked a nationwide controversy about end-of-life decisions. See, for example, "Physician-assisted Suicide" by John Shotwell, *Kentucky.com, Lexington Herald-Leader* (11/10/14).

The controversy seemed to me unwarranted since I find no fault with Brittany's heartfelt parting message to us: "My Right to Die with Dignity at Age 29," *CNN* (11/2/14). Why should she have to suffer a long, painful and expensive death because of other people's religious and ideological beliefs (which she did not share)? Making end-of-life decisions for oneself, after careful consultation with professionals, family and friends, is, or ought to be, a basic human right. Just as troubling, why should she have to move from California to Oregon, with all its consequent expense and aggravation, in order to act on her decision? What are the legitimate interests of the State, if any, that would justify infringement upon her right to die?

The issue of individual choice has been painfully real to me ever since my failed spinal fusion in December 2012 made my back pain much worse. Except for one painful sciatica event when I was in extreme pain, I had never seriously thought about suicide as a viable option. Fortunately the pain subsided within a day, but my search for a more effective pain killer raised similar issues.

I want my docs to feel free to let me make my own decisions about pain killers and when and how to die. Who else should make these decisions? If one oxycontin pill can make me float above my bed in a high rather than severe pain, think of what new and improved meds could do if legally permissible. And I want to make the call about when my life is no longer worth living. This way I will shed my mortal coils in relative comfort and dignity. Laws that stand in the way of this right to decide one of life's most important decisions need to be revised or jettisoned.

So too docs should be held harmless when they prescribe pain medication requested by senior citizens. The prior chapter detailed my unfortunate journey within the best health care system in the world in dealing with my chronic back pain which was intensified by a failed spinal fusion. I declined oxycontin and Percocet because they caused plumbing problems. The less potent tramadol which is my primary pain medication, works for only about half of my back pain. Therefore I was encouraged one day to read that the FDA had approved Zohydro—a pain killer reported to be ten times more effective than other approved pain medications.

Zohydro

According to *Wikipedia,* Zohydro is the trade name for hydrocodone bitartrate and hydrocodone is a semi-synthetic opioid synthesized from codeine, one of the opioid alkaloids found in the opium poppy. The FDA approved Zohydro ER over the objections of its own advisory review panel which voted 12 to 2 against approval due to concerns about its potential for substance abuse.

I called Primary Physician #6's office to request a Zohydro prescription. I was told that he was on an extended leave of absence. What do I do now? Wait for him to return? Find a new primary physician even though that would take substantial time and paperwork to achieve? Fortunately, I knew that Primary Physician #6's boss who owned the clinic was a Harvard Medical School graduate. Playing this card, I asked his assistant if Dr. RF would approve a Zohydro prescription for me. The response was referral to pain specialist, Dr. Shannon Blau. When Dr. Blau's office told me that under no circumstances would he approve Zohydro for a patient, I renewed my request to Dr. RF.

I figured that part of his concern must have been litigation and so I offered a CYA cover: I would sign waivers and/or participate in clinical trials. Still the answer was No, but Dr. RF proposed an alternative plan. He would accept me into his personal limited patient group (requiring an additional fee from me each quarter) and we could work together to try some other traditional non-addictive medications that might work better than tramadol to relieve my back pain. But he would not prescribe Zohydro because it had not been proven to be non-addictive. What? I am a seventy year old man with unfixable A-fib and debilitating back pain due to an unsuccessful spinal fusion and you won't prescribe a new pain killer because it might be addictive? Is addiction worse than living in 24/7 pain? Maybe for the doctors and others not experiencing the pain, but not for me and I doubt it is for other patients in serious pain. Much needs to change in our medical system, but a sensible incremental start would be laws designed to protect doctors from litigation when they prescribe pain killers in cases such as mine. I would go a big step further and apply the same logic to other medical situations.

My request for a Zohydro prescription became moot when a few weeks after approving Zohydro, the FDA reversed its decision. Zohydro would make for an interesting chapter in a book about the FDA drug approval process and related politics. See, for example, "A New Pill 10 Times Stronger than Vicodin," *The Daily Beast* (4/23/13), and "Why Did the FDA Approve a New Pain Drug? by Cathryn J. Ramin, *New Yorker* (12/2/13). If my docs would have written a Zohydrol prescription for me in the window when it was legal, perhaps I would have found it created plumbing problems like oxycontin or other unacceptable side effects. Perhaps I would have declined the drug when its pros and cons were fully explained to me. But the point is, the decision was arbitrarily removed from my control. In large part because I have not been able to find an effective pain killer, I decided to opt for a surgical remedy as described in the previous Chapter 25.

"It's Your Pain Talking"

My experience is sobering in realizing how quickly and extensively an individual can lose control over his/her body. In addition to this experience with Zohydro, the prior chapter (pp. 217-218) relates my experience with Primary Physician #6 who unilaterally decided not to honor my requests to send my medical records to Berlin's Charité Hospital and local neurosurgeon, Dr. Choi, so that I could consider all my options, because he concluded it was "my pain talking!" I realized that I had lost a key part of my humanity. Whatever I said would be dismissed since it was not me talking, but my pain. How demeaning is that? If Primary Physician #6 can dismiss what I am saying as simply my pain talking, perhaps the whole world can do the same. Perhaps this and the other books I am writing in pain the last eighteen months can be dismissed as simply my pain talking? No one should be able to dismiss another's voice by concluding it is just the pain rather than the individual talking. I can and will listen to advice from professionals, but the ultimate decision about pain killers and even euthanasia ("to be or not to be?") should be mine, not theirs. Free choice is nowhere and at no time more important than when the individual is suffering so much and the quality of life so poor. At this important point in one's life I don't want the Tea Party or right wing or even the medical profession or my family telling me that I should not have this choice. Think of the arrogance and indignity involved in any other conclusion. The ultimate irony of course is that the very persons and entities who claim to be the guardians of free choice (many Republicans and the right wing) are the very ones fighting to oppose it for others. Not only for life/death decisions, but also for other key decisions. What arrogance to think that they, rather than the individual involved, should make these decisions.

I normally would keep my health matters to myself. My colleague and friend, John Gearen, is correct; who wants to hear "organ recitals" when there is so much else to do and report? But

I offer my organ recitals and related observations here in the hope that they can help effect necessary changes in our health care system. The most important of these would be guarantees that the individual has the right to make the ultimate decisions about risking and ending his or her life.

Marijuana

My tramadol relieves about half of my back pain for three hours at a time and I am grateful for that relief. The only pain killer that is almost 100% effective for me is marijuana. I have avoided drugs all of my life but at one point during the summer of 2014 my chronic back pain was so energy draining that I accepted my friend Nash's offer to try some of his weed. About 7 pm one evening after Nash explained how to light up and smoke, I took three tokes (puffs) of his marijuana, and within five minutes almost all of my back pain was gone! It was the most wonderful feeling to be free of back pain and I thank the powers that be that marijuana is now legal in Colorado. Not only was the weed effective but it lasted until the next morning (about 12 hours), and probably is not toxic like other pain killers. I immediately applied for a medical marijuana card and first used it at Sacred Seed in Denver to buy marijuana drops for the tongue (cost almost $100 for 4 ounces). I purchased the drops because smoking burns my throat and I was hoping that the drops would not cause the high I experience from smoking. When smoking marijuana I, like most, lose my ability to complete a sentence; funny at first, but not so much after that since I am not able to continue my writing or other work. Therefore I don't often resort to my stash of marijuana, but it is a great relief just to know that I can smoke a joint if my back pain becomes unbearable. I cringe when thinking about all the politicians and Greedheads who combine forces to block marijuana legalization in so many other states and thereby deprive so many who could benefit from its pain relieving qualities. Of course the resistance should not be surprising given so many others would lose their profitable alternatives if a better pain killer is found and legalized.

Making an ultimate call about life itself ("to be or not to be") is complex. Were it not so, we would have found better solutions long ago. Advocating the individual right to make end-of-life decisions, for example, is easy compared to the reality many face when Alzheimer's or similar memory loss renders the individual incapable of rational choice.

This memoir would not have been written if it were not for my pain (mental and physical) and my need to find a distraction from it. Had I turned to a poison pill for relief, rather than writing for distraction, this memoir and other books I am writing would not be possible. In my case the writings may have value only for a few, in other cases the impact on society could be great, but I submit never great enough to override the individual's fundamental right to make ultimate life and death choices about themselves by themselves. I can live even if uncomfortably so, with my tramadol-controlled back pain. Others are not so "fortunate."

Stem Cell Therapy

At one point when discussing progress in stem cell therapy with Primary Physician #6, he said that in Germany stem cell treatment was mandatory prior to hip replacement because it was so much more affordable for the national health plan than hip replacement. Yes, just inject some stem cell oil or jelly into my hips and back, enabling them to self-cure. But the major money in U.S. medicine, he continued, has been directed into the competitive expansion of hospitals which in Colorado's case explains the many empty hospital beds throughout metro Denver. In fact it proved to be a moot point in my case as several docs later confirmed that stenosis, the reason I could not walk or even stand for more than 4 or 5 minutes, is not treatable by stem cell therapy. It would have saved me a lot of time and aggravation if Primary Physician #6 could have told me this at the outset.

I asked Primary Physician #6 if he thought "the Broomfield stem cell specialist" might be able to help. Dr. Christopher Centeno of Regenerative Sciences and the Centeno-Schultz clinic in Broomfield, Colorado reportedly had developed promising stem cell treatment for arthritic hips and knees, but the FDA had subsequently shut down most of his experiments as too risky and against the law. See Jame Moye's article "Power Play" in *5280 Magazine* (August 2011) for details. So full implementation of promising stem cell remedies in the United States will be left for a future generation.

Steroid Injections

My back pain got so bad I decided to do what I had resolved never to do: submit to another back surgery. I went back to Primary Physician #6 for a referral to another different (one chance is enough for any particular surgeon) neurosurgeon. This time Primary Physician #6 insisted that I try steroid injections first. He confided that he also had such severe L-4-5 back pain that it almost ended his career. He said Rick Schwettmann was the doc who saved his career with timely steroid injections and that the first few injections helped him manage his back pain for nine years. I was skeptical, but also desperate and willing to try anything. At my first visit with Dr. Schwettmann I remember being irritable because I had been told by one of his assistants that I needed to get copies of my prior x-rays to bring to the visit. I spent most of a morning to track them down, and then noticed that the x-rays were visible on Dr. Schwettmann's computer screen and so my time securing them had been wasted. I also was a bit annoyed that Dr. Schwettmann seemed unconcerned about answering questions that I thought were relevant, like the cause of my new sciatica attacks. He just kept poking and probing, concluding that all lumbar levels L1-5 plus S1 were a problem but he thought he could help me with steroid injections. Dr. Schwettmann wanted a new MRI to supplement the old MRI and x-rays, so it was not until several weeks later that I received the first set of steroid injections.

The injections into my back caused only minor pain and the relief was immediate. Walking out of Porter Hospital I felt zero pain, probably because of the sedatives. The next morning was the test. I could not believe it. Most of my back pain was gone. Getting out of bed always increased my pain level. That morning I stepped out of bed easily. I had my life back. My attitude improved. Suddenly I wanted to do things that I had procrastinated on before. I pruned some deadwood out of my backyard fruit trees. I symbolically planted some new flowers in my garden and groundcover for my back yard. New life; life with little pain. How wonderful it is! Even if the relief had dissipated in a day, the one pain free day would have been worth it because it would prove that a remedy was possible. In fact the injections wore off within six weeks and I was told that only three sets of injections per year were allowed. Another brick wall in my search for a remedy for my chronic back pain, but at least I had been allowed to make the call to opt for steroid injections and secure temporary relief.

End-of-Life Choice

I realize the issues are complex and I have much to learn about them, but I think most individuals want to be in control of end-of-life decisions that affect them. It seems a logical proposition, but of course is complex in implementation. For a start, I don't want my family or friends or doctors or the state to decide when and how I die. Thank you all for your concern and I welcome your input so I can make a fully informed decision, but that should be my decision to make. If you are not convinced, see Javier Bardem's moving performance in "The Sea Inside" (2004), *The Diving Bell and the Butterfly* (2007) by Julian Schnabel, or *Google* "assisted-suicide movies" for a surprisingly long list of movies dealing with this issue. If I decide to prolong my life in a death bed, I want strong pain killing medication. Given my eye-opening experience of being denied the strongest pain killing medication when suffering 24/7 from debilitating back pain at age 72 because it might become addictive and had not yet been fully tested, I have this nightmarish vision of suffering horrible end-of-life pain, and I hear the doc outside my hospital room dismissing the nurse's plea with, "Sorry, that medication may be the best, but it could be addictive, and has not yet been fully tested."

In addition to strong pain killers, I want to exit this life listening to a mix of my favorite music: Elvis gospel, Leonard Cohen, Kris Kristofferson, Emmy Lou Harris, Mahalia Jackson and Beethoven's Fifth and Ninth. To me Elvis and Mahalia gospel music and Beethoven symphonies represent some of the finest accomplishments of the human spirit and as such satisfy and reinforce my humanistic religion. They provide immense comfort at all times but especially in the most difficult times. I don't care if the religious lyrics are totally contrary to all my beliefs since I find them comforting—a version of the almost universal need to believe that there is life after death, and the rationale for tolerance for those who find comfort in supernatural beliefs. So if in doubt, my living will representative should keep the mix playing quietly until my final breath even if not sure I can still hear anything—a hedge against the locked-in syndrome so well depicted in *The Diving Bell*. Anyone in that helpless situation would appreciate a few "butterflies" as distraction.

Others of course would want a different mix of music with their personal favorites, but a small amount of preparation in creating a mix would seem to provide great end-of-life comfort for almost everyone. And don't skimp on effective pain killers. This is my general concept and I and others need help in the intelligent and empathetic implementation of the medication/mix concept. Let's face the issues openly and honestly and intelligently. There is no shame and much reason to do so.

The Colorado End of Life Options Act

Partly the result of Brittney Maynard's heartfelt plea and her husband's subsequent efforts to publicize this injustice, California passed a death with dignity act later in 2015. Colorado's proposed Death With Dignity bill did not even make it out of committee in 2015 due to vigorous opposition by religious groups, but a revised version re-titled "The Colorado End-of-Life Options Act" will be introduced in 2016. If passed, this law would allow terminally ill adult Coloradans the right to obtain life-ending medication if their suffering becomes unbearable. A large majority of Coloradans (68%) support this option, but the bill will generate considerable opposition from the forces that defeated the prior version in 2015. As with single payer health insurance discussed in Chapter 25 (ColoradoCare pp. 226-227), legislation at the state level might succeed in the near future on several issues when comparable national initiatives would likely be non-starters.

CHANCE

For most of my life I have been skeptical of supernatural explanations of worldly events. As detailed in pages 42-43 of Volume I of *ARR*, as a teenager I rejected my mother's indefensible Christianity and the *Bible* underpinning it. Although my thinking was far from the sophisticated analysis depicted in later works by Christopher Hitchens (*God Is Not Great*) and Richard Dawkins (*The God Delusion*), I had concluded that religion is Santa Claus for adults. Occasionally, however, I, like many others, experience events that seem to defy rational scientific explanation. One example was the picture of my mother which had fallen on the day of her death, as detailed at pages 130-31 of Volume I. Also, on a more general level, most of my career in education law could be defined as an attempt to bring some qualitative balance to a national media obsessed with standardized tests and other education outcomes which can be quantified. As some student protesters proclaim: "We are more than numbers." Similarly the quote often attributed to Albert Einstein: "Not everything that matters can be counted, and not everything that can be counted matters." It seems intuitively obvious to me that both quantitative and qualitative assessments are necessary in evaluating students, teachers, schools and most human activity, including election of our President and other politicians.

Beginning sometime in the spring of 2014 I began to experience a multitude of positive events, both large and small, that seemed to defy rational explanation and could not be easily dismissed as random chance. Here are a few—offered as Exhibits:

Exhibit 1: 830 Leyden Land Sale
After more than twenty years trying, selling a small piece of dirt at a handsome profit

This is a long story that is hard to make short, but worth the space in my opinion because so many unlikely events happened within a suddenly condensed time frame. For over twenty years I had been trying to sell a small piece of vacant land I owned adjacent to the big Denver Victorian at 838 Leyden Street (photo page 48) where I had lived from 1979 to 1988. The 4,800 square foot renovated three-plex that I purchased for $150,000, however, took up most of the normal size lot where originally it had followed the Montclair pattern of one big house on an entire city block. World War II housing demand reinforced by returning veterans resulted in the big Victorian houses acquiring nine modest (under 1,000 square feet) ranch houses as neighbors on the same block.

Therefore I owned a big three-story Victorian house with a small claustrophobic back yard. I would often look over the fence separating my big house at 838 Leyden from the small house at 830 Leyden which had an enormous back yard. One day I saw the owner of 830 Leyden doing yardwork in his large backyard. I offered to buy the back one third of his lot so that I would have a big house on a big lot, and he would have a lot proportioned to his small house, plus a substantial check to deposit in his bank. He declined, but said he would sell me the entire property for $50,000. I thought about his counter-offer for a few days and then agreed when he offered $40,000 seller-carry financing.

Within days I removed the east-west cedar fence between our backyards and repositioned it to create a north-south fence line and a huge back yard more proportionate to my big Victorian. I offered the small house at 830 Leyden for a below market value rent in return for tenant assistance like yard maintenance and had only two tenants in twelve years until I sold it in 1992 for $65,000. Therefore the one-third lot at the back of 830 Leyden represented my remaining profit on 830 Leyden. More than dollars, the expanded back yard created a "wow" effect for visitors not expecting such. Over time I created a rose garden with brick paths connecting two fountains which could be lighted at night. It was a little oasis that Pam and I enjoyed for many years and attractive enough to be the wedding setting for one of my tenants.

After tiring of the commute to and from my work near the Denver Tech Center, I purchased the 4,800 square foot 1974 suburban house at 6048 South Locust Circle in 1988 for $155,000 (only a few miles from PLE offices at 8085 South Chester Street). After building floor-to-ceiling custom bookcases for both downstairs and upstairs libraries, a lower and upper deck, and other improvements, Pam and I moved into our spacious "new" digs. The three units at 838 Leyden Street rented easily until I had my first vacancy in 1996 and decided to sell (a mistake!). I gave the buyer, Trev Palmer, the option of buying the one third 830 Leyden lot for $10,000 in addition to the $250,000 he agreed to pay for 838 Leyden and closed in October 1996. Since I thought the extra land added huge value, I was surprised that Trev declined. He explained that he planned to renovate and flip 838 Leyden and so could not afford the additional $10,000. Then Trev and his wife fell in love with their renovated Victorian and occupied it themselves for fourteen years. For almost twenty years after selling 838 Leyden I tried to sell my 830 Leyden land to the four adjacent property owners;

each wanted the land but said they could not afford it. One of my brothers told me I should just give the land away since no one would ever want to buy the small landlocked piece of "worthless dirt."

Fast forward to about 2009 when Trev put the renovated Victorian up for sale for an astonishing $950,000, and eventually sold to a young professional couple NM & SM for $743,000 in 2010. I offered to sell them my 830 Leyden land for $50,000, and was surprised that they declined since the City and County of Denver's legally required actual value for the land had increased over the years to $68,600. I argued that the $50,000 was a fraction of the added value given Zillow's $1 million estimated value of 838 Leyden without my land. Also, I pointed out that owning the one-third lot meant that they would control the destiny of the entire lot at 830 Leyden since no one could scrape the house and build a McMansion, as was starting to happen nearby, without the entire lot. SM, however, thought the city's appraised value of $68,600 as well as my $50,000 price was too high, did her own research and concluded the real value was somewhere between $15,000—$30,000—clearly too big a gap to bridge.

So impasse until January 2014 when the city of Denver inexplicably lowered its actual valuation of my land to $44,000 (in a rising property market) and more than doubled my tax obligation. I asked for an explanation and a city official told me that my one-third lot had been reclassified as owned by a non-resident of Denver (I lived in Centennial about 15 miles away) and therefore taxed at a higher rate. I was so upset by what seemed to me indefensible discrimination against non-resident owners of Denver property that I considered organizing non-resident owners for a class action suit against the City and County of Denver.

After cooling off, and tired of the whole controversy, I offered to sell my land to NM & SM for the newly appraised $44,000 if they met my terms of a seller-financed five year carry in order to minimize my taxable gains. I gave them ten days until 2/21/14 to decide and on the last day they sent me a Purchase & Sale Agreement for $44,000 without my specified owner-carry terms. Had they included the terms I had emphasized were important to me, I would have signed the same day. Instead I decided to write a counter-offer the next morning with my terms at $44,000.

As I was writing up the counter-offer the next morning, I received a phone call from John Crays who said that Cory Staples, the owner of the 830 Leyden house, had decided to sell and wondered if I also would be interested in selling my 830 Leyden property so that he could put the two parcels back together again. What is going on here? After trying for almost twenty years to sell my 830 Leyden land, suddenly I had a written offer and an inquiry on alternate days. John explained that he looks for small houses in the area to buy for investors so the houses can be scraped and new larger houses built. He just happened to be passing by 830 Leyden the day before when Cory, who rarely is home during the day, answered the doorbell. Would Cory be interested in selling? Yes, as a matter of fact Cory had just decided to sell 830 Leyden and was planning a move to Washington. Talk about luck; I had suggested several times over the years that Cory should buy my land so that eventually a big house could be built on a full size lot, but Cory replied it was a moot point since he liked his small house, did not mind a smaller yard and never intended to sell.

The negotiations were difficult because all parties had different interests, but John persisted and closed the deal on May 30, 2014. Cory received $250,000 and I $55,000, so John's investors paid $305,000 for the restored full size lot—plus costs to scrape the house and pay John his commission. The serendipitous events meant that I received an $11,000 windfall—the difference between what John delivered and the amount I would have received from the couple next door if they had put seller-carry terms in their $44,000 offer. They accused me of "backing out of our agreement," but of course no agreement had been reached since they never met my terms. Not only did they lose the huge "wow" factor of a big back yard, they lost control of the destiny of the 830 Leyden lot next door. Within months, a McMansion replaced the little house, blocking sunlight and condemning their big Victorian house to a tiny backyard forever.

Of course I was delighted with my $11,000 windfall. After being frugal all my life, I figured at age 72 I deserved the subsequent buying spree of antiques, Persian rugs, bronzes and other treasures that found new homes at my house and also the MODWE and Star houses. Plus I had $44,000 with which to renovate these two furnished executive rentals. It is still hard to believe after all those years I sold the little piece of "worthless dirt" for $55,000. It almost makes me believe in some supernatural force looking out for my interests (an absurd thought). If there were such, however, why didn't he/she/it blow down the little house at 830 Leyden the night before I sold? Had that been the case, owning one-third of the land for which the investors paid over $300,000 would have entitled me to at least $100,000 rather than "only" $55,000.

Exhibit 2: Scoring my "dream homes" against the odds

I was able to buy both of my dream houses even though they came on the market at the same time and my income was below conventional bank standards. (See pp. 98-100 and 100-108 for details.)

Exhibit 3: Collector Cadillac

I was able to buy a 1981 Cadillac Eldorado collector car with only 31,000 original miles (as a back-up for my 1995 Toyota 4-Runner) for only $2,400 one Saturday at an estate sale where I had purchased some collectible books. I only went to the sale because I knew it included some collectible books marked down on the last day of the sale. Again, a serendipitous purchase against great odds.

Admittedly Exhibits 1, 2 and 3 involve "chump change" for many, but for me they are significant examples of fortuitous beneficial events. Over the next several months literally scores of small fortuitous events occurred one right after another, encouraging me to consider, against my better judgment, whether there might be some supernatural force involved.

Exhibit 4
Writing four books and creating a website in 2014

Before January 2014 I was not thinking of writing a book or creating a website. Then some unfortunate events lit a fire and, to change metaphors, jump started me on a manic writing spree. I look back at 2014 and am amazed that I had been so productive. Of course the amount of writing is not an indicator of quality, and that is open to the judgment of readers and thus remains an open question.

Hot Hands Fallacy

Then I made the "mistake" of mentioning the unusual bundling of fortuitous events to my friends Prentiss Willson and

Lee Dembart. They responded by asserting that I had fallen victim to "the Hot Hands fallacy"—the idea that everything in our lives is governed by random probabilities when we think that other explanations are possible. The game of basketball provides the case in point. In basketball, most of us think that some teams or individuals get hot hands and that accounts for streaks of above average successful shots or winning games. In my thinking and experience, I am "guilty" of the hot hands fallacy because I have observed so many times how a team can enter the zone of improbability by inspiring teamwork or whatever and thus break free of the chains of probability. In other words, "momentum" is not just a concept, but real. Lee and Prentiss argue that streaks of so called hot hands are really just like all other random events that sometime by chance just merge to create streaks (confusing us who think of it as hot hands) but average out over time to be just a normal event that gets cancelled out by the law of averages in the long run.

I recently sent an e-mail to Lee (one of the smartest persons I know) saying that I still have some reservations about the hot hands fallacy and have not got there—yet. I'm tossing Lee a bone by indicating that someday I too will "get it" and join the ranks of the knowledgeable. He writes back saying that I should not be forced to a conclusion just because he (and others in the know) are so firmly convinced that the concept of "hot hands" is a widespread fallacy. I need to, he continues, arrive at that conclusion by myself rather than be influenced by others. I find this somewhat annoying because of the implied superiority of his sense that he is right and those who don't understand it the same way "just don't get it." We have been at this point in the argument before, and I have been similarly annoyed before and when I express my annoyance at his certainty, Lee apologizes, but only because that is the gentlemanly thing to do. In his own mind he knows he is right. We love to debate and discuss complex classic issues like this—it is so stimulating to do so with good friends over a beer or two on a Saturday night.

The best I can reason to this point is that Lee and Prentiss and the other "believers" in the hot hands fallacy are right because they define the terms in such a way that it has to be right. It becomes a kind of tautology—by definition it is true because it has been defined that way. As such, it is not a great insight into a great issue, but simply a mind game of defining the terms. He who defines the terms, wins. If you define the terms over such a long period of time (almost inconceivably long given our life spans) then by law of averages and probability hot hand streaks and similar events inevitably happen.

My point is that we live our lives within a short time span (less than a hundred years; less than a minute in the cosmic time period) and therefore reasonably come to conclusions based on time and space that we can understand rather than the incomprehensible time and space that telescopes and microscopes show is reality. Hamlet: "There are more things in heaven and earth, Horatio/Than are dreamt about in our philosophy." I have tried to make this point with Lee and Prentiss several times before, but I am not sure they "get it"—or have even heard my point, being so preoccupied, as most of us are, with formulating the next point that we don't even hear or listen to the one being made by our fellow armchair philosopher.

So I get annoyed sometimes in this debate with Lee and Prentiss, and then it hits me: so too must the religious objects of my condescension feel annoyed with me when they detect the superiority of my conclusion that "religion is Santa Claus for adults." In Volume I of *ARR*, I tell about Mark riding his bicycle as a kid with eyes closed and crashing into a tree. When asked why he was pedaling with eyes closed, the dazed Mark replies, "I wanted to see how far I could get." The answer: Not very far. I smugly conclude that this is a metaphor for Mark's life because as a missionary his whole career and life as I see it is a journey with eyes closed. But I go on to point out how admirable it is that Mark and Jeannie have forgone most worldly possessions and comforts to pursue their beliefs (bringing truth to the ignorant former East Germans who were brainwashed by Communism before God brought the Wall down through his agent, Ronald Reagan.) So here I am doing to Mark what I see Lee doing to me, and need to remember the sage conclusion of a great poet:

ON KNOWING

Some divide religious philosophy
Into believers in eternity
And atheistic negativity
And yet they are so very much alike
In being positively sure they're right
And in knowing that they know they know
Although the real division one can show
Is between their absolute certitude
And all those who have been forced to conclude
That life does elude such exactitude
And remains immersed within mysteries
Beyond reach of our ideologies.
Therefore not knowing isn't just politic
But the logic for turning agnostic.

This little poem reflects my belief that both sides in this eternal debate are too certain they are right given the reality of all that remains unknown (and some would say "unknowable"). But Prentiss in response made a good point: are both sides equally open to changing their minds? This is a huge difference because I think Prentiss and Lee and most agnostics and atheists are open to changing their minds when scientific evidence is presented. In my experience, many theists are not open to changing their minds except to the very limited extent of acknowledging that science has uncovered another fact that can be explained by the hand of God.

After my amateur discussion above about natural and supernatural explanations of the world, I found a discussion of these issues in a book I serendipitously found at an estate sale a few days before writing this chapter. In the Introduction to *An Intelligent Person's Guide to Atheism* (2001), Daniel Harbour summarizes the debate that Prentiss, Lee and I (and countless others historically) engaged in about natural versus supernatural explanations:

> "Almost everyone has had discussions about whether God exists. They usually follow the same well-beaten path. A theist points to a wonderful, remarkable occurrence, such as a beautiful coincidence and claims that it provides evidence of God. An atheist responds that coincidences provide no solid evidence, then points to an appalling, remarkable occurrence such as a disaster and claims that it provides evidence against God. The theist retorts that disasters and God are hardly incompatible, appealing perhaps to a divine plan or to divine inscrutability. And so the gainsaying goes, back and forth. However, after several such discussions, most people reach the same conclusion: one cannot prove that there is a God and one cannot prove there is not. As this is a point beyond which argumentation

cannot progress, the question of belief is left to the individual's discretion, or indiscretion, as the case may be, and atheists and theists settle for an accommodating compromise, each thinking the other wrong, but unassailably so." (p.1)

Indeed, I think, the accommodating compromise makes sense by avoiding further conflict and why not let the theists enjoy the comfort of their delusions? There surely is great advantage in "the opiate of the people," given an almost universal need for such, even if it is just wishful thinking. Harbour has a convincing answer.

Harbour's book is so full of insights that I am tempted to quote at even greater length, but instead settle for the following thought, and recommend the book to readers like me who may find it unusually helpful:

"So, while the atheist is not debating the worth of religion, while he or she is being accommodating, the theist is busy influencing politics and society on the basis of his or her beliefs. The atheist's unilateral withdrawal from the argument leaves the opportunity and power to shape society in the hands of the opponent." (p.4)

The irony of my pain/writing has been noted. If Liz had not left me, I would not be writing this or any of the other positive life changes I enjoy today. Her departure which is one of the worst experiences in my life has stimulated some of the best. In addition to jump starting a manic phase of writing which has been very productive and satisfying, many other pieces of my life have turned surprisingly positive. Prentiss points out the obvious: if there is a beneficial supernatural explanation behind all my positive experiences in 2014, why did she/he/it undercut my health in such a painful way? I haven't yet figured out a convincing answer to that question, but I'll keep trying.

GOALS

As we glimpse our various destinies
It seems one of life's little ironies
We spend our youth in goal formulation
And the rest of life in pursuit of them
Even when they don't give satisfaction
So consider a minute this light verse
Don't marry your goals for better or worse
Or someday you will surely come to rue
Forgetting the gist of the gypsy's curse
Wishing that all of your dreams come true.

Author's upstairs library

Chapter 27
LIFE IS UNFAIR:
CAN OLD WHITE MEN HELP?

In proportion as the structure of government gives force to public opinion, it is essential that public opinion should be enlightened. —George Washington

Life Is Unfair

How many times have we heard that? If there is some supernatural force in the universe, IT started unfairness with prehuman oil deposits in our geology. And then much, much, much later continued that unfairness by giving men a sex drive strong enough to perpetuate the species. Therefore those who advocate for fairness are doing so against the natural history of our world.

Can Old White Men Help?

Goodhead humans have defined "fair" as giving everyone equal opportunity. But creating a level playing field is a political ("democratic") construct that tries to change the natural order of our world. In that world the lot of almost everyone depends on where they were born. The most egregious example is the contrast between the few born on top of huge reservoirs of oil, and the many born on top of endless sand. So too, the "fate" of you and me is the product of where we were born. See discussion of Choice v. Chance in Chapter 26. I emphasize this difference to underscore the difficulty of Goodheads trying to make life more democratic while the Greedheads fight to maintain and enlarge their unfair advantage. The odds are not encouraging for Goodheads, but old white men can help improve the odds.

As I page through the first volume of *A Rhodes Retrospective*. and proof-read a draft of this second volume, I realize how much old and dead white men dominate the pages, and so I added this chapter as justification.

White men, living and dead, are on the wrong side of history these days when minorities and feminists and others have organized sufficiently to blame white male Greedheads for their troubles. And of course this is historically true but should not lead those harmed by living and dead white men to overlook the Goodhead white men who have in the past and can in the future offer valuable support.

Most of the living old white men discussed in this book are "Goodheads," including me if I may be so presumptuous, and can be enlisted to support progressive causes, including those designed to make our democracy work better. For example, it deserves repeating (often) that the civic standard is based on the founders' (all old white males) concept that the primary purpose of education is to prepare students to participate effectively as citizens in our constitutional democracy. Indeed, our Constitution is designed to make our democracy work. This in turn requires the informed and active citizens that the civic standard is designed to develop. Sounds simple enough, but of course is incredibly difficult given multipurpose confusion among supporters of public education and powerful interests supporting the prevailing business standard of competing in the global economy.

Here are just a few of the old white male Goodheads I have had the privilege of knowing as discussed in this memoir, who I think could still unite with and benefit other progressive leaders and organizations in their current battles with the Greedheads: Bill Bradley, Ben Heineman, John Gearen, Richard Danzig, Bill Drayton, Michael Rebell, Harry Lewis and Prentiss Willson. Although I haven't discussed any of this with any of them, I'm sure they will thank me profusely for volunteering them for additional public services! The point of course is not just about these few who are mentioned as exemplary Goodheads in my book, but the hundreds of thousands of other old white male Goodheads who should not be dismissed just because they are old, white and male. I am not raising this as a legal issue about age, race or gender discrimination, but rather as a political and practical argument. Given the natural state of our world as unfair, you young and strong Goodheads who are following in our footsteps will need all the help you can get to take control from the Greedheads, and in our remaining years we probably can help improve your small chances of doing so.

Other dead old white male Goodheads discussed in this book already have done more than their share: Ollie Rekow, Claude Dziuk, John Monro, James Conant, Henry Chauncey, Archibald Cox. Note that Conant and Chauncey were blue blood WASPS, who contributed to shaping a new meritocracy out of the ruins of their New England aristocracy, as discussed at pages 25-31 in *Bobos in Paradise* (2000) by David Brooks. So was John Monro who implemented the transformative Conant/Chauncey plan with financial aid programs imitated by colleges and universities across the country, and Archibald Cox who provided a Goodhead example for the country in speaking truth to Nixonian power.

No need to repeat given the number of mentions throughout this book, but I'm incorrigible on the subject: The old white dead men who just happened to be our founders and gifted us the Constitution and core values which are the envy of most of the world (if we can overlook that "little" matter of exclusion of African-Americans and women from participation in the new democracy), and form the basis of the civic standard. In conclusion, let me emphasize the obvious by paying tribute to another old white dead man whose muse of fire gave us a lifetime's work exploring the mind and heart of humanity like none other before or after: William Shakespeare, aka Edward de Vere, 17th Earl of Oxford.

LATE BLOOMERS

His teacher considered him dim witted
But all of mankind then benefitted
When Edison's electric bulb of light
Enabled us to see through darkest night.

Before he defined relativity
The greatest mind of our century
Young Einstein was expelled without degree
From his high school in Munich, Germany.

So too Michael "Air" Jordan on his way
Proving himself best in the NBA
Before realizing his skywalking dream
Was cut from his high school basketball team.

Their proof of late blooming mind and body
Shows there still may be hope for you and me.

UPPER CUT*

There is a barber on East Colfax Ave
A strip for winos and those who don't have
The wherewithal to change down on their luck
And merchants trying to make an honest buck
Plagued by deadbeats begging for drink and eat
Frustrating efforts to clean up their street.

After clipping the hair of business men
The barber sketches with pencil and pen
Varied faces of the street once again
But most of all faces of the red men
Who once roamed proud and free across this land
Now busted for extending empty hand
Or not having a place to sleep or stand.

In Chief Joseph Irontooth's sunken eyes
You see the young brave both strong and wise.
Creviced cheeks of Richard Risingsun show
That his bright sun set many moons ago.
From once proud tribes of Comanche and Sioux
Today they panhandle just to make do.
Do Richard and Joe drink away their shame

And try to forget the sur part of their name?
Perhaps all men are really much the same
And drawing beneath their wrinkles and their pain
The barber's portraits help us better see
These beaten men's inherent dignity.
Thus the barber of Colfax clips away
Trimming hair and prejudice day by day.

* Poem dedicated to Walter Young,
Author's former barber.

Chapter 28
CHANGING MY WILL

"The Education of a Man is Not Completed Until He Dies." —*Robert E. Lee (1807-1870)*

In Chapter 11 of Volume I of *A Rhodes Retrospective*, I hoped to encourage kindred-spirit Goodheads to discuss and advance the civic standard as the basis for reform of public education in the United States. Since the standard website/blog template allowed for three subject areas, I added Politics/Business and Health Care to Education since I also wanted to promote research and discussion in those troubled areas. The civic standard is an example of a big concept that could change the entire field of education, but all proposals that could make our democracy work better, regardless of scope, are potential subjects.

I was thinking "inside the box" and assumed MODW should seek 501 (c) 3 certification in order to attract tax deductible contributions. This approach did not satisfy my goals for MODW, and so I changed my will to a traditional will where my family would acquire most of my estate. This too seemed a questionable decision since my family is deeply divided along religious and political lines (skewing right wing as my youngest brother Mark is a missionary who supports Trump). The typical family will provides incentive for family to hire an estate sale company to sell all estate assets as quickly as possible so proceeds can be distributed to family. The typical estate sale company charges 40 percent for its services, and further reduces prices in order to attract buyers. Thus over 50 percent of the estate value is lost at the outset. This also is not what I want for the fate of my estate.

Now as I write this in August 2023 I have come up with an approach aligned with my values by thinking "outside the box." I want to transfer 100% of my small estate to Make Our Democracy Work Enterprises, Inc. ("MODWE"), but with directions to the MODWE Board of Directors to hold rather than sell estate assets after I die. The new goal will be to continue the existence of MODWE by NOT selling estate assets if possible. We will not seek 501 (c) 3 certification, and will pay property taxes on the big house at 6048 South Locust Circle ("the MODWE Center") and other expenses from approximately $132,000 in MODWE liquid funds. The rationale is that once an estate item is sold, capital gain taxes are due, and lawyers and accountants further deplete assets by arguing over taxes due. We of course welcome donations from those who do not require tax incentives.

By not selling estate assets, no tax is due, and the MODWE Board of Directors can continue holding the MODWE Center and its contents, as well as the adjacent rental at 6459 E. Maplewood Avenue ("the MODWE House") indefinitely into the future. Therefore I encourage the Board of Directors which will have complete control of all my assets after I die to negotiate with my tenants at the MODWE House (John and Kim and their children Hunter and PennyLane) to extend the lease for another five years, and in five year extensions thereafter so no estate taxes are due. I see it as win-win because the tenants will not be burdened by the conventional mortgage needed to purchase the MODWE House, and my estate including the MODWE Center and its contents can continue indefinitely as my legacy.

Donald Trump

Volume II of A Rhodes Retrospective published in January 2015 contains no reference to Donald Trump. He had announced his candidacy for president on November 15, 2014, but few of us took him seriously. My friends and I assumed that he had entered the race to embellish his brand, and had no chance of becoming President of the U.S. Like many, I underestimated the extent of anger at the status quo which had become deadlocked and almost nonfunctional. The anger was stimulated in part by many publications like that of Thomas Picketty depicting the extent of income inequality in the U.S. I did not realize that my anger as outlined in Volume 1 was also shared by many of those on the right who also did not want to continue with a deadlocked political system. Trump appealed to and ultimately controlled most of these discontents, and the result was that Trump was voted in as the 45th President of the United States of America. And the greatest threat to our democracy in the history of the U.S.A.!

But MODWE will continue as its Board of Directors pursue the goal of perpetuating MODWE by leasing rather than selling estate assets after my death, and the ultimate goal of supporting any common-good cause they want with any surplus over and above carrying costs for the MODWE Center.

The MODWE Center

I purchased the big house at 6048 So. Locust Circle (now the MODWE Center) in Centennial out of bank foreclosure in 1988 for $155,000. At the time I was simply looking for a new primary residence near the offices of Pendleton Land and Exploration near the Denver Tech Center where I had accepted a new job. The big house was "a white elephant" built by Mr. Fredericks as home for his large family in the Palos Verdes subdivision where he was a major developer. But hard times forced him to turn the house over to the bank. The white elephant was twice the size of other Palos Verdes homes: 4,800 square feet on the first and second floors, and an additional 1,800 square feet of finished basement. I found the size attractive because it could contain my huge book, art, and antiques collection. I installed extensive wood shelving for my books, added two decks, and made other "improvements" over time which would not appeal to a typical buyer in the neighborhood.

To almost every room I added books, art and antiques, and over time I came to love my white elephant—not for its dated architecture, but because of what I had made of it. Some visitors were appalled by "the clutter," but others loved the house as much as I did. "Best house ever," enthused one visitor who was delighted to see his children pick their own books to keep from my collection of children's books in one second floor bedroom. Now I am gratified to have created an estate plan which will enable the MODWE Board of Directors to keep the house and its contents as is, and the MODWE House, indefinitely. And perhaps also perpetuate my advocacy for The Civic Standard: The primary purpose of public education is to prepare students to participate effectively as citizens in our constitutional democracy.

The long narrow porch at the front of the big house did not mean anything to me when I purchased it in 1988, but over the years became my favorite part of the house. With a growing "forest" of Blue Spruce in the front yard, I could watch activity in the cul de sac with privacy because no one could see me. Except in the colder months I often would sleep comfortably all night on the sofa on the porch when the house was too warm (never using the air conditioning, thinking it wasteful for a single guy).

Waterless Landscape Experiment

Most of the big house's half acre lot is in the back yard and was covered in thirsty Kentucky bluegrass which I maintained at great expense for over thirty years. The private back yard looked good but was primarily used by McDuff, our wonderful German Shepherd mix and Bones, our brilliant Australian Shepherd (see bookplate at first page of this book). The one time it was well used was for my niece Sara's wedding to Nathan Jespersen, and more than 50 guests enjoyed the bluegrass setting.

About three years ago I started an experiment to turn the back yard into a no-irrigation landscape by letting it go to seed and then regularly pulling bad weeds such as:

1. Gallium Aperine. Gallium Aperine, by far the worst weed in my yard, grows to about 18 inches tall with attractive blue/purple blossoms in the summer that turn into nasty burrs in the fall which stubbornly stick to any clothing or animal fur they contact (like velcro).

2. Myrtle Spurge. Myrtle Spurge is a low-growing perennial with fleshy blue-green stems and leaves. Some homeowners like Myrtle Spurge because they are not aware that this attractive plant is a toxic invader in Colorado. Because it is an invasive non-native plant Myrtle Spurge is a Colorado A-List species noxious weed requiring eradication on all lands public and private.

3. Thistle. Thistle is the common name for a group of plants with sharp prickles on leaves. Grows to 4-6 feet tall, and is an aggressive invader which strangles defenseless lawns.

4. Bindweed. Bindweed (with white flowers) is one of the most persistent and difficult to control weeds that inhibit growth

of other plants. Bindweed's interconnected root system defies pulling and most control efforts.

5. Dandelion. Dandelion is a hardy perennial weed promoted as a "toxic", as a diuretic, and food source. This toxic weed with bright yellow flowers is also very difficult to control.

6. Silver Lace Vine, a Japanese invader that attracts the dreaded Japanese Beetle so harmful to Colorado gardens and lawns.

Except for dandelion and bindweed, these bad weeds can be easily pulled when the ground is wet after a heavy rain or enhanced sprinkler or hose watering. Even so the task is onerous because they grow in such large numbers and need to be hand pulled one at a time.

My hope is that the remaining "good weeds" and flowers and ground cover will offer a viable alternative to grass yards requiring irrigation. Good weeds, plants, and flowers in my back yard include:

1. Vinca. Vinca (aka Perwinkle) is an attractive ground cover that grows to about 10 inches tall with dark green year around and blue blossoms in the spring. I would like to cover my entire yard with Vinca, but it needs some shade to survive. With some shade it is an aggressive grower.

2. Veronica. Veronica is both a weed and a cultivated plant. After drab winters, Veronica is a short ground-cover that gives a splash of color with its dark green foliage and light blue blossoms. It prefers sun and attracts butterflies and other pollinators.

3. Aster. Grows to about 3 feet tall, with light blue/purple flowers in the fall. I have islands of Aster throughout the back yard, and they look great around statuary.

4. Sunflower. Grows about 5 feet tall with bright yellow

flowers in fall.

5. Holly. Holly with its dark green foliage and red fruit is cultured as an ornamental which persists into winter and make for popular Christmas decorations. Holly also is the name of a beautiful Renaissance woman with homes in Centennial and Buena Vista, Colorado.

6. Milkweed, a butterfly favorite. Grows to 3-4 feet high in dry soils. Produces a milky sap and star shaped blooms.

My goal is not to xeriscape (expensive) or simply reduce the water currently used, but a landscape that can survive on only natural rainwater and snowmelt. I may need assistance with this experiment from the Colorado Department of Agriculture or some other entity with a similar goal.

"Hot Hands" Redux

I described the unlikely events leading to the sale of one-third of a lot at 830 Leyden Street in Denver (see pages 264-268). This led to a challenge from my friend Prentiss Willson and his friend Lee Dembart accusing me of falling for "the hot hands fallacy." Now in 2023 I am experiencing a similar series of events that I consider not explainable by probability theory. It starts with the sale of the Star House which I was able to sell to a realtor for $650,000 AS IS (see page 99-100). The AS IS provision is huge because it enabled me to get a competitive price for the Star House without having to repair and market the property or pay the usual commissions. I figure the AS IS provision saved me over $100.000, considerable time, and a great deal of "brain damage."

The Star House sale within a few weeks led to Junkaholics (720.257.8790) agreeing to clear most of the excess books and other "clutter" in the MODWE Center basement which were taking up so much space as to make the basement unusable. Jorge and Roberto cleared enough space to enable me to park my car inside the garage for the first time in over twenty years. It was painful to see Jorge and Roberto toss so many of my beloved books into their dumpster, but mitigated somewhat by the fact they kept so many books and other contents for themselves, and assured me some of the books were destined for their community book program.

The improbable AS IS sale of the Star House for a good price generated some cash and opportunity for me to be "the bank" with a $280,000 note which in turn helps to generate a monthly $500 surplus cash flow to sustain the "no sale" concept which is key to my revised MODWE plan. See Appendix A: Sample Budget.

Another example surprised me when Tim Brynteson, Paul Brynteson's lawyer son at the Otis & Bedingfield law firm in Loveland, Colorado, volunteered to take Paul's place as Personal Representative ("Executor") of my will. This change substantially increases the odds of MODWE surviving through the next generation of Americans, and leaves Paul free to focus on his Director role. Paul is Number 40 in the team photo of the 1961 Montevideo High School basketball team (see page 89 of Volume 1).

Also improbable were the events surrounding my need to clear all deadwood, including several trees, from my yard. On September 21, 2023 I almost accepted a $4,400 bid from a tree company, but at the last minute decided to wait overnight until I had a chance to review its insurance policy. The next morning Ubaldo Castenada of Beaver Tree Services knocked on my door stating he could give me a great price for the work since his crew, now waiting in my driveway, did not have any work scheduled that day. He provided proof of insurance—and an offer of $2,600 for the tree work, and $400 to trim all the junipers around my house (which were not included in the prior $4,400 bid).

Also improbable were the events that developed when Holly Schutz and her conservative husband LeRoy (a recently retired geologist from Neumont Mining Company) hosted an 80th birthday party for me at their riverside "mansion" in Buena Vista. A few days before in the Lifetime Fitness pool I told Patty Werner that the best birthday gift I could imagine would be a recording of my list of 130 favorite songs which could be looped to me on my death bed. Patty took the concept to her conservative computer-savy husband Anthony, and after much work, with an assist from Mark and Marjorie Johnson, they produced a thumb drive and alternative 7 CDs which made the best gift ever a reality. Our joyful experience at the 80th birthday party forced me to reconsider my attitude towards conservatives who hold right wing political and religious beliefs. We can engage, and even help each other at times. As a mixed group we had a great time without the conflict of arguing about our opposing religious and political beliefs.

Last, but certainly not least, my athletic club Lifetime Fitness just installed three Hydro-Massage chairs which all members can enjoy at no additional charge.

Favorite Songs

Preparing and comparing favorite songs proved to be great fun. My initial list had "The Last Farewell" by Roger Whittaker as Number 1, but soon replaced by Bette Midler's cover of "The Rose." Kris Kristofferson, Leonard Cohen, and Eric Bogle get multiple songs on my list. Johnny Cash's "Cadillac" somehow is included, but I always disliked that song. Linda Ronstat's "I'll Never Marry" made my list, but her duet with Johnny Cash is a better version. I deleted Garth Brooks' "Friends in Low Places," and

Merle and Holly Schutz

added Little Richard's "Tutti Frutti." Dear Reader, what is your favorite song(s)?

Bridging Differences

We will never start to bridge differences if we never associate with each other. A first step may be to acknowledge that the other side's views are worthy of serious consideration. Abortion offers a timely example since the right wing opponents have a strong argument, as do we with opposing views. Abortion, the decision about whether a fetus will live or die, and under what conditions, raises profoundly difficult questions that go to the very heart of our shared humanity. The primary difference between the sides is who should make the ultimate decision: the mother or the state? That each side has different views on how to deal with abortion does not alter the fact that they are at the heart of a profoundly difficult issue.

So too on a personal level I need to examine the opposing views of my family, and this requires engaging with them in spite of our differing religious and political views. If Patty and Anthony can manage to survive their differences over twenty years of raising two children, then I should be able to get along with my family as well. I can engage with my family, and also justify my decision to exclude them from my will in favor of MODWE.

The complexity of trying to bridge differences is underscored by the excellent dialogue reported in "Naomi Klein on her Doppelganger (and yours)" (Naomi Wolf) by Sean Illing, Vox, September 2023.

For example, Naomi Klein notes that the conspiracy theorists may get the facts wrong, but they often get the feelings right. People like Steve Bannon are very good at sensing the grievances and fears of the left wing and then offering them a counterfeit vision of emancipation.

Although I do not believe in God, readers will note that one of my favorite maxims is "Man Plans, God Laughs," emphasizing how little we control our lives. Another ironic example is that after all of my capitalist money-making ventures with several apartment buildings and two private corporations as General Counsel, I made the most money from my investment in two single family rental houses. I find it almost inconceivable that if there is some supernatural force governing the universe (unlikely), IT would care about prayers or praise, but probably has a keen sense of humor—and irony.

NOW & THEN

As the darkness closes in

Shut your eyes to dream again

Of endless summer days when

Limbs were strong and body thin

Running free of all discipline

The whole world was yours to lose or win

And never looking back to where you'd been.

MAKE OUR DEMOCRACY WORK ENTERPRISES, INC. SAMPLE BUDGET

Estimated Income and Expenses of Make Our Democracy Work Enterprises (MODWE):

The following Expense and Income estimates as of today (September 25, 2023) of course will change over time. Both Expense and Income will have increased when my revised will is implemented.

Estimated Monthly Expenses

Property Taxes estimated $5,000 annual divided by 12 =	$ 417
Insurance estimated $3,000 annual divided by 12=	$ 250
Excel Electric & Gas estimated $1,500 divided by 12=	$ 125
Water estimated minimal payment $432 divided by 12–	$ 36
Sewer estimated $400 divided by 12=	$ 35
HOA dues $60 annual divided by 12=	$ 5
Misc. Landscape estimated $240 divided by 12=	$ 20
Repairs estimated $1,200 divided by 12=	$ 100
Cleaning estimated $600 divided by 12=	$ 50
Misc. estimated $864 divided by 12=	$ 76

Total estimated Monthly Expenses: $1200

Estimated Monthly Income

Mike Penny Payments on Star House $14,664
    divided by 12= $ 1222

6459 E. Maplewood Ave Rent Payments $28,800 divided by 12
$2,400 month less $1,900 month to Wells Fargo Bank =
    $500 surplus $ 500

Total estimated Monthly Income = $ 1722

Liquid Assets

Alfa 1/Schwab High Cap per Lee Busto: $100,000
Cash in MSM Checking Account: $ 20,000
Other Bank of West/BMO Check Accts: $ 12,000
Other?

Total Liquid Assets: $132,000

Appendix B
PUBLICATIONS BY MERLE STEVEN McCLUNG

BOOKS

1. THREE FARCES: THE TIM & FANNY SHOW, WHITE COLAR TIME, DOCTOR SPERM, Half Court Press, (2014).

2. A MUSE OF FIRE: A PLAY ARRANGED FROM THE WORKS OF SHAKESPEARE, Half Court Press, (2015).

3. A RHODES RETROSPECTIVE: MY EDUCATION, VOL. I, Half Court Press, (2015).

4. A RHODES RETROSPECTIVE: MY CAREER, VOL. II, Half Court Press, (2016).

5. A RHODES RETROSPECTIVE: MY CAREER, VOLUME II REVISED EDITION, Half Court Press (January 2024).

6. CLASSIFICATION MATERIALS, Editor, Harvard Center for Law and Education (1973 Revised Edition).

7. STUDENT CLASSIFICATION MATERIALS: 1976 SUPPLE MENT, Editor, Harvard Center for Law and Education (June 1976).

8. SEARCHING FOR THE TRUTH ABOUT "TRUTH IN TEST ING LEGISLATION," with Rexford Brown, Education Com mission of the States (1980).

9. POVERTY AND PROTEST: A CASE STUDY IN METHODS OF SOCIAL CHANGE, Editor (1969 manuscript).

10. HANDBOOK OF STUDENT RIGHTS AND RESPONSIBILI TIES, Editor, Connecticut State Dept. of Education (1977).

BOOK AS STEVEN McMANN (pseudonym)

11. METAPHORS: A REVERSE LOVE STORY, Volume 1, Half Court Press (2014).

UNPUBLISHED THESES

12. SHAKESPEARE'S PLAINSPEAKER: AN APPROACH TO CORIOLANUS, Harvard College Department of English, (1965).

13. ABILITY GROUPING: THE PRACTICE OF MAXIMIZING STIGMA AND MINIMIZING EXPOSURE IN PUBLIC SCHOOLS, Harvard Law School, Third Year Paper for Professor Frank Michelman, (1972).

NEWSLETTER

14. FOOTNOTES, Numbers 1-8 (1979-1981), Editor & Director, Law & Education Center, Education Commission of the States (ECS), Denver, Colorado.

WEBSITE

15. MAKE OUR DEMOCRACY WORK.COM, Founder, Author, Editor (2014—present).

AMERICAN OXONIAN ARTICLES

16. MILES COLLEGE: A CHANCE FOR BIRMINGHAM'S BLACK STUDENT? (April 1970).

17. THE WORLD'S FIGHT: RHODES SCHOLARS AND ASHOKA SOUTH AFRICAN FELLOWS, (Winter 1992).

18. Book Review of David Bornstein's HOW TO CHANGE THE WORLD: SOCIAL ENTREPRENEURS AND THE POWER OF NEW IDEAS (Winter/Spring 2004).

LAW REVIEW ARTICLE

19. COMPETENCY TESTING PROGRAMS: LEGAL & EDUCATIONAL ISSUES, FORDHAM LAW REVIEW (May 1979).

PRESENTATION

20. THE PROFESSIONAL RESPONSIBILITY OF TESTING ORGANIZATIONS: ONE LAWYER'S VIEW, a paper and presentation delivered to the Educational Testing Service (ETS), Princeton, N.J. (September 25, 1980).

COMPETENCY TESTING ARTICLES

21. COMPETENCY TESTING: POTENTIAL FOR DISCRIMINATION, Clearinghouse Review (September 1977).

22. LEGAL IMPLICATIONS OF INTELLIGENCE AND COMPETENCY TESTING, Proceedings, The National Conference on Testing: Major Issues, City University of New York (November 1977).

23. ARE COMPETENCY TESTING PROGRAMS FAIR? LEGAL?" Kappan Magazine (February 1978).

24. COMPETENCY TESTING AND HANDICAPPED STUDENTS, with Diana Pullin, Inequality in Education (March 1978).

25. DEVELOPING PROFICIENCY PROGRAMS IN CALIFORNIA PUBLIC SCHOOLS: SOME LEGAL IMPLICATIONS

PUBLIC SCHOOLS: SOME LEGAL IMPLICATIONS AND A SUGGESTED IMPLEMENTATION SCHEDULE (a paper presented to the California State Department of Education, August 1978).

26. LAWYERS, COURTS AND EDUCATIONAL POLICY: THE REAL CASE OF MINIMAL COMPETENCE TESTING—A RESPONSE TO GETZ AND GLASS, The High School Journal (March 1979).

27. LEGAL AND EDUCATIONAL ISSUES IN COMPETENCY TESTING, The Education Digest (January 1980).

THE CIVIC STANDARD PUBLICATIONS

28. PUBLIC SCHOOL PURPOSE: THE CIVIC STANDARD, Phi Delta Kappa Fastback Number 503 (2002).

29. THE CIVIC STANDARD: AN ALTERNATIVE TO NO CHILD LEFT BEHIND, Education Week (December 3, 2008).

30. REPURPOSING EDUCATION, Kappan Magazine (May 2013).

MISC. ARTICLES

31. PREVENTIVE LAW AND PUBLIC EDUCATION: A PROPOSAL, Journal of Law & Education (January 1981).

32. SCHOOL CLASSIFICATION: SOME LEGAL APPROACHES TO LABELS, Inequality in Education (July 1973).

33. STUDENT RECORDS: THE FAMILY EDUCATIONAL RIGHTS AND PRIVACY ACT OF 1974, Inequality in Education (July 1977).

34. DEVELOPING STUDENT RECORDS POLICY: THE MASSACHUSETTS EXAMPLE, Inequality in Education (July 1977).

35. THE LEGAL RIGHTS OF HANDICAPPED SCHOOL CHIL-DREN, Educational Horizons (Fall 1975).

36. "DO HANDICAPPED CHILDREN HAVE A LEGAL RIGHT TO A MINIMALLY ADEQUATE EDUCATION?" Journal of Law & Education (April 1974).

37. THE PROBLEM OF THE DUE PROCESS EXCLUSION: DO SCHOOLS HAVE A CONTINUING RESPONSIBILITY TO EDUCATE CHILDREN WITH BEHAVIOR PROBLEMS?" Journal of Law & Education (October 1974).

38. THE RIGHT TO LEARN, TRIAL Magazine, (May/June 1974).

39. ALTERNATIVES TO DISCIPLINARY EXCLUSION FROM SCHOOL, Inequality in Education (July 1975).

40. EQUAL EDUCATIONAL OPPORTUNITY AND THE LAW: AN OVERVIEW, The National Children's Directory, M.L. Bundy Ed. (1977).

INDEX OF POEMS
By Merle McClung

ABOUT THE AUTHOR

Merle McClung is a former Harvard basketball star, Rhodes Scholar and "Goodhead" lawyer. He lives in a big box in Centennial, Colorado surrounded by more than 10,000 books collected since graduating from Harvard Law School in 1972. Likely epitaph: "He always had room for another book."

If you enjoyed *Volume II of A Rhodes Retrospective: My Career*, read *Volume I of A Rhodes Retrospective: My Education*. Available from *Amazon.com*.

Table of Contents, *ARR Vol. I*

SPECIAL OFFER

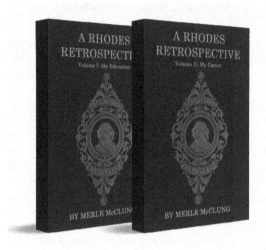

**A Rhodes Retrospective Volume I and II Set
direct from the author at a discounted price of $35.**
(Save $15)

**For more information, go to
MakeOurDemocracyWork.com/Books**

Volumes I and II are also available separately
from Amazon for $24.95 each.

Other books by Merle McClung:

Metaphors: A Reverse Love Story
(by pseudonymn Steve McMann)

Three Farces:
The Tim & Fanny Show • White Collar Time • Doctor Sperm

A Muse of Fire:
A Play Arranged from the Works of Shakespeare

Available from *Amazon.com*

Go to
www.MakeOurDemocracyWork.com
Create the Change You've Been Waiting For

Follow Merle's Blog
and join the discussion.

Merle McClung, Executive Director
Make Our Democracy Work Enterprises, Inc.
6048 South Locust Circle
Centennial, CO 80111
Landline Phone 303.290.9725

Editor:
David T. Kennedy

Specializing in writing, editing, programming, graphic design and website development. Contact me to collaborate on your next creative project.

dave@dkennedy.io
dkennedy.io
720-813-5177

Design:
Pamela McKinnie/Concepts Unlimited

So you want to publish your book!

It's amazing how easy it is in today's world to publish and sell your own book. Publishing a book positions you as an expert in your field and adds value to your seminars and consulting. Books can tell your story, raise money for your non-profit, promote your business and serve as a legacy. For more than 25 years Concepts Unlimited has been helping authors distinguish themselves with well-written, beautifully designed books—many of which have won international awards and made it to "Best Sellers" lists. We handle the cover and custom interior design and successfully navigate the publishing and marketing process to produce the book of your dreams. Contact us for a free one-hour consultation.

conceptsunlimited@estreet.com
www.ConceptsUnlimitedInc.com
www.PamelaMcKinnieArt.com
303-918-9416

Made in USA - Kendallville, IN
61390_9780692628317
01.23.2024 1349